Foreign Words

KRITIK

German Literary Theory and Cultural Studies
Liliane Weissberg, Editor

*A complete listing of the books in this series
can be found online at http://wsupress.wayne.edu*

© 2005 BY WAYNE STATE UNIVERSITY PRESS,
DETROIT, MICHIGAN 48201. ALL RIGHTS RESERVED.
NO PART OF THIS BOOK MAY BE REPRODUCED WITHOUT FORMAL PERMISSION.
MANUFACTURED IN THE UNITED STATES OF AMERICA.

09 08 07 06 05   5 4 3 2 1

LIBRARY OF CONGRESS CATALOGING-IN-PUBLICATION DATA

BERNOFSKY, SUSAN.
FOREIGN WORDS : TRANSLATOR-AUTHORS IN THE AGE OF GOETHE / SUSAN BERNOFSKY.
P. CM. — (KRITIK, GERMAN LITERARY THEORY AND CULTURAL STUDIES)
INCLUDES BIBLIOGRAPHICAL REFERENCES AND INDEX.
ISBN 0-8143-3222-6 (CLOTH : ALK. PAPER)
1. TRANSLATING AND INTERPRETING—GERMANY—HISTORY—18TH CENTURY. 2. TRANSLATING AND INTERPRETING—GERMANY—HISTORY—19TH CENTURY. 3. TRANSLATING AND INTERPRETING—PHILOSOPHY. 4. KLEIST, HEINRICH VON, 1777–1811—CONTRIBUTIONS IN TRANSLATING AND INTERPRETING. 5. HÖLDERLIN, FRIEDRICH, 1770–1843—CONTRIBUTIONS IN TRANSLATING AND INTERPRETING. 6. GOETHE, JOHANN WOLFGANG VON, 1749–1832—CONTRIBUTIONS IN TRANSLATING AND INTERPRETING. 7. LITERATURE—TRANSLATIONS INTO GERMAN—HISTORY AND CRITICISM. I. TITLE. II. KRITIK (DETROIT, MICH.)
PT289.B423 2005
418'.02'094309033—DC22
2004019246

∞THE PAPER USED IN THIS PUBLICATION MEETS THE MINIMUM REQUIREMENTS OF THE AMERICAN NATIONAL STANDARD FOR INFORMATION SCIENCES—PERMANENCE OF PAPER FOR PRINTED LIBRARY MATERIALS, ANSI Z39.48-1984.

Foreign Words

Translator-Authors in the Age of Goethe

SUSAN BERNOFSKY

WAYNE STATE UNIVERSITY PRESS
DETROIT

For my parents,
my sister,
and my beloved Don

Contents

PREFACE *ix*

1.
From Homer to Shakespeare:
The Rise of Service Translation
in the Late Eighteenth Century *1*

2.
The Translation as a Doppelgänger:
Amphitryon by Molière and Kleist *47*

3.
Hölderlin as Translator:
The Perils of Interpretation *91*

4.
The Paradox of the Translator:
Goethe and Diderot *139*

Coda:
From the Nineteenth to the Twenty-First Century *193*

ABBREVIATIONS *197* NOTES *199* BIBLIOGRAPHY *221*
INDEX *231*

Preface

THIS IS A BOOK about translation history and practice. It has protagonists: three great early-nineteenth-century German authors who were translators as well. It is also intended as an introduction both to a period in which translation began to play an unprecedented role in literary culture and to the theoretical perspectives from which this period can now most productively be viewed. The turn of the nineteenth century was a golden age of translation as an art form with respect both to the quality of the translations being produced and to the seriousness with which they were received. Indeed, the turn of the nineteenth century saw the emergence not only of modern translation in the form in which we know it today but of modern translation theory as well.

Studies of the developments in literary translation during this period are often dominated by the buzzword *Romanticism*. There is good reason for this: the key text of translation theory dating from this time was the work of a card-carrying *Romantiker*, Friedrich Schleiermacher; his friend and ally August Wilhelm Schlegel produced what were beyond all doubt the most influential translations of the age, *Die Werke Shakespears*, which immediately became one of the core texts of Romantic literature. The revolution in literary translation they helped initiate centers around what I call "service translation": translation in which the translator strives to subjugate his own authorial intention to that of the author of the original text, a mode of translation that had not previously been practiced. The contributions of the Romantics to both the practice and theory of translation will be discussed at length in the first chapter of this book ("From Homer to Shakespeare: The Rise of Service Translation in the Late Eighteenth Century"). In the three chapters that follow it, I turn to the spectacular achievements of the great translator-authors who followed in the Romantics' wake, producing important works of translation in the first half-dozen years of the nineteenth century.

The three figures of the *Goethezeit* (Age of Goethe) whose work I will analyze in depth—Heinrich von Kleist and Friedrich Hölderlin as well as Goethe himself—were all "strong" translators who placed their own unmistakable imprint on the works they translated. In a sense, this is a claim that can be made of all translation; the notion that there might be such a thing as a neutral, merely accurate rendering of any work of literature is a fallacy. But it is *as authors* that these particular translators translated the way they did, intervening in the constructions of the original texts, and their translations are marked by literary concerns that can be found elsewhere in the oeuvre of each. They were authors in the sense of the auteur directors in film.[1] As such, their work as translators is deserving of study quite independent of all period concepts. Translation of this sort—I will call it "authorial translation"—is defined not by the translator being an author in his own right, but by his active shaping of the translated text in a particular direction. Authorial translation is not the antithesis of service translation; rather, it depends on it, as authorial intent in translation can be recognized as such only after a norm of fidelity to the original has been established. None of the three translator-authors whose authorial translations will be investigated here was a member of the Romantic circle, yet the sorts of translation they practiced can best be understood when viewed against the backdrop of the advances in the field of translation that preceded their work, advances clearly owed to the Romantics.

In the case of Kleist, the translator's authorial interventions are relatively straightforward: after producing a translation of the first two acts of Molière's play *Amphitryon* whose fidelity to the aims of service translation is nothing short of virtuosic, Kleist writes his own third act, one that thoroughly undermines Molière's authorial intentions. In the process—and via a series of minute interventions at other points in the text—Kleist manipulates the doppelgänger-driven plot of Molière's comedy to produce a tragicomedy that thematizes the translation process and subverts the original/copy relationship. His work is a hybrid of service translation and its diametrical opposite: the outright erasure of the original through its replacement by a new text.

Hölderlin's translations of Sophocles' tragedies *Oedipus Rex* and *Antigone* present a more complex constellation of issues. On first glance, Hölderlin's work appears to be an extreme case of service translation, with sentences attuned to Greek syntax to the point of risking outright incomprehensibility. Walter Benjamin names him as the ideal of the translator working to achieve a hybridization of languages, using the patterns of one to enrich the other. Yet at the same time, Hölderlin's understanding of tragedy causes him to make decisive alterations in Sophocles' text, which then provide the basis for his interpretations of the plays. The key moments in these texts turn out to be not Sophocles' but Hölderlin's.

Of the three authors whose translations are discussed here, Goethe is the most difficult to categorize. In his novel *Wilhelm Meister*, he advocates a pre-Romantic form of translation, freely shaping the translated text to conform to the presumed wishes of the audience. Yet even in his early translation of Denis Diderot's "Essays on Painting," in which he revises Diderot's thought in nearly every line, he clearly assumes a (service-oriented) responsibility vis-à-vis the original text that prompts him to identify and account for his changes as he makes them and to translate with meticulous precision wherever not otherwise noted. In contrast, Goethe's translation of Diderot's *Le neveu de Rameau* nearly a decade later is full of authorial interventions in a text that is on the whole a masterpiece of service translation. For all his differences from—and disagreements with—Diderot's thought and worldview, he succeeds in creating a language in German that is remarkably Diderodian. At the same time, the discrepancies between the original and the translation in both these cases bear witness to a far-reaching debate on the nature of artistic representation in which both authors were participants.

This book is a tribute to the art of translation. It concerns itself first with the emergence of modern translation as we know it today, but then turns to the practitioners who broke the rules, the "bad," the prodigal translators who hopped the fence of fidelity to enter into a realm of autonomous, emancipated translation that became itself a mode of original art, of discovery. This new mode—deliberately skewing a work to a particular end—enjoys renewed theoretical interest at

PREFACE

the turn of the twenty-first century,[2] making these great nineteenth-century virtuosi even more important as forebears. Though we might not directly emulate the work of these renegades today, they have played a crucial role in defining literary translation as it can and does exist for us now.

The research for this book was begun and completed in Berlin with the help of two generous grants from the Alexander von Humboldt-Stiftung. I would like to thank my dissertation advisor, Stanley Corngold, who helped see an earlier version of this project into the world, as well as series editor Liliane Weissberg, who offered invaluable guidance and support for its expansion into the present form. I am grateful to Franz Kempf, Laurie Dahlberg, and Tabatha Ewing for their constructive readings of parts of the manuscript, to Anne-Lise François and Lutz Koepnick for their advice and encouragement, and to Aimée Ergas and Tom Broughton-Willett for their expert editing and indexing.

Excerpts from an earlier incarnation of chapter 1 appeared under the title "Schleiermacher's Translation Theory and Varieties of Foreignization: August Wilhelm Schlegel vs. Johann Heinrich Voss" in *The Translator: Studies in Intercultural Communication* 3:2 (1997); an abbreviated version of chapter three, "Hölderlin as Translator: The Perils of Interpretation," was published in *The Germanic Review* 76:3 (2001).

1
From Homer to Shakespeare: The Rise of Service Translation in the Late Eighteenth Century

The tradition of German authors who were active as translators dates back to well before the dawn of the Age of Goethe, but it was only near the end of the eighteenth century that the labors of authorship and translating came to be sufficiently differentiated for their combination in a single person to seem in any way remarkable. The translation norm in the late seventeenth and early eighteenth centuries had been largely what is now referred to in German as *Nachdichten*, in English, retelling or paraphrase. The translator was at liberty to alter the tone, style, diction, or form of a work, even to delete certain passages or add new ones of his own if he thought it would improve the final product. In a very real sense, these early translators were themselves the authors of the texts they produced, and there were a number of prominent literary figures among them. Friedrich Gottlieb Klopstock translated Homer; Christoph Martin Wieland translated plays by Aristophanes, Euripides, and Shakespeare; Johann Christian Gottsched translated Racine's *Iphigenia*, Leibniz's *Theodicee*, and B. Le Bovier de Fontenelle; Luise Gottsched translated Addison, Pope's *Rape of the Lock*, and Moliére's *Misanthrope;* Johann Jacob Bodmer translated Milton's *Paradise Lost*, Pope's *Dunciad*, and Samuel Butler's *Hudibrast;* and Gotthold Ephraim Lessing translated two plays by Diderot.

CHAPTER 1

The final decades of the eighteenth century witnessed a sea change in the dominant mode of translation, one that decisively shifted the relationship between authors and their translators. The intent of the original author began to determine the shape of the translated text, giving the author an unprecedented authority over the translator's work. This change can be observed not only in individual translations but also in the critical and theoretical responses to them—reviews in which translators were criticized for their deviations from the original texts and, beginning in the early nineteenth century, theoretical essays arguing for the role to be played by faithful translations in the aesthetic education of a nation. The translator's work acquired a new scholarly component previously reserved for translations from classical languages, a responsibility vis-à-vis both the language and the cultural context of the original text. The turn-of-the-nineteenth-century translator's task, then, involved as much diligent study as poetic inspiration. These new translators were no longer authors in their own right for whom the foreign text was primarily a source of raw material and inspiration, but rather skilled craftsmen putting their talents at the service of a foreign author. They were, as I will be referring to them throughout this book, "service translators," not because they did not themselves write original works of their own (many of them in fact did so) but because in the translation process they subordinated their talents to the authority, the perceived artistic intention, of another.

The term *service translation* intersects with and complements Lawrence Venuti's term *foreignizing translation*, without doubt one of the most powerful ideas about translation to emerge during the 1990s. Venuti's *foreignizing*, described in his 1995 book *The Translator's Invisibility*, was inspired both by the theories of Schleiermacher, which will be discussed at length later in this chapter, and by Antoine Berman's notion of an "ethics of translation" that entails "bringing out, affirming, and defending the pure aim of translation as such," "defining what 'fidelity,'" and, above all, developing a "non-ethnocentric translation."[1] "Foreignizing" translation stands in opposition to the "domesticating" sorts of translation whose aim is to "bring back a cultural other as the same, the recognizable, even the familiar," and includes a range of strategies by means of which translators impact the development of literature in their own mother tongues.[2] Foreignizing most often involves the deliberate use of cultural references and linguistic structures specific to the work being translated and its original language, but the translator can also develop different sorts of techniques for "disrupting the cultural codes that prevail in the target language" so as to "signif[y] the difference of the foreign text."[3] These techniques may consist of the use of unexpected vocabulary items or syntactical structures chosen to signal the translated text's difference from its new literary and cultural context, or even simply a choice of text that subverts expectations for work in a certain genre or from a certain language, country, or continent. Service translation, by contrast, while it also privileges those characteristics of the translated text that reveal its origins in another language and culture, strives above all to emulate the characteristic features of the individual original work (style, tone, diction, imagery, metaphor, and poetic and/or narrative form). Its aim is to provide not merely an index of difference but a specific sense of the nature of this difference and the ways in which a particular language and culture manifest themselves in a particular work.

Foreignizing, ethical translation has become a linchpin in most recent discussions of turn-of-the-nineteenth-century translation theory and practice, and it provides a useful link between the work of these early translators and their present-day counterparts. That I have chosen to frame my argument in different terms marks a conscious deviation from a strictly Venutian approach, which would preclude all suggestion of a hierarchical relationship between authors and translators.[4] But for purposes of my discussion, terms linked to the notions of service and authorship most clearly represent the issues at stake in the work of the figures I am investigating. The distinction between foreignizing and service translation, for example, is useful in discussing translators like August Wilhelm Schlegel, whose highly service-driven translations are foreignizing to only a moderate degree. The term *service translation* serves also to distinguish the work and intentions of these turn-of-the-nineteenth-century translators from those working at the turn of the twenty-first century for whom foreignizing translation is, as it were, a political tool, a means to escape the position of "invisibility" that is in fact nothing other than the legacy of their service-translator forebears. Finally, it is important to note that a translation's functioning in a service mode in no way precludes its being foreignizing as well.

This thumbnail sketch cannot, of course, do justice to what was a complex development spanning several decades. In the course of this chapter I will be describing in far greater detail the principal developments and events that served to effect a dramatic change in the funda-

CHAPTER 1

mental understanding of translation during this period. Only when viewed against this backdrop—the newly forged standard of fidelity that had emerged by the beginning of the nineteenth century—can the achievement of the three translator-authors to whom this book's final chapters are dedicated be judged. As will be seen, all three of these figures—Kleist, Hölderlin, and Goethe—exercised certain rights of authorship in their translations, but in none of the three cases does this represent a return to early-eighteenth-century translation norms. Rather, the particular forms of authorial translation that govern their work became possible only after a standard of service translation had been established. All three of these translating authors deviated from the norms that had implicitly come to govern the translator's work by the time they began their translations, and assessing the extent to which they did so requires an understanding of the standards that were then the status quo.

The establishment of service translation as a norm was in large part the achievement of the early Romantics: the *Athenäum* circle around the Schlegel brothers, including Friedrich Schleiermacher, Novalis (Georg Philipp Friedrich Freiherr von Hardenberg), and Ludwig Tieck. Many of the critical discussions of translation method were carried out in the form of literary skirmishes in various journals between the members of this circle and their adversaries. Indeed, the most accomplished service translator of this period was beyond all question August Wilhelm Schlegel, whose translations of seventeen of Shakespeare's plays became canonical as soon as they began to appear in 1797 and remain so today; and the foremost theorist of service translation was Schleiermacher. While the three sets of translations to be examined in depth in this book are not themselves Romantic works, they would not have been possible without the contributions of the Romantics who preceded them.

This introductory chapter, then, first describes the rise of service translation that paved the way for the appearance of the new authorial translations early in the nineteenth century, then turns to the problem of establishing a theoretical basis for the work of the authorial translator.

THE SHIFT IN TRANSLATION THEORY

We can date the beginning of the rise of service translation to the appearance of Johann Heinrich Voß's translation of Homer's *Odyssee* in hexameter verse in 1781. This well-received—at least initially—and

THE RISE OF SERVICE TRANSLATION

widely read volume prompted a number of published responses that gave new direction to the ongoing debate about what constituted "faithful" translation. The ethically weighted term *faithful* (treu) was introduced into the discussion of translation by critic Georg Venzky in his "Bild eines geschickten Übersetzers" ("Portrait of a Skillful Translator"), which was published in Johann Christian Gottsched's influential journal *Critische Beyträge* in 1734. For Venzky, the faithful translator was the author's advocate in ways that would come to be judged unacceptable by later critics: he might "assist" his author by deleting or altering passages he found objectionable, or translate poetry as prose for the sake of clarity. The product of the translator's work, in Venzky's view, might even surpass the original text in quality. Venzky's position was typical of those underlying many of the critiques of translations published by Gottsched in the *Beyträge* throughout the 1730s. It also reflected widespread translation practice at the time, which involved not only the production of translations that would be considered by later standards unacceptably loose but also translations of translations. There had been a decline in the study of foreign languages other than French during the first half of the century, and a large number of Greek, Latin, English, and Spanish works were routinely "translated" into German from their French translations, resulting in texts whose link to their originals was tenuous.[5]

In general, quantity outstripped quality in the translations of this period. Gottsched himself complained, "Die Uebersetzungssucht ist so stark unter uns eingerissen, daß man ohne Unterschied Gutes und Böses in unsre Sprache bringt: gerade als ob alles was ausländisch ist, schön und vortrefflich wäre"[6] (The translation mania has proliferated to such an extent among us that good and bad works alike are being translated into our language as though everything foreign were necessarily beautiful and admirable[7]). In 1740, French critic Éléazar de Mauvillon provoked a flurry of defensive replies with his widely publicized charge that the Germans were *only* translators: they had produced, he said, no memorable literary works of their own and now were mangling those of foreign writers with their inferior translations.[8]

These criticisms soon began to prompt serious critical responses addressed to both the mode of the translator's work and its purpose. The stakes for judging the "fidelity" of a translation were raised with the appearance of Breitinger's *Critische Dichtkunst* (1740), in which he demanded that the translator avoid the "periphrastic coldness"

5

CHAPTER 1

(periphrastische Kaltsinnigkeit) that produces a dull effect (Mattigkeit). Rather,

> Man muß nicht bloß ungefehr dasjenige sagen, was der Urheber gesagt, sondern auf die Weise und mit dem Nachdruck, wie er es gesagt hat. Des Uebersetzers Pflicht ist, daß er neben den Gedancken auch die Form derselben liefere.⁹

> One must not only say approximately the same thing the author said, but in the same way and with the same emphasis with which he said it. The translator's duty is to deliver, along with the thoughts, the form in which they appear.

This standard of fidelity—one that includes not just the "content" of the text per se but the form in which it is communicated, the ordering of the thoughts, and the placement of emphasis—anticipates the demands for fidelity that were to become standard around the turn of the nineteenth century. The question of the criteria to be used in judging translations played a role in the so-called *Zürcher Literaturstreit*, the quarrel (largely about the relative importance of the imagination and rationality in poetic works) between the Swiss and Leipzig schools that pitted Bodmer and his compatriot Johann Jacob Breitinger against Gottsched. By the early 1740s, Gottsched himself had accepted his Swiss opponents' criteria for judging translations and used them to question the quality of translations published by Bodmer and Breitinger themselves.

Despite the presence of these proposed critical standards for literary translating, few of the translations produced between 1740 and the late 1760s came close to fulfilling the task set by Breitinger. For one thing, the practice of paying authors and translators for their work, which had begun in the late seventeenth century and become more widespread in the eighteenth, encouraged a number of lesser talents to try their hands at it. As Lessing complained,

> Unsere Übersetzer verstehen selten die Sprache; sie wollen sie erst verstehen lernen; sie übersetzen, sich zu üben, und sind klug genug, sich ihre Übungen bezahlen zu lassen.¹⁰

> Our translators rarely understand the language [from which

THE RISE OF SERVICE TRANSLATION

they are translating]; they translate for practice and are clever enough to get paid for these exercises.

Lessing's own translations of Diderot's plays (*Le fils naturel* and *Le père de famille*, published in 1760) were an exception to the general trend in these decades. They were in fact quite service-oriented and nonetheless enjoyed at least as much popular success as Lessing's own plays;[11] but they were prose dramas, and by far the greatest variation in approaches to translation was to be seen in translations of verse.

A number of conditions that existed in this period encouraged the proliferation of mediocre translations. Translators were generally paid by the signature (rather than according to the quality of their work), and often they were placed under severe time pressure by their publishers to complete translations of works that had appeared in other languages—above all French—fast enough to avoid having their work preempted by some other translator/publisher team. This extreme form of competition developed because of pre-copyright practices: publishers could apply for the "privilege" of being the sole publisher of a book in an individual state (there being as yet no politically unified German nation), but even when they held such "privileges" they were in danger of being undercut by cheaper, or more rapidly produced, editions published in neighboring states, or even by locally produced illegal reprints. Literary piracy was rampant. Only in 1773 did it become illegal to reprint a book without permission within a given state (the first such law was in Saxony)—and even then certain states continued to encourage the practice of unauthorized reprinting because it boosted local economies. The first work to be granted a legally binding copyright valid in all the German states was the definitive edition of Goethe's works in 1828. The English government, by way of comparison, began granting authors copyright protection of their works in 1710, and the copyrights paid to English authors throughout the eighteenth century far exceeded those received by their German counterparts.[12]

By the mid-1770s, translations accounted for a good one-third of the new books offered for sale at the Leipzig Book Fair each year—and this despite the fact that translations were affected by the new laws governing reprints. According to the laws in some states, translations could be interpreted as reprints of the original texts (which were sometimes printed locally) unless the translator deviated substantially from the

7

original, supplied notes, or otherwise added his own material. And new translations of previously translated books—even those that had been translated poorly—were considered reprints of the first translations as long as copies of the original edition remained unsold. Bad translations, then, could be attacked by critics on two grounds at once: both for ruining the work of good authors and for making it inaccessible to better translators.[13] Indeed, translations during this period were subjected to the most exacting critical scrutiny in journals such as the *Allgemeine Deutsche Bibliothek,* founded in 1765, in which, for example, a translation by Gottsched prompted one critic to speculate "ob der Übersetzer das Gedicht selbst oder die deutsche Nation bey den Ausländern habe lächerlich machen wollen"[14] (whether the translator was trying to make the poem itself appear ridiculous, or to make the German nation look ridiculous to foreigners). Principally these reviewers demanded that translations be "verständlich und schön"[15] (comprehensible and pleasing). They were to present the information contained in the books clearly, if need be with footnotes.

Meanwhile three figures writing in the 1760s and 1770s— Heinrich Wilhelm von Gerstenberg, Johann Georg Hamann, and Johann Gottfried Herder—began to speak of translation in ways that would eventually provide the basis for the translation theory of the turn of the century. In 1769, Gerstenberg divided translations into two categories: those made for a lay public, which he described in terms that amount to "comprehensible and pleasing," and those intended for well-educated readers interested in historical matters. In a review of a Bible translation, he wrote of this latter category of translations in a way that anticipates the sorts of questions raised by Schleiermacher.

> Alle Ausdrücke des Originals, welche den Geist und die Denkungsweise des biblischen Verfassers oder seines Volks oder seines Zeitalters karakterisiren, muß der Übersetzer buchstäblich übertragen, wenn er treu seyn, und mich völlig in die Lage des Schriftstellers versetzen will. [. . .] Desgleichen, alles was zum Styl des Verfassers gehört, aufs genaueste und wörtlich im Deutschen ausdrücken, damit man den Ton des Originals nicht verliere.[16]
>
> All the expressions in the original that characterize the spirit and the way of thinking of the Biblical author or his people

or his age must be literally translated if the translator wishes to be faithful and to transport me completely into the writer's situation. . . . Similarly, everything that forms part of the author's style should be expressed precisely and verbatim in German so that the tone of the original is not lost.

Yet Gerstenberg was careful to specify that his demand for literal translation did not extend to "idioms"; the verbatim translation was something that belonged "unter den Text und nicht in den Text"[17] (beneath the text, not in the text). Hamann, too, noting the difficulty of representing one language with another, spoke of the necessity of the translator's compensating with "Abweichungen und Ersetzungen oder Äquationen"[18] (deviations and replacements or equivalents) for differences between cultures and languages. All languages, he wrote, are based on a common language—the language of nature—and all writing is a sort of translation "aus einer Engelssprache in eine Menschensprache, d.h. Gedanken in Worte—Sachen in Namen—Bilder in Zeichen"[19] (from a language of angels into a human language, i.e. thoughts into words—things into names—images into signs). In the end, however, both Gerstenberg and Hamann wrote of a translation practice that reacts with resignation to the fundamental untranslatability of texts; both the emphasis on the sameness of languages (Hamann) and the incommensurability of idioms (Gerstenberg) imply a translation practice that, in the end, is little more than a theoretically more enlightened reliance on the "comprehensible and pleasing."

Herder's perception of translation had developed by the 1770s from a position similar to that of Gerstenberg and Hamann to the conviction that a poem could not survive separated from the form particular to it. Whereas earlier he had declared the hexameter an inappropriate form for the German language, now he spoke of the importance of translating Homer into German hexameters.[20] At the same time, he was developing his theories on the interrelation between language and nation—ideas that would serve as a basis for Schleiermacher's work on the topic. "Jede Nation," Herder wrote, "hat ein eigenes Vorratshaus ihrer zu Zeichen gewordenen Gedanken"[21] (Every nation has its own storehouse of its thoughts that have become signs)—the language of a nation gives rise to its thought just as its thought gives rise to its language. Finally he arrived at the formula: "La langue c'est nation" (Language is nation).[22]

CHAPTER 1

Herder was stronger as a translation theorist than as a translator. The fragments of Shakespeare he published in the first volume of his collection *Alte Volkslieder* in 1774, accompanied by a note in which he claims to have found them among the papers of a deceased friend, do constitute an attempt to reproduce the formal properties of the original. But the Shakespeare they present is a melodramatic creature of the *Sturm und Drang*, bristling with exclamation points and reduced to an assemblage of fraught moments (such as Hamlet's monologue, which becomes a "Probe einer schauderhaften Metaphysik über Tod und Leben"[23][a sample of a horrific metaphysical reflection on death and life]). Yet Herder's views on translation provide the most important bridge between the theory of the eighteenth and nineteenth centuries.

The development to be observed in the theoretical understanding of translation during the second half of the eighteenth century shows a distinct movement away from the perception of a text as information—"content," story—to be communicated to the reader in some form of the translator's choosing. In translation practice, the corresponding development took place in two steps. First came the basic concession to poetic form: the understanding that prose and verse are such different modes of expression that translating a verse text into prose must necessarily distort it beyond recognition. This led to attempts to translate verse texts into verse forms (which often differed from those of the original text). Second came the conviction—accompanied by the awareness of the cultural specificity of languages and texts enunciated by Herder and soon to become the basis of Schleiermacher's theory—that the essence of a literary text is inextricably tied up not only with its form (hexameter, blank verse, etc.) but also with its style, tone, and syntax and with the way in which these attributes figure within the text's original language. The result, at the turn of the century, was the birth of service translation.

THE SHIFT IN TRANSLATION PRACTICE

The pivot around which the turn to service translation practice took place was the pioneering work of Johann Heinrich Voß, which was first lauded, then reviled, and in the end again lauded by translators working in a school that he was—unintentionally—instrumental in producing. In 1781, when translation practice was still generally governed by the principle of "comprehensible and pleasing," Voß published a translation of Homer's *Odyssee* in hexameters that was widely praised not only for the philological thoroughness of his work but also for his skillful use of the verse form. His was the first German Homer in trochaic hexameter not immediately rejected for the awkwardness of its verse—in contrast to the earlier attempts published in 1776 and 1778 by Leopold Graf Stolberg and Bodmer.[24] The hexameter form had failed to establish itself in German despite its striking and celebrated use by Friedrich Gottlieb Klopstock in his *Messiade* (which appeared in installments between 1748 and 1773, with a complete book publication following in 1780);[25] and the original hexameter work Voß published soon after his volume of Homer appeared, *Luise: eine ländliche Idylle* (1795), was acknowledged by Goethe as the model for his 1797 *Hermann und Dorothea*.[26]

Admittedly there are criticisms to be made of Voß's translation. For the sake of preserving both line length and number of lines he excluded a significant number of words and phrases, while at other points incorporating filler phrases of his own that do not always sit well in Homer's text. His desire for fidelity to the original sometimes resulted in unwittingly comic phrases, particularly in Homer's ornamental epithets, such as "weitumschauende Gegend" (wide-gazing region), "blutgeschändete Mutter" (blood-defiled mother) and "segelberühmte Phaiaken" (sail-renowned Phaeacians).[27] Yet Voß's *Odyssee*, unlike those that had preceded it, was translation in the modern sense, an attempt to render both the form and content of the original work in something akin to their original relation.

The main impact of Voß's work on the field of translation, however, was to come a dozen years later with the appearance of his volume *Homer's Werke* in 1793, which contained both *The Iliad* and a heavily revised version of his *Odyssee*. The revision served to make the text conform more closely to the syntax of the Greek original. In book 6, for example, Voß revised the lines

> Liebes Kind, was bist du mir doch ein läßiges Mädchen?
> Deine kostbaren Kleider, wie Alles im Wuste herumliegt!
>
> Dear child, what a careless girl are you to me [in my view]?
> Your precious clothes, how everything lies about in disarray!

to read:

CHAPTER 1

> Welch ein läßiges Mädchen, Nausikaa, bist du der Mutter!
> Dein Gewand, wie liegt es in Wust, so gepriesener Schönheit;[28]
>
> What a careless girl, Nausicaa, you are to the [your] mother! Your garment, how it lies in disarray, of such praiséd beauty!

August Wilhelm Schlegel, reviewing the translation in 1796, wrote that Voß had attempted to adhere to the Greek syntax "nicht so nah wie möglich (dieß wäre sehr zu loben), sondern so nah wie es in unserer Sprache unmöglich ist" (not as closely as possible [which would have been laudable], but as closely as is impossible in our language; SW 10:163), and Klopstock quipped that if the original text were ever lost, it could be reconstructed with the help of Voß's translation (10:136). In later years, Voß continued to revise his Homer translations even further, making them converge more and more on the line structure of the original text. His Vergil of 1799 and above all the Shakespeare translations he published in the 1810s display similar characteristics.[29] For Voß, the German tongue had come to seem a virtually transparent medium for communicating the structure of the original language.

The encounter between Voß and Schlegel—Voß's revised translation and Schlegel's mammoth review of it, which occupies a full seventy pages in his collected works—marks the crucial turning point in late-eighteenth-century translation. Schlegel vehemently rejected Voß's work, but the confrontation with the principles of translation Voß represented were clearly fundamental to his own development as a translator, and it was in conversation (if not conflict) with Voß's work that Schlegel developed his own principles of translation, which were to influence the translations of his fellow Romantics. The earliest translations produced by Schlegel, largely in collaboration with his teacher and early mentor Gottfried August Bürger, had still belonged to the eighteenth-century norm. But a year after his review of Voß's translation appeared, Schlegel began to publish the Shakespeare translations—clearly work in a new mode—that would soon establish his reputation as the greatest translator of the age.

The extent to which Schlegel's new style of translation—lines of blank verse closely matched to their originals—constituted a break with the past can immediately be seen by comparing his Shakespeare translations with the earlier editions available in German: those of Wieland

THE RISE OF SERVICE TRANSLATION

(published between 1762 and 1766) and of Johann Joachim Eschenburg (1775–82). All of Eschenburg's translations, and all but one of Wieland's, rendered Shakespeare's lines in prose. Even in the one play Wieland translated in verse, *A Midsummer Night's Dream*, the German lines are linked only loosely to the corresponding English ones, and passages tend to become significantly longer in the translation. Compared to these earlier translations, the kinship between Schlegel's work and that of Voß is clearly evident.

While Schlegel never wrote a text explicitly outlining his theoretical approach to translation, his review of Voß's *Odyssee* contains a number of statements from which a theoretical standpoint can be extrapolated. Schlegel's principal objection to Voß's mode of translation is that Voß distorts the German language impermissibly in attempting to follow the syntax of the Greek original. Translation is always, Schlegel writes, a twofold project, simultaneously "eine Dollmetschung des Griechischen" and "eine Uebertragung ins Deutsche" (SW 10:149; a translation of the Greek and a translation into German). This sounds like a reiteration of the eighteenth-century demand for "comprehensible and pleasing" translations, but Schlegel adds to this a new conception of fidelity that deviates markedly from the eighteenth-century notion of literal correctness with regard to meaning (such as was proposed by Venzky). Instead, Schlegel calls for a translation that takes into account the text's sensual properties.

> Der Eindruck, den eine dichterische Darstellung machen soll, hängt endlich nur dem kleinsten Theile nach von dem Sinne der Wörter und Redesätze ab, in so fern der Verstand ihn ausmitteln kann: durch den lebendigen Hauch der Rede, durch eine Fülle beseelter Töne nimmt die Poesie [. . .] die ganze Empfänglichkeit des Menschen in Anspruch. (10:121)

> The impression that a poetic representation is to make is, finally, dependent to only the smallest extent on the meanings of the words and phrases, as they are available to the understanding: through the living breath of speech, through an abundance of animate sounds . . . , poetry absorbs man's full receptive powers.

This language is alive ("living," "animate"); it lives in the impression it makes on the reader. Schlegel's view of language as something all but possessed of physical characterstics differs not only from Venzky's standpoint but also from that of Breitinger, since Breitinger's "excellent model," which is to be reproduced "in just the same order, connection and context," is a pattern not of sounds but of "concepts and thoughts": abstract ideas rather than the corporality of speech. Schlegel's "living breath of speech," on the other hand, though he does not explicitly say so, implies a cultural specificity of language such as was described by Herder.

For all his criticisms of Voß's translation, Schlegel clearly agrees with Voß on one major point: that a translation must simultaneously take into account both the meanings of the words being translated and the text's formal characteristics. And five years and sixteen Shakespeare plays later, in 1801, Schlegel would publish a partial retraction of his original critique, explaining "Wenn man den Zweck will, muß man auch die Mittel wollen" (SW 10:182; If you want the ends, you also have to want the means).[30] He conceded, in other words, that it was not possible to attempt to translate both the form and the content of a text without being prepared to accept the fact that the finished product was likely to turn out looking different from a text that had been written originally in German. The reading public, too, he wrote, was meanwhile becoming accustomed to Voß's translations and increasingly willing to accept the principles behind them (10:183). Yet what he really seems to want is a text that displays cultural and formal acumen without sacrificing either clarity or beauty; and this is the difficult goal which he sets for himself and achieves astonishingly often in his own translations.

Meanwhile the drafts of Schlegel's manuscripts in the late 1790s reveal a revision process that shows him moving closer and closer to Voß's principle of syntactical equivalence in his work on the texts. This process can be readily observed in the translation of Ariel's famous song (act 1, scene 2, Shakespeare 1816:28) from *The Tempest*:

> Full fathom five thy father lies;
>   Of his bones are coral made;
> Those are pearls, that were his eyes:
>   Nothing of him that doth fade,
> But doth suffer a sea-change,

> Into something rich and strange.
> Sea-nymphs hourly ring his knell:
> Hark, now I hear them,—ding-dong-bell.

Schlegel's final translation of the song, published in 1798 in the third volume of his edition, uses a bold inversion of noun and possessive pronoun to copy the rhythm of the first line in English:

> Fünf Faden tief liegt Vater dein.
> Sein Gebein wird zu Korallen,
> Perlen sind die Augen sein.
> Nichts an ihm, das soll verfallen,
> Das nicht wandelt Meeres-Hut
> In ein reich und seltnes Gut.
> Nymphen läuten stündlich ihm,
> Da horch! ihr Glöcklein—Bim! bim! bim![31]

The "anglicizing" literalness of the translation belies the fact that Schlegel arrived at this version through a revision process that at points led him quite far from the syntax of the original. The opening lines of an earlier version recorded in his manuscript, for example, are considerably less literal in this sense:

> Fünf Klafter tief der Vater dein
> Liegt am Meeresgrund; erstarrt
> Zu Korall' ist sein Gebein,
> Jedes Aug 'ne Perle ward.

And a still earlier version of the translation, published in Schiller's journal *Die Horen* in 1796, deviates even further from the English syntax and rhythms:

> Tief in Meeresgrund gefallen,
> Liegt dein Vater wohl bewahrt.
> Sein Gebein wird zu Korallen,
> Jedes Aug 'ne Perle zart.[32]

CHAPTER 1

The singsong quality of this earliest version is produced by the strict regularity of its trochees. Schlegel has copied the rhyme scheme of the original, but not its rhythms, and Shakespeare's dense first line (five of its eight syllables are stressed) has been stretched to two. This song is all too light where Shakespeare's lines are heavily weighted, difficult to read aloud rapidly. Schlegel broke up the regular meter in the second version, but his enjambments produce an effect quite different from that of Shakespeare's weightily end-stopped lines. His final version of the translation puts much heavier emphasis on the sounds of the original poem. The first set of rhymes, *dein/sein*, mimics the long *i* (*lies/eyes*) that dominates in the first lines of Shakespeare's poem after an initial interior off-rhyme with *five*. Schlegel, recognizing the importance of this interior rhyme for establishing the sound patterns in the poem, preserves it, though he is unable to fit it into the same line: instead he repeats the vowel with *Sein Gebein* in the second line. "Sein Gebein wird zu Korallen" was already present in the 1796 version, but the line reads quite differently in its new context. Rather than moving quickly toward its rhyme-word *Korallen*, in echo of *gefallen*, the line is now slowed midstride by the interior rhyme with its emphasis on *Gebein*. The slow solemnity of the poem's tone is further underscored by the heavily alliterative opening line, whose four *f*-sounds in German (counting the *f* in *tief*) mimic the sound structure of the English. And the curious phrase "Vater dein" of the opening line, which sounds unfamiliar in German but is not copied directly from the English, has been maintained from the poem's second version in which it is syntactically accounted for by the continuation of the sentence in the following line. Schlegel's decontextualizing of the phrase—and the addition of the rhyme words *Augen sein*—dramatically alters the feel of these lines.

While this series of revisions serves to bring the syntax of the translation into close correlation with its original, as did Voß's revision of his Homer lines, there is nonetheless a significant difference between them. Schlegel's changes are not only syntactical but also, and above all, concerned with the sounds of the text, the melody and rhythms of its phrases, in short what Schlegel called "the living breath of speech." The extent to which questions of syntax were also, for Schlegel, questions of rhythm is apparent everywhere in his revision process, even in the case of as simple a line as "Sir, I would speak with you" (*The Merchant of Venice* 4.2.12), which appears in no fewer than five different versions in his manuscripts:

Herr, ich muß mit euch sprechen.
Ich muß euch sprechen, Herr.
Herr, laßt euch etwas sagen.
Ich wollt' euch etwas sagen, Herr.
Herr, noch ein Wort mit euch.[33]

The progression of these lines, too, is telling. The first, and most syntactically literal version (with *would* rendered monosyllabically as *muß*, rather than as *möchte* or *wollte*) falls short rhythmically, with the line pausing awkwardly after *Herr*. The second avoids this problem by shifting the address to the end. But saying *Sir* or *Herr*, presumably to get that character's attention, only *after* the request for an audience makes little sense, or, at the least, produces a significant change in tone, which Schlegel reverses in the third variant. But this version, with *laßt*, sounds too much like a command—and so, for that matter, does the *muß* of the first and second variants. Schlegel returns to a more literal version of the English text in his fourth attempt, reinstating the literal *wollt'*, but this produces a line far more cumbersome than Shakespeare's. The last variant, which appears in the final version of the play, departs from these more literal renderings but preserves the rhythm of the original line and closely approximates the tone of the English request, a petition neither commanding nor suppliant. At the same time, it is the most syntactically faithful: like the original, it begins with *Sir* and ends with *you*.

There is a difference, then, between the sort of formal/syntactical fidelity practiced by Voß and that of Schlegel. Where Voß focuses on prosody, on the metrical patterns of the original, Schlegel is more attentive to sound and rhythms, the style and tone of the work he is translating. One could say that the two agreed in principle on the way translations should be made, but that Schlegel was more skillful in putting these principles into practice. At the same time, neither one of them was an outstanding author in his own right. Both published original works—Voß, *Luise: ein ländliches Gedicht in drei Idyllen* (*Luise: A Bucolic Poem in Three Idylls*), and Schlegel, the play *Ion*—but neither authored texts that are still read today. In Schlegel's case, the fact that he was not known as an author has diminished his fame as a translator as well: his translations are generally spoken of only as part of the so-called Schlegel-Tieck Shakespeare edition and are assumed by many to

CHAPTER 1

have been a collaborative effort.[34] In fact, not one of the plays in this edition was translated by Ludwig Tieck. (He edited Schlegel's translations—for the worse, by most accounts—and supervised the production of additional, initially anonymous translations by his [Tieck's] daughter, Dorothea, and Wolf Graf Baudissin. Schlegel's only real collaborator on his translations was his own wife, Caroline, who received no credit for her work.) But Tieck, like Wieland, was himself a respected author, and so his name sold books and continues to do so. On the other hand, Tieck did prove himself as the translator of other work: his 1799 translation of Cervantes's *Don Quixote*, which has deservedly remained in print, as well as prose works by Henry Fielding (such as the *History of the Life of the Late Mr. Jonathan Wild*, translated in collaboration with his friend Hagemeister—an excellent translation that carefully follows the twists and turns of Fielding's sentences) and two works by Ben Jonson, *Volpone or The Foxe* and *Epicoene or The Silent Woman*.

Other prominent figures who produced service translations in the first half of the nineteenth century include Schleiermacher (Plato's works, 1804–10), Friedrich Baron de la Motte Fouqué (Cervantes's play *Numancia*, published anonymously in 1810), Joseph Freiherr von Eichendorff (a collection of Calderón plays, 1846–53), Georg Büchner (two plays by Victor Hugo, 1835), and—perhaps surprisingly—Wieland. Although his translations were indeed unquestionably eighteenth-century work, he later became convinced of the necessity "den Affekt auszudrücken, der in der Form liegt"[35] (expressing the emotion that lies in the form). Introducing his translation of a speech by Isokrates in 1796, he writes:

> Was meine Uebersetzung dieser Rede betrift, so habe ich darüber nur wenig zu sagen. Beynahe wär ich versucht, mich zu entschuldigen, daß ich mir dabey zum Gesetz gemacht, mich so genau als nur möglich war, an meinen Autor anzuschmiegen, mich vor jeder Versuchung, ihn verschönern zu wollen, zu hüten, und ihm selbst in dem, worin ich mit Dionysios von Halikarnaß seinen Stil für tadelhaft halte, so nahe zu kommen, als die Verschiedenheit der Sprachen nur immer zulassen wollte.[36]

As for my translation of this speech, I don't have much to

say about it. I'm almost tempted to apologize for having made it my rule in this translation to stick to my author as closely as possible, resisting all temptation to beautify him, and even in those passages in which, like Dionysios of Halikarnass, I find his style deficient, I attempted to follow him as closely as the differences between the languages allowed.

The translations of Aristophanes and Euripides that Wieland published in his journal *Attisches Museum/ Neues Attisches Museum* between 1796 and 1809 stand firmly in the service tradition. They are in metrical verse throughout, and Wieland's lines are only slightly less compact than, say, those of the mid-nineteenth-century Aristophanes translations by Ludwig Seeger that have become canonical (whereas Wieland's translations of these works have been forgotten).[37]

In any case, regardless of the mode—service-oriented or not—of the translator's work, it is unquestionably true that the translator who is also a writer enjoys a certain cachet in the popular imagination, an almost fetishized status unavailable to the one who "only" translates. The antiquarian bookseller in Berlin from whom I purchased my edition of Schlegel's Shakespeare translations apologized for not having Wieland's in stock. We trust writers to know about writing—surely this is not unreasonable—and there is a strong tradition, even in English, of great authors who also translate: from John Dryden to Alexander Pope to Richard Wilbur. But the question remains how successfully the particular desires and designs of authorship can mold themselves to the constraints on creative production the translator's task entails.

Meanwhile, in the eighteenth and early nineteenth centuries, becoming a translator was a way of becoming an author for some to whom authorship—whether for want of talent, because of the gender barrier, or for other reasons—was denied. This was the case for many of the hack translators who provoked the scorn of Mauvillon and Lessing in the mid-eighteenth century. Translation as a form of authorship also played a special role among women with literary talent, who in this period still had great difficulty finding acceptance (and publishers) as authors in their own right. Some female writers were able to publish anonymously (Benedikte Naubert, Dorothea Schlegel, Therese Huber), under pseudonyms (Karoline von Günderrode), or under their husbands' names (Caroline Schlegel-Schelling, Dorothea Schlegel,

Therese Huber).³⁸ Even Luise Gottsched, known as a literary figure during her lifetime, stood to a great extent in her husband's shadow and assisted him on his own projects.³⁹ Some women (Victoria von Rupp and Christiane Friederike Huber) gave themselves out to be the translators or editors of works they had in fact authored.⁴⁰ But even as translators, women did not always get credit for their labors. Henriette Herz published translations from the English under Schleiermacher's name. Henriette Schubart translated anonymously for a volume edited by Sophie Mereau-Brentano, who previously had published her own work and translations anonymously. August Wilhelm Schlegel's wife Caroline received no credit at all for her work on all or virtually all of his Shakespeare translations—a collaboration still rarely acknowledged despite the fact that Schlegel's still unsurpassed late-nineteenth-century editor and commentator Michael Bernays speaks of it at length.⁴¹ And even as late as the 1830s, Dorothea Tieck's now-canonical Shakespeare translations—service translations!—were appearing under the name of her father, Ludwig, along with those of Wolf Graf Baudissin. In a sense, this access to the world of literary activity without public acknowledgment could be only a partial fulfillment of the desire for authorship. But difficult as it was for women to enter the scene as translators, it was still easier for them to do that than to be accepted as authors in their own right. Dorothea Schlegel translated Mme. de Staël's *Corinne, ou l'Italie* and, together with Helmine von Chézy, an epistolary novel by Barbara Juliane Freiin von Krüdener. Sophie Mereau-Brentano translated the letters of Ninon de Lenclos and Boccaccio's novel *Fiammetta* (which has since been revised by others and reprinted several times), as well as publishing an adaptation of Mme. de La Fayette's *La Princesse de Clèves*.

Schlegel and Voß were themselves not quite authors in the full sense of the term, but this is not what made them service translators. Rather, they became this through their (shared, if contested) ambition to show their readers, as far as possible, the text in accordance with the original author's wishes. In matters of structure as well as content (and, in Schlegel's case, sound, voice, timbre), they took their cue from the original texts in a way that seems by no means radical today but certainly was so at the time. If we are not surprised by this development in translation, it is because we are its heirs: modern translation was born at the turn of the nineteenth century, and all good translators today work in this tradition (or have special reasons not to).

These early service translators were immediately plagued by a dilemma that continues to plague translators today: perfect translation in this mode is, strictly speaking, impossible. In one of the numerous reviews of translated books that Schlegel contributed to the journal *Allgemeine Litteratur-Zeitung* between 1796 and 1799, he wrote that

> die Aufgabe des poetischen Übersetzers ist eine ganz bestimmte, und zwar eine solche, die ins Unendliche hin nur durch Annäherung gelöst werden kann, weil er mit ganz verschiednen Werkzeugen dasselbe ausrichten soll. (SW 12:140)

> the task of the poetic translator is a quite specific one—a task that can infinitely approach its solution [but never reach it], because he is to perform the same thing with different tools.

Aspiring to achieve the "same thing with different tools" is the key to service translation. The translator's text is to reproduce the sounds, structures, and resonances of its original despite the fact that the medium in which the translator is working is a language of its own, with its own rules, structures, and cultural context and history. Clearly such a success cannot be achieved outright, but it can be approximated, and it is the closeness of the approximation that reveals the translator's skill, indeed his artistry.

That even Schlegel's translations, then, are not perfect examples of service translation lies in the nature of the task: it is a goal for the translator to strive toward, but one that can never fully be achieved. Beyond this, the specific ways in which Schlegel's translation changes the nature of Shakespeare's texts has been discussed largely in terms of his Romanticism. In his book *The Experience of the Foreign*, Antoine Berman argues that Schlegel was drawn to qualities in Shakespeare that were *already* Romantic: the Romantic ideal of poetic universality according well with the "manifold registers of his [Shakespeare's] language—rhetorical, poetic, philosophical, political, popular, etc."[42] Shakespeare, for the Romantics, stood in such salutary contrast to French-influenced classicist writing as to prompt Friedrich Schlegel, originator of the notion of "organic poetry," to ask whether the works of Shakespeare should be judged as art or as nature.[43] And, as Schlegel declared, "Nein, er ist uns nicht fremd: wir brauchen keinen Schritt aus unserm Charakter herauszugehn, um ihn 'ganz unser' nennen zu dürfen" (SW 7:38; No, he is no stranger to us: we don't have to take even a single step outside our character to be able to call him "completely ours"). Other critics, like Andreas Huyssen, emphasize the ways in which Shakespeare's plays *became* Romantic in the process of being translated into German:

> The high value placed on poetic translation seems logical only when one considers that, in the end, even a classical work must necessarily become Romantic in translation, since every poetic translation is characterized by the fundamental early-Romantic categories of progressivity and infinite approximation. He who wishes to Romanticize the world must also Romanticize—his fidelity to the letter and sense of the foreign text notwithstanding—precisely this work itself, whether it be classical or Romantic, "objective" or "interesting."[44]

On either reading, it is quite clear that the Shakespeare of Schlegel's German is no longer the same author he was in English. Shakespeare was criticized in eighteenth-century Germany for his lack of refinement in humor as well as dramatic structure,[45] and Schlegel's translation is somewhat more genteel; he toned down some of the bawdier passages, and on the whole made his lines more metrically regular.[46] To this extent, his Shakespeare really is a creature of the Romantic movement.

Schlegel's twofold approach to translation, the close approximation of the impossible task of creating sameness out of difference, is perhaps most clearly articulated in his critique of the discussion of translation in Goethe's novel *Wilhelm Meister*:

> Eine poetische Übersetzung, welche keinen von den charakteristischen Unterschieden der Form auslöschte, und "seine" [Shakespeares] Schönheiten, so viel möglich, bewahrte, ohne die Anmaßung ihm jemals anderes zu leihen; welche auch die mißfallenden Eigenheiten seines Stils, was oft nicht weniger Mühe machen dürfte, mitübertrüge, würde zwar gewiß ein Unternehmen von großen, aber in unserer Sprache nicht unübersteiglichen Schwierigkeiten sein.[47]

> A poetic translation which would not erase any of the characteristic differences of form and would preserve "his" [Shakespeare's] beauties inasfar as possible, without ever presuming to give him others; and which would also translate the displeasing characteristics of his style, which would surely often require just as much effort, would admittedly be an undertaking of great difficulty, but one whose difficulties are not unsurmountable in our language.

These remarks are apropos of the scene in Goethe's novel in which Wilhelm Meister takes it upon himself to produce a new translation of *Hamlet,* one that in his view will improve on the play by trimming some of the distracting background incidents: "äußer[e] Verhältnisse" (external matters) such as the uprising in Norway, the war against Fortinbras, and so forth. The only function of these incidents, as Goethe has Wilhelm explain, is to hold together the important scenes; they harm the unity of the play and are "höchst fehlerhaft" (gravely flawed).[48] Admittedly, *Wilhelm Meister* appeared in 1795–96 (though Goethe had begun work on an earlier version of the novel a good decade before) in a period when Goethe had only just begun to occupy himself seriously with the topic of translation. And even so, he has his Wilhelm translate faithfully in at least one sense, in the scene in which Hamlet addresses his father's ghost:

> Seine Übersetzung dieser Stelle kam ihm sehr zu statten. Er hatte sich nahe an das Original gehalten, dessen Wortstellung ihm die Verfassung eines überraschten, erschreckten, von Entsetzen ergriffenen Gemüts einzig auszudrücken schien. (MA 5:323)

> His translation of this passage served him well. He had adhered closely to the original, whose syntax seemed to him particularly well suited to express the constitution of a surprised, frightened mind gripped with horror.

At least in this one passage, Goethe's Wilhelm is a service translator who sets out to follow his original with the rigor of a Voß (whose work Goethe will, years later, cite as an important model of how to translate, as discussed in chapter 4 of this book). Admittedly, Wilhelm's application of the Voßian principles is imperfect. He translates:

> Sei du ein guter Geist, sei ein verdammter Kobold, bringe Düfte des Himmels mit dir oder Dämpfe der Hölle, sei Gutes oder Böses dein Beginnen, du kommst in so einer würdigen Gestalt, ja ich rede mit dir, ich nenne dich Hamlet, König, Vater, o antworte mir! (MA 5:322)[49]

> Be thou a spirit of health, or goblin damn'd,
> Bring with thee ayres from heauen, or blasts from hell,
> Be thy intents wicked, or charitable,
> Thou com'st in such a questionable shape,
> That I will speake to thee, Ile call thee *Hamlet*,
> King, father, royall Dane, ô answere mee
>   (*Hamlet* I:4)[50]

There are several shortcomings to Goethe/Wilhelm's translation. A range of terms (*of health, wicked, charitable*) are simplified into *good* and *evil*, and the translator circumvents the difficulty of translating both *royall* and *king* in a single line (in German *königlich* and *König*) by simply omitting the first of them. And, as Hans-Jürgen Schings notes in his commentary on the novel, Goethe preserves the mistranslation of *questionable* as *ehrwürdig* (*honorable*) introduced by Wieland in his translation, although Eschenburg's translation had meanwhile appeared with the word correctly rendered in the sense of "amenable to being questioned" (MA 5:779n). Moreover, Goethe's translation is in prose.

Schlegel's commentary is concerned not so much with the niceties of translation in this passage (beyond regretting that the translation is not in verse) as with the notion that the translator might take it upon himself to improve on a text in the process of translating it—to act, in other words, as an author. And this handful of sentences from his essay on *Wilhelm Meister* is the closest he comes—since he wrote no texts devoted specifically to translation theory—to formulating a manifesto of service translation, an approach he implicitly defended in his many reviews of others' translations and which, in large part, he practiced himself.

This approach would develop, in the early nineteenth century, into what would come to be understood as Romantic translation theory. Goethe and Wilhelm von Humboldt wrote important essays on the topic, but by far the most significant contribution to the field was made by Friedrich Schleiermacher in his series of lectures on translation.

Romantic Translation Theory

Of the works of translation theory written in German during the first two decades of the nineteenth century, three soon became canonical and are still widely read today: Schleiermacher's "Über die verschiedene Methoden des Übersetzens" ("On the Different Methods of Translating," 1813), Wilhelm von Humboldt's introduction to his translation of Aeschylus's *Agamemnon* (1816), and Goethe's note on translation from his *West-östlicher Divan* (*Western-Eastern Divan*, 1819). Of these three texts, Goethe's has been the most broadly influential. It was cited by Walter Benjamin in his seminal essay "Die Aufgabe des Übersetzers" ("The Task of the Translator"), and thus entered at least indirectly into much of the twentieth-century translation theory that came out of literary criticism. (In Douglas Robinson's 1991 *The Translator's Turn*, for example, Goethe's contribution to the field of translation is described as one of the major paradigm shifts in the German tradition—along with the work of Martin Luther and Martin Buber before and after him.) Schleiermacher's lecture on translation, on the other hand, was long neglected by critics writing in languages other than German, and it would perhaps have remained so if Lawrence Venuti had not devoted a chapter to it in *The Translator's Invisibility*. Of all the works of Romantic translation theory in German, Schleiermacher's contribution is by far the richest, as well as the most extensive. It serves well as a bridge between turn-of-the-nineteenth-century theory and the far more politicized approach to translation that has dominated, especially among English-language theorists, since the 1980s.

Schleiermacher's study posits the existence of two central, diametrically opposed approaches to translation: "Entweder der Uebersetzer läßt den Schriftsteller möglichst in Ruhe, und bewegt den Leser ihm entgegen; oder er läßt den Leser möglichst in Ruhe und bewegt den Schriftsteller ihm entgegen"[51] (Either the translator leaves the author in peace as much as possible and moves the reader toward him; or he leaves the reader in peace as much as possible and moves the writer toward him). In the first instance, the translation serves to present the work with as few alterations (paraphrases, cultural adjustments) as possible. Such a work makes no pretense to being an original text. The translator allows certain marks of foreignness to remain, both in his language use (word choice and syntax) and in details that might strike target-language readers as unfamiliar. In the second, the translator aspires to show us the work "wie es sein würde, wenn der Verfasser selbst es ursprünglich in des Lesers Sprache geschrieben hätte"[52] (as it would be had the author himself written it originally in the reader's tongue). Leaving aside the peripheral forms of translation Schleiermacher rejects outright (interpreting, paraphrase, and imitation),[53] the translator is asked to make a choice between defamiliarizing the language of the translation for the sake of the original or abandoning certain aspects of the original to facilitate its assimilation into the new linguistic and cultural context. Schleiermacher discusses both methods at length, and concludes that the former is the only truly suitable one. Schleiermacher assigned no specific name to his method of choice, but I will follow Venuti's lead throughout this book in referring to it as foreignizing translation, while keeping in mind that the term has a wider range of meaning in Venuti's own theoretical writings.

Like human beings, Schleiermacher writes, texts are shaped by the language in which they originate, and thus it is impossible to make a translated text appear native to its target language (the language into which it is being translated) without changing its nature dramatically. Such a translation would have to account for the two different histories of the original and target languages and their actual and projected influence on the shape of the text, something clearly impossible "als bis es gelungen ist durch einen künstlichen chemischen Prozeß organische Produkte zusammenzusetzen"[54] (until we have succeeded in assembling organic products through an artificial chemical process). Saying a translation is the book the author would have written had he written his book in the target language, Schleiermacher writes, is like offering to show someone the picture of a man as he would look if he had had a different father.[55] This is an understanding of texts that is both genetic and psychological. Texts are organic; they grow within the closed environment of a particular language.

The utopian part of Schleiermacher's project is "durchaus ein Verfahren im großen, ein Verpflanzen ganzer Litteraturen in eine Sprache"[56] (clearly . . . a large-scale operation, the transplanting of entire literatures into a single tongue). This massive project can succeed

THE RISE OF SERVICE TRANSLATION

only as the joint effort of many translators working in the same mode, so that the sum of their translations will give readers a sense, if indirectly, of various foreign languages. The reading public can be taught receptivity only through a large number of examples. Schleiermacher's theory could, in principle, hold for readers in any language; but he writes specifically about the Germans, who he says are so receptive to the foreign that they can be said to have a calling:

> Eine innere Nothwendigkeit, in der sich ein eigenthümlicher Beruf unseres Volkes deutlich genug ausspricht, hat uns auf das Uebersezen in Masse getrieben; wir können nicht zurükk und müssen durch.[57]

> An inner necessity, in which a peculiar calling of our people asserts itself clearly enough, has driven us to translation *en masse;* there is no turning back, we must keep forging on.

Communicating a "feeling of foreignness" in a translation means giving a sense not only of the texture of writing in that language but also of what it would mean to have grown up speaking it.[58] To accustom the reader to foreign texts is thus to engage him in a communal process of becoming more open to other cultures. When Schleiermacher valorizes certain forms of translation and criticizes others, he is thinking not only of serving the particular authors being translated but also of fostering the development of an internationally oriented cultural literacy, a sort of national aesthetic education.

Schleiermacher's theory is not highly developed with regard to its application. Whether he intended the foreignness of the translated text to pervade each of its lines, or whether the foreign elements were to be occasional reminders of the text's foreign origins, is nowhere specified. While this circumstance may be somewhat frustrating for the literary historian eager to pin down Schleiermacher's intentions, it allows the translation theorist a great deal of leeway in making use of this highly fertile material. Schleiermacher's own translations—notably of Plato—display a high degree of foreignizing language throughout, particularly with regard to syntax, yet his view of this sort of translation extended to works (such as those of Schlegel, whom he names explicitly) whose foreignizing tendency is much less pronounced.

Schleiermacher's text is the most sophisticated formulation of ser-

CHAPTER 1

vice translation, though he does not speak of translation explicitly in these terms. A side effect of his politicized understanding of translation is to remove from the process *all* authority on the translator's part. The translator in this utopian vision is subordinated not only to the author he is translating but also to the "large-scale undertaking" in which he is a participant, the transplantation of "entire literatures" into the German language. Certainly he is to make a mark on the texts he translates, but this mark is not to be his *own* authorial stamp, but rather that of the original author and the original language, both of which he counterfeits to the best of his abilities. He is to mark the text with the signs of the cultural specificity of the text it refers to—but he is not to sign his name to it. This translator is indeed to be invisible, but not quite in the Venutian sense (which will be discussed in the next section of this chapter). In Schleiermacher's vision, he will be invisible as an individual authorial personality, but as *function* (since the text is to wear the marks of its own translatedness) he will be very much in evidence. A corollary of this view is that it goes without saying that the translator must never make alterations in a text (as did so many eighteenth-century translators) to make it fit more naturally into its new cultural and linguistic surroundings. It is precisely its marks of foreignness that give the text its full value. (This is also a basic credo of post-colonial translation theory, which will also be discussed in the next section of this chapter.)

Views similar to Schleiermacher's are expressed in the note on translations included in Johann Wolfgang von Goethe's commentary to his *West-östlicher Divan* of 1819, which will be briefly introduced here and discussed at length in chapter 4. Goethe describes the history of translation as falling into three "epochs" that are both developmental and chronological: 1. the translations of Luther that seek to please the reader's ear (not necessarily in the manner of the original) and communicate a content; 2. those of the eighteenth century, in particular Wieland and the French, that address the foreignness of original texts but always bring them back to their own ground, demanding "durchaus für jede fremde Frucht ein Surrogat das auf seinem eignen Grund und Boden gewachsen sey" MA 11.1.1:263; for every foreign fruit there must be a substitute grown in their own soil (TT 61); and 3. translation "wo man die Uebersetzung dem Original identisch machen möchte, so daß eins nicht anstatt des andern, sondern an der Stelle des andern gelten solle" (MA 11.1.2:264; to achieve perfect identity with the original, so that the one does not exist *instead of* the other but *in the other's place*, TT 61, my italics). This final stage corresponds to Schleiermacher's foreignizing translation that "moves the reader toward the writer." Like Schleiermacher, Goethe speaks of the need to accustom the reading public to translation of this sort: for him as well, translation is to serve an educational function, though he does not elaborate on the aim such education would have. More explicitly than Schleiermacher, he emphasizes the extent to which foreignizing translation mediates the original for the translation's reader:

> Eine Uebersetzung die sich mit dem Original zu identificiren strebt nähert sich zuletzt der Interlinear-Version und erleichtert höchlich das Verständniß des Originals, hiedurch werden wir an den Grundtext hinangeführt, ja getrieben und so ist denn zuletzt der ganze Zirkel abgeschlossen, in welchem sich die Annäherung des Fremden und Einheimischen, des Bekannten und Unbekannten bewegt.[59]

> A translation that attempts to identify itself with the original ultimately comes close to an interlinear version and greatly facilitates our understanding of the original. We are led, yes, compelled as it were, back to the source text: the circle, within which the approximation of the foreign and the familiar, the known and the unknown constantly move, is finally complete. (TT 63)

The translation, then, is to be transparent: a medium whose purpose is to lead the reader to the "Grundtext," the ground or source text that would appear most perfectly in the (impossible) interlinear translation. This is another way of expressing what Schlegel called "performing the same thing with different tools." For both, this is an endeavor in which perfection can be infinitely approached but not achieved.

Wilhelm von Humboldt, the third important Romantic theorist of translation, differs from both Goethe and Schleiermacher in cautioning against what he sees as laboriously foreignizing translation, since

> eine Uebersetzung um so abweichender wird, je mühsamer sie nach Treue strebt. Denn sie sucht alsdann auch seine Eigenthümlichkeiten nachzuahmen, vermeidet das bloß All-

gemeine, und kann doch immer nur jeder Eigenthümlichkeit eine verschiedene gegenüberstellen.[60]

the more a translation strives toward fidelity, the more it ultimately deviates from the original, for in attempting to imitate refined nuances and avoid simple generalities it can, in fact, only provide new and different nuances. (TT 56)

A "Farbe der Fremdheit" (color of foreignness, foreign flavor) is inevitable, Humboldt writes, but the reader's awareness of the text's foreignness (*Fremdheit*) must never be allowed to distract from the experience of the foreign (*das Fremde*) that gives the text its character.[61] That is, the reader must be drawn into the world of the foreign text—one not transplanted to his own locale—without being reminded at every moment of the text's spatial, temporal, and cultural distance from the site of his reading.

An important point made by Humboldt that neither Goethe nor Schleiermacher addresses is the contribution of translation to the development of the translator's own language—not just his own linguistic skills but the whole range of possibility available to writers in this language. The translator, Humboldt writes, aids the "Erweiterung der Bedeutsamkeit und der Ausdrucksfähigkeit der eigenen Sprache"[62] (increases the expressivity and depth of meaning of one's own language; TT 56). This is to become a central issue for Walter Benjamin (though he does not cite Humboldt) in "The Task of the Translator," which will serve as a bridge between Romantic thought on translation and late-twentieth-century theory. Benjamin's essay is concerned for the most part not so much with the problems of translating particular texts as with a sense of what the practicing translator can contribute to the development of a language. For Benjamin, languages are not divergent but convergent. Despite their differences and historical circumstances, they are "einander in dem verwandt [. . .], was sie sagen wollen"[63] (interrelated in what they want to express), and it is the translator's task to bring them closer together.

The Romantic translation theorists, then, provide a fully formulated basis for drawing conclusions for translation practice from the cultural/national grounding of languages as well as texts. These theories, for which Herder was the important progenitor, themselves inspired a wide range of late-twentieth-century theories, in large part thanks to the mediation of Benjamin.

Benjamin and the Legacy of Romanticism in Twentieth-Century Translation Theory

Walter Benjamin's essay on translation was written to accompany his translations of Baudelaire's *Tableaux parisiens,* which appeared in 1923 (whereas the essay itself was probably completed in 1921). At the heart of Benjamin's essay is what he calls "die reine Sprache" (pure language). This is not some ideal notion of language before Babel but rather the infinitely remote convergence of all languages at the "messianische Ende ihrer Geschichte" (GS 4.1:14; messianic end of their history[64]). In Benjamin's understanding, the world's languages are gradually becoming more similar to one another. While their difference from one another defines them as independent systems of communication, it is a difference that cannot be upheld. This is a story not of history per se but of the history of languages (the end of *their* history). Languages will cease to exist as individual systems at the point of their mutual convergence in pure language:

> In dieser reinen Sprache, die nichts mehr meint und nichts mehr ausdrückt, sondern als ausdrucksloses und schöpferisches Wort das in allen Sprachen Gemeinte ist, trifft endlich alle Mitteilung, aller Sinn und alle Intention auf eine Schicht, in der sie zu erlöschen bestimmt sind. (4.1:19)

> In this pure language—which no longer means or expresses anything but is, as expressionless and creative Word, that which is meant in all languages—all information, all sense, and all intention finally encounter a stratum in which they are destined to be extinguished. (TT 80)

Pure language is infinitely articulated, infinitely expressive, and thus free of all ambiguity. In it, there is no longer any difference between what is meant and what is said.

The process by which the developmental vectors of individual languages converge toward one another is nothing other than the translation process seen in terms of foreignizing impulses. If the translator translates in such a way as to cause one particular language to function according to patterns typical of another, he is making a contribution to the development of his language and fulfilling the translator's "Aufgabe," his assignment or task. It is the work of the translator that causes these vectors of development to bend toward one another, and it is this bending that makes possible, in the infinitely distant (messianic) future, the convergence of all languages in pure language.

Paul de Man has noted that this conception of history and futurity is "not temporal but is the correlative of the figural pattern and the disjunctive power which Benjamin locates in the structure of language."[65] The development of language occurs over time, but for Benjamin it is not this temporality that is important but rather the mechanisms (such as translation) through which this development takes place. De Man's understanding of Benjamin's use of the word history in this context, affirming the mechanisms implied in the "disjunctive power," ought to have precluded his much remarked-on misreading of the word *Aufgabe* in the sense of "giving up."[66] Reading this pun into Benjamin's argument, de Man emphasizes the impossibility of the translator ever producing a perfect translation, a classically Romantic concern, though not a problem Benjamin addresses.[67] De Man appears to consider the development of languages through translation something that happens naturally, of its own accord ("Pure language is perhaps more present in the translation than in the original"[68]), rather than something that must be made to happen by the translator working with particular attention to the differences between languages, and which may fail to occur should the *translator* not go about his *task* in the proper way. Benjamin's conception of "pure language" as the eventual, projected product of the translator's labors is influenced by Rudolf Pannwitz's *Die Krise der europäischen Kultur*, which calls for the translator to work actively to make his language "suffer the shock of the foreign language" and "widen and deepen his language through the foreign one" (TT 8).

In Benjamin's understanding of translation and of the translator's task, the key to the convergence of languages lies in the use of syntactical patterns unfamiliar in the translator's language. Benjamin does not explicitly spell out the line of reasoning on which this position is based, but it can be inferred from other parts of his argument. Early in his essay he speaks of the phenomenon Schleiermacher calls the *Irrationalität* of language: the lack of identity between corresponding elements of different languages (which also recalls Leibniz's observation "daß wohl keine Sprache in der Welt sey, die ander Sprachen Worte jedesmahl mit gleichem Nachdruck und auch mit einem Worte geben könne"[69] [that there is surely no language in the world that can reproduce the words of other languages in every case with the same emphasis in a single word]). Thus, in Benjamin's example, we should be conscious of the discrepancies between the German word *Brot* and the French *pain*: "das Gemeinte [ist] zwar dasselbe, die Art, es zu meinen, dagegen nicht" (GS 4.1:14; As to the intended object . . . the two words mean the very same thing [but] the modes of intention in these two words are in conflict[70]). The difference is largely one of cultural context, the fact that the Frenchman and the German, hearing their respective words for bread, can be expected to have a number of overlapping but by no means coextensive associations. Since these cultural associations belong to a history that is constitutive of language use in any particular context, it is not possible for them to be altered, that is, for individual words to be approximated further to one another. What is—at least in theory—flexible in a language is the way individual words are joined together in grammatical structures: the way in which, for example, the Frenchman will say "le pain de mon père" (the bread of my father), whereas an American has a choice between this form and a preceding possessive: "my father's bread." These structures are fixed by convention and linguistic history, but not, perhaps, by necessity. Does the fact that one cannot now say "my father's bread" with that syntax in French mean that one will never be able to do so? To approximate one language to another, for Benjamin, is to import such structures gradually. Pure language, which resides in the messianic future because it can never be achieved as such, represents the moment at which all languages embrace the structures of all others, when it is only the individual words that differ. But will not these, too, then come to resemble one another, to become each other? Languages become more alike not by shedding levels of complexity, the particular structures that shape their linguistic character, but by exporting these structures while importing others—in other words, by becoming increasingly complex and thus increasingly expressive. Pure language is the opposite of Esperanto.

The key image in Benjamin's essay is that of an arcade:

Die wahre Übersetzung ist durchscheinend, sie verdeckt nicht das Original, steht ihm nicht im Licht, sondern läßt die reine Sprache, wie verstärkt durch ihr eigenes Medium, nur um so voller aufs Original fallen. Das vermag vor allem Wörtlichkeit in der Übertragung der Syntax und gerade sie erweist das Wort, nicht den Satz als das Urelement des Übersetzers. Denn der Satz ist die Mauer vor der Sprache des Originals, Wörtlichkeit die Arkade. (GS 4.1:18)

True translation is translucent; it does not conceal the original, does not block the light from falling upon it, but allows pure language—as if intensified though its own medium—to shine upon the original all the more fully. This may be achieved, above all, by a literal rendering of the syntax, which proves the word rather than the sentence to be the primary element [Urelement] of the translator. For the sentence is the wall before the language of the original, and literalness is the arcade.[71]

When Benjamin writes that the *word*, not the *sentence*, is the true medium of the translator, he is thinking not so much of isolated words (such as *Brot* or *pain*), but of words in context. (We should remember that the word *Wort* in German can also mean a brief utterance of more than one individual word: a phrase.) Paul de Man notes an opposition in Benjamin between the words *Wort* and *Satz* that parallels the one between *letter* and *word*; in each case, the smaller unit does not contain a portion of the meaning of the whole.[72]

For Benjamin, translation as it is usually understood is like a wall constructed in front of the original that blocks it from view. Eighteenth-century translation is opaque; it presents a surface parallel to that of its original and covers it over. The original can become visible only when gaps have been made in the outer wall of the translation, and this, for Benjamin, can happen only by means of syntactical structures taken over from the language of the original that serve to disrupt the surface of the translation. Through the spaces made by these ruptures or gaps, bits of the original can be glimpsed, just as one can see the back wall of an arcade or covered sidewalk from the street by looking through the spaces between the arches that only partially screen it from view. The arcade is a useful metaphor for Benjamin, in that its regular pattern of supporting structures with empty space in between can be compared to the view of a sentence as a series of linked structures (phrases and clauses). It also suggests that the reader of the translated sentence will experience the text of the translation much the same way as the flaneur experiences a particular street.[73]

"Pure language" enters into Benjamin's metaphor of the translation as an arcade in the form of a light source: "True translation is translucent; it does not conceal the original, does not block the light from falling upon it, but allows pure language—as if intensified through its own medium—to shine upon the original all the more fully." The same gaps in the syntactical structure of the translation that allow the observer (reader) to glimpse portions of the original text make it possible for the rays of light emanating from pure language (as from a sort of stylized sun) to penetrate through to the original. This metaphor reveals the inaccuracy of de Man's suggestion that "pure language is perhaps more present in the translation than in the original."[74] Pure language is not a quality of language but a relational construct: it is the marker of congruence between languages, it illuminates syntactical parallels.

Paradoxically, Benjamin's own translations of Baudelaire are not good examples of the sort of translation he advocates. They display Benjamin's own skill as a poet far better than they do any great concern for the syntax of Baudelaire's lines. This is surprising in view of the fact that this essay was published as an introduction to his translations, but not when one considers that Benjamin's essay is finally more concerned with the development of the German language than with the desire to have good translations of particular works into German. (Benjamin, the translator of Baudelaire, intent on how best to convey in German the nature of the poems he loved, was perhaps not quite the same thinker who stepped back from these translations to gain the theoretician's distance.) Yet one reason why Benjamin's essay has had such an impact on later generations of translators and translation theorists alike is precisely because his comments on translation are of such great practical use, whether or not they were so intended.

Consider, for example, a recent essay by poet and translator Christopher Middleton entitled "Translation as a Species of Mime":

> For a mime, the key to his performance is the rhythm of his breathing (as for a dancer). The rhythm of his breathing is the ghostly system through which his essential image is channeled, to become the dynamic of his gestures, his indi-

CHAPTER 1

vidual body articulated as motion. For the translator, this breathing is *the syntax which makes the words ring true*. Without the right syntax, even the rightest words can lack appropriate bonding.[75]

Middleton goes on to invoke Benjamin's notion of the aura (something pertaining, in this context, to an original text and largely lost in translation) as part of his explanation of why the translator, translating, must—through syntax—exaggerate the style of the original: "It is precisely the distance of the numinous that calls for the hyperbolic gestures." Middleton's comments on syntax as a key tool of translation point back to Benjamin, who was, to my knowledge, the first translation theorist to write explicitly of syntax. Schleiermacher, though his theory would seem to require this, does not. In a sense, then, Benjamin has, intentionally or not, filled in the gaps of Schleiermacher's theory: he takes it to the logical conclusion that makes it relevant to the practical work of translators for whom Schleiermacher's utopian goals might seem foreign indeed. "Translate with attention to syntax so as to give a better sense of the original text" is a more practical directive for a translator than "leave the writer where he is and move the reader toward him."

It is curious that, given the concerns of his essay, Benjamin should invoke as his acknowleged model not Schleiermacher or Humboldt but Goethe. Benjamin's ideas on translation, however, do not so much follow those of Goethe as revise them. Where Goethe writes that the aim of translation of the third epoch is to *put itself in the place* of the original (which might invite comparison with the metaphor of the wall in Benjamin's model of undesirable translation), Benjamin redefines what being in the place of the original might consist of. Certainly he emphasizes not only that one word can never fully be replaced by the corresponding element of another language but also that the words of a translation have a different relation to the text's subject matter than do those of an original: the words of the original, he writes, are the organic complement of its sense, like the flesh and rind of a fruit, while the language of a translation is draped around its content like royal robes (GS 4.1; TT 76). It is this pair of metaphors that inspires some of the most illuminating reflections in Jacques Derrida's essay "Des tours de Babel." These metaphors, or "A-metaphors," as he calls them (with "A" suggesting both "amphore" and "ammétaphore"),[76] point to the

THE RISE OF SERVICE TRANSLATION

difference between nature and art; it is by means of the latter that the sense, the naked body of the king, is concealed from view.[77] On Derrida's reading (itself a sort of "translation," as he asserts at several junctures), Benjamin's essay tells the story of a translation in which what is at stake is "neither reception nor communication nor representation"[78] but a series of transactions, a debt/responsibility, which the translator's work is an attempt (inevitably imperfect!) to repay.[79] Finally, the key work of translation is theological: it is in the translation of the Holy Scripture that the perfect union of word and sense—meaning that does not mean anything beyond the specific speech act, as in prophecy, in other words "pure language"—is reached.[80] And it is this emphasis on interlinear translation as an ideal that points back through Benjamin's text on translation to that of Goethe.

Like Benjamin, Antoine Berman, writing in the 1980s, takes the theses of the Romantic translation theorists as the basis for a moral imperative of translation. For Berman, the translator's responsibility is not, as for Benjamin, that of a shaper of his native tongue, but rather that of one in a position to offer resistance to the violence inherent in the translation act itself. Translation, for Berman, is situated at the crossroads of the "appropriationary and reductionary injunction" (the tendency of one culture to assimilate or domesticate the works of others) and the "ethical aim" of making it "an opening, a dialogue, a crossbreeding, a decentering".[81] Thus Berman reiterates Schleiermacher's desire to see the translator function as a cultural mediator, a go-between whose aim is to unite cultures rather than erase their difference.

Through the mediation of Benjamin's essay, Goethe's notes on translation have become influential in late-twentieth-century thought on translation. In *The Translator's Turn*, Douglas Robinson reads Goethe's text through Benjamin's notion of languages progressing to the messianic end of their history and conflates Goethe's idea of the translated text striving to occupy the same place as its original with Benjamin's pure language, which will come to exist the moment all languages occupy the same position.[82] This conflation is not entirely accurate; Benjamin, unlike Goethe, is concerned more with the translator's contribution to the development of language per se than with the successful translation of a particular work. But it is nevertheless true that Benjamin and Goethe have a very similar notion of progress: striving toward the infinitely distant goal of being able to express in one language precisely what has been expressed in another. In fact, the all-encompassing nature of Benjamin's "pure language" makes it akin to Goethe's "Weltliteratur." For Robinson, both Benjamin's and Goethe's projects have a redemptive aspect: the translator's task is to undo the damage done at Babel.

The most productive reflection of Romantic translation theory in the late twentieth century appears in Lawrence Venuti's book *The Translator's Invisibility*, in which Venuti considers the historical tendency of the aesthetic communities of certain languages (notably English and French, both of which have a strong colonial tradition) to discourage translations that bear, syntactically or in other ways, the mark of their translatedness. For the translation not to look like a translation, the translator must become invisible—hence the book's title. This "invisibility" is a condition against which the translator must struggle, both for the sake of his own work and artistry, and to preserve and support the less dominant cultures in whose demise he would otherwise be guilty of collaborating. Translation thus plays an integral role in the phenomenon of globalization and as such has the potential to be either beneficial or detrimental to cultures lacking the basis for global domination. Venuti's translator, practicing his art, is a political activist: his foreignizing translation strategies disrupt the target language reader's reception of the translated text, making it impossible to misconstrue the text's status as foreign body in the target-language culture. By dovetailing his discussion of translation strategies with that of the political context in which the translator's work is performed, Venuti fills out and extends the political ramifications implied in Schleiermacher, whom he credits as the first theoretical proponent of the foreignizing impulse in translation.

Related lines of thought have been explored by translation theorists working with post-colonial approaches.[83] Though it is rare for Romantic theory to be evoked explicitly in these works, even in passing—references to Benjamin are far more frequent—they belong to the same group of arguments, which they update to account for a late-twentieth-century political context. Gayatri Chakravorty Spivak, in her important essay "The Politics of Translation" (1993), has warned of the dangers inherent in the project of foreignizing if the translator is not up to all aspects of her task:

> [D]epth of commitment to correct cultural politics, felt in the details of personal life, is sometimes not enough. The

history of the language, the history of the author's moment, the history of the language-in-and-as-translation, must figure in the weaving as well.[84]

In a move that recalls Scheiermacher's desire to have the language of the translation communicate the language and world in which the work originated, Spivak warns of the risks of producing "a sort of with-it translatese, so that the literature by a woman in Palestine begins to resemble, in the feel of its prose, something by a man in Taiwan."[85] Doing it right is not impossible—a "right" that is utterly individual, one that must be sought out, learned anew for every project of every translator—but it is difficult, even more so, Spivak's descriptions suggest, than many translators can bear to imagine. But of course it stands to reason that in the project of communicating to a foreign audience the nature not only of a people, a culture, but also of an individual writer at an individual "moment," the stakes are high. "Doing it right" is also at issue in Kwame Anthony Appiah's "Thick Translation" (1993), which calls for a mode of translation that will include (if necessary with the help of footnotes and annotations) the information needed to "locate the text in a rich cultural and linguistic context"—in short, to "preserve for us the features that make it [the translated text] worth teaching."[86] This emphasis on the pedagogical aspect of the translator's task again recalls Schleiermacher's "large-scale undertaking." Appiah's definition is so acute because it takes into account the different sorts of demands that will (and should) be made on literary translations, depending both on where the language and culture of the original text stand in relation to those of the translation and on what the important features of the original text are: is it Joyce's "Jabberwocky," a work of philosophy, or a collection of Akan proverbs? "There is," Appiah insists, "no definite set of desiderata,"[87] only the hope that the translator's work will display resourcefulness, cultural sensitivity, and sound pedagogical instincts.

These ideas are situated in a broader context of translation theory in Tejaswini Niranjana's *Siting Translation: History, Post-Structuralism, and the Colonial Context*, a powerful study of the ways in which the practice and phenomenon of translation remain inextricable from the complex of issues surrounding the legacy of colonial domination, as translation conventionally "depends on the Western philosophical notions of reality, representation, and knowledge. Reality is seen as something unproblematic, 'out there'; knowledge involves a representation of this reality; and representation provides direct, unmediated access to a transparent reality."[88] Investigating the role of historical consciousness in Benjamin's work on translation and the responses to this work by de Man and Derrida, Niranjana is left doubting the suitability of deconstruction to address political issues, leading her to call for new, more critical approaches to translation theory and to translations that "attempt to deconstruct [essentialist anti-colonial narratives], to show their complicity with the master-narrative of imperialism."[89]

The issues discussed by Venuti, Spivak, Appiah, and Niranjana, as well as others such as Harish Trivedi, Susan Bassnett, and Maria Tymoczko—the location of power in the translation act, what it means for one language to be replaced by another one that has perhaps greater international influence, the loss of both individual and national voices in translation, and possibilities for establishing more benign modes of translation that respect and further the multiplicity of voices—can reasonably be said to constitute the cutting edge of thought on translation. There is no doubt that translation studies, to maintain its legitimacy as an intellectual enterprise, must address these problems and seek to propose at least tentative measures for remedying the wrongs it discovers. This is the task of the translation theorist for the dawn of the twenty-first century.

The role that the present volume has to play in this larger project is one of establishing a historical background for this theoretical work, tracing the roots of these newly spotlighted issues back to origins that have not yet been adequately studied. Because this work requires the examination of individual translators and translations, my approach here will be largely philological, but always with an eye to how these analyses fit into the larger context of a historical development with its attendant issues.

The most important point of reference for my notions of service and authorial translation is Venuti's concept of foreignizing, as discussed at the beginning of this chapter, particularly as it applies to the work of individual translators working in the context of a given literary establishment. While one might be tempted to suppose the practice of authorial translation would best serve to emancipate the translator from the status quo, this is not necessarily the case. Foreignizing translation, originally the invention of translators who were decidedly *not* authorial in their approach, serves to emancipate the work of the foreign-language author vis-à-vis the fixed literary standards associated with the target language into which his work is being translated. The translator who achieves this emancipation in the author's name is simultaneously asserting his own presence (by means of non-conformist language use in his own language) and erasing it (by allowing the original work to speak as directly as possible to the reader of the translation, minimizing the act of mediation). Foreignizing and service translation thus intersect but do not coincide. Foreignizing translation in the strictest sense, the bending of one language to account for the characteristics of another, is the single most important technique available to the service translator, whose voice, however, will be shaped by other factors as well, such as fidelity to aspects of the original text *not* determined by its original language: the author's particular stylistic traits, use of metaphor, allusion, and so forth, that is, the attributes that together make the text "worth teaching."

The authorial translator, on the other hand, is likewise asserting his own presence (at the expense of the foreign author). Is he also playing into the hands of the literary establishment, and thus, implicitly, the social/cultural/political/economic establishment that surrounds him? In the case of eighteenth-century translation, this was certainly true, but in the work of the post-1800 translators to be examined in the following chapters, the matter is far from clear-cut. In each of these instances, the authorial interventions—in fact, subversive acts—seem more likely to shock the reading public than to fulfill its expectations. In any case, the nineteenth-century authorial translators whose work will be discussed here practiced foreignizing translation, just as did, for the most part, the service translators who preceded them.

SERVICE TRANSLATION: A SUMMATION

Romantic translation, then, both in theory and practice, can be characterized as service translation. It was also very much a product of Romantic thought, part of Friedrich Schlegel's quintessentially Romantic project of *Universalpoesie* (universal poetry) whose goal was to unite all disciplines and all genres: "Poesie und Prosa, Genialität und Kritik, Kunstpoesie und Naturpoesie" (poetry and prose, genius and criticism, art poetry and nature poetry).[90] Romantic translation shared in the universalizing impulse behind this enterprise, which by its very nature could be always only a work in progress, never an achieved goal, and it played an important role in the assimilation of Dante, Boccaccio, Cer-

CHAPTER 1

vantes, Shakespeare, and Calderón into the Romantic canon as ready-made literary forebears. If these foreign writers were to inspire a new generation of Romantic artists, their work had to be made available in German translations that gave a clearer sense of the nature of their texts than had been the case in eighteenth-century translation. For the Romantics, developing new methods of translation was an important consequence of the desire for literary cross-pollination.

At the same time, it must be remembered that service translation was from its beginnings a goal, not a product. Every translation involves some degree of interpretation, and every act of interpretation carries consequences. As Foucault has taught us, the one who controls meaning controls power—especially when the meaning thus "controlled" is taken to be objective. Hence, as Vincent Crapanzano has pointed out in his fascinating double study of religious fundamentalism and judicial constitutionalism in the United States, one finds an obsession with the notion of literalism in both the religious and the legal spheres. Although even the most "literalist" reading of an original text clearly involves interpretation of some sort, it is clear that substantially more moral authority can be claimed for a text that is at least ostensibly *not* the product of interpretation. The most potent power is that which is exercised surreptitiously. An interpreted law or a translated Bible passage has the greatest power if those subject to them believe they can be taken at face value. No one trusts a fun house mirror, but what if you could convince people that what they are seeing is a mirror free of distortion, one that shows the truth?

Yet service translation remains in most cases the best shot we have at gaining access to works written in a language we do not understand. As Venuti has pointed out, foreignizing translation remains a much-beleaguered enterprise. But with translations whose prose bears the marks of cultural otherness (or is suspected of doing so) often lambasted as "translatorese," regardless of actual quality and above all in the languages with the strongest colonial tradition behind them (English and French),[91] service translation has firmly established itself as the gold standard. In the English-language tradition, this did not take place until the final decades of the twentieth century. (Before this, many were still translating like Helen Lowe-Porter, who, though she performed a great service to many readers with her many translations, is famous for chopping Thomas Mann's long sentences into bite-sized bits.) Now that it is established, service translation is a tradition that

42

will be difficult to shake; it will surely remain as a standard to be transcended, sidestepped, riffed on, but always returned to.

Just as contemporary translation theory has been shaped by Romantic thought on translation, our practical sense of what comprises a good translation is part of the twentieth century's Romantic legacy. The idea that what we do when we translate is to attempt to replace every part of the original text with something written in a new language that corresponds to the original as closely as possible in both form and content, and that takes into account the structural and cultural differences between the languages in question, may now seem too obvious to warrant discussion (though how exactly this principle translates into practice remains a difficult point). It is, however, a conception of translation (and of text) that could not have existed before the advent of ideas like Herder's "Der Genius der Sprache ist auch der Genius von der Literatur einer Nation" and "Das Wort erzeugt den Gedanken" (The spirit of language is also the spirit of the literature of a nation; the word produces the thought).[92] The understanding of words as constitutive (and not merely expressive) of meaning, the belief that national difference is, among other things, a linguistic phenomenon—these were the preconditions for the views on translation developed by Goethe, Humboldt, and Schleiermacher, and they remain central two hundred years later.

Does service translation—the rise of the "invisible" translator, in Venuti's terms—anticipate the "death of the author," which Roland Barthes was to proclaim in 1968? Paradoxically, yes and no. For Barthes, the author's demise consists in the realization that all writing is, in a sense, copywork, that every text is "made of multiple writings, drawn from many cultures and into mutual relations of dialogue, parody, contestation," a multiplicity that is focussed not in the author but in the reader.[93] This recalls Novalis's utterly Romantic claim "Am Ende ist alle Poesie Übersetzen" (In the end, all poetry is translation)—originality is an illusion.[94] Like the Barthesian author, the service translator is a link in the chain of intertextual history. For Barthes, however, the author's absence from the text is a matter of structural necessity, not conscious choice on the part of the writing subject (which could hardly be construed as that which elects its own absence). The translator-author withdraws actively, as it were, from the translated text—an exercise of authority, and one that arguably requires more artistry than does "presence." The service translator, by standing back from the text, would make the original author appear to be the author in the Foucauldian sense of the one responsible for it ("Texts, books, discourse, really began to have authors . . . to the degree to which the author could be punished"[95])—but in fact this denial of authority is tricky. The *fatwa* that targeted Salman Rushdie's translators as well as the author himself after the publication of *The Satanic Verses* held the translators jointly responsible for the text's contents—yet no one would identify the book's content as having *arisen* in the translation process. The balance of relative authority between original author and translator is further complicated in the case of authorial translation.

Authorial Translators in the Early Nineteenth Century

As has been demonstrated in the preceding sections, there was a long tradition in German of translators who altered the texts they translated to suit their own tastes or the presumed tastes of their readers. But this sort of translation is far removed from the work of the great authorial translators that will be examined in the following chapters. Admittedly, both sorts involve deviations from the original text. But it was only after the establishment of service translation as a norm that the encroachment on the "authority" of the original authors by these authorial translators—intentional, carefully orchestrated interventions that constantly returned to the baseline of service translation—became possible in this form. Only after it became a standard expectation for translators to strive to make their work "the same" did it become interesting—as a specifically aesthetic endeavor undertaken to achieve some particular end—to make it different. While the lack of fidelity in eighteenth-century translation was coincidental and unremarkable, in the nineteenth century it became a matter of art. Thus, while none of the translator-authors examined in detail in this book are Romantics, strictly speaking, all three are indebted to the work of the Romantic translators who preceded them. It is only against the backdrop of this earlier work that their achievements can properly be judged.

These three translator-authors are anomalies, exceptions. The majority of their contemporaries who translated did so in a service mode. Thus, they do not constitute a "development" in translation history, much less a movement. Their work as translators was as individual as their work as authors, and it is difficult to say whether or not, as translators, they engendered literary heirs. If they did, these, too, will be anomalous, at best related to, say, the twentieth-century practice of writers producing "imitations" of foreign-language texts, in which the original serves largely as a springboard for a text of the "copyist's" own (such as those by poet Robert Lowell). But the important characteristic for defining these "authorial" translator-authors is that the work they produce *is* for the most part a model of service translation. They play with our expectations, giving us the original author's text seemingly just as it was in the original, but in each case decisively, subversively skewed.

As will be apparent in my analyses of these works, translation theory and actual translations are often as not at odds with one another, even when they have the same authors. This has never been truer than now, when the branches of theory associated with translation studies (there are many) have become so diverse as to support dozens of journals, university press book series, half a dozen academic organizations, and a handful of internet discussion forums. Translation theory concerns itself with linguistics, with training simultaneous interpreters, with theological questions relevant to Bible translation, with issues of national identity and cultural specificity, not to mention feminism, post-colonialism, deconstruction, psychoanalysis, and aesthetics. Very little of this is of much use to the translator laboring at her desk a week before deadline—in the short term, that is. In the longer term, translation theory is invaluable to the translator who sees her craft as existing within an intellectual, as well as literary, historical context. There may be no one right way to translate, but there are innumerable wrong ways, and translation theory allows us a more explicable basis than intuitive aesthetic commonsense for talking about the choices we make. Translation theory is also a useful testing ground for ways of talking about literature in general, particularly about how writing (and thinking about writing) is affected by cultural, social, historical, and political circumstances. Translation is a form of reading that leaves a particularly durable trace: the written translation serves as a record of how one highly engaged reader has encountered a text. It is, as Spivak has written, the most *intimate* act of reading.[96] In the analyses that follow, the translations of three highly talented readers as well as writers will offer lessons of their own, not only in translation but also in reading itself.

2
The Translation as a Doppelgänger: *Amphitryon* by Molière and Kleist

Heinrich von Kleist's *Amphitryon: Ein Lustspiel nach Molière* (*A Comedy After Molière*) is not a translated text on every page, but it differs from eighteenth-century adaptations in that the vast majority of the text—almost all of the first two acts—is a work of extreme service-translation fidelity, rendering the sense, tone, and cadence of Molière's lines with exceptional accuracy. The *nach* of its title implies not only "in the manner of" or "in imitation of" Molière, but also *Amphitryon* in a post-Molièrean, post-Enlightenment age, when the comedy of manners has ceased to be a socially relevant form, and Kleist's text is marked throughout by a multivalent ambiguity. On the one hand a model of the most faithful translation, it turns radically away from the authorial intent expressed in Molière's *Amphitryon: Comédie,* and thus it is exceptionally well suited for examination as a work of authorial translation.

Molière's 1668 interpretation of the Amphitryon myth assumes a basic equilibrium in the state of the world. Prank-playing gods can knock things out of kilter—as Jupiter, out of lust for the virtuous Alcmena, assumes the guise of her husband, Amphitryon—but the humans in their hands are, finally, in good hands, and order can always be restored. The play concludes with a grand spectacle of resolution, with Jupiter explaining his ruse and promising compensation for any harm done. In Kleist's play (written most likely in 1803 and published in 1807),[1] the potential of the gods to do unintended harm—not to mention the chaos explicitly planned by Jupiter—is far greater, and at the end of the play there is a strong sense that very little has been put to rights. Alcmena, rather than being whisked off stage as in Molière, is placed, explosively, at the center of the action. By the time Jupiter has given his final address and the curtain drops, she has been restored to her legal husband, but with what may prove to be grave psychological damage (the play ends before the full consequences of her disorientation become apparent, leaving the spectator free to fear the worst). Meanwhile, Amphitryon himself has been severely rattled in his sense of personal identity. In short, Molière's *Amphitryon* has become, in Kleist's hands, a play very much as Kleist might have written it *without* the use of Molière's text as a template, and as such it challenges the primacy of Molière's play as original text. A more complete appropriation is hardly imaginable.

To avoid confusion in the discussion that follows, the word *translation* will be used to refer only to those lines of Kleist's play that have direct antecedents in Molière's text, even if they are significantly transformed in their new contexts. Otherwise I will speak of the *adaptation* of individual passages and scenes. In these terms, Kleist's play is an adaptation of Molière's play that includes a translation of most of it. Molière's play is itself an adaptation of a work by Plautus (inspired in part by Rotrou's 1636 adaptation, *Les Sosies*), but Molière is not to Plautus as Kleist is to Molière. The difference lies in the nature of the critical distance Kleist brings to Molière's text. Not content merely to update or modernize the older work, he creates an adaptation capable of standing beside its original as a subversive double, a model of an anti-classicist aesthetic. My analysis will address the ways in which Kleist used his translation as a tool to serve his own aesthetic, literary, political, and philosophical ends, and how he was able, by the most subtle shifts in the lines he translated, to produce scenes that seem far less the work of Molière and far more his own.

In particular I will be tracing a thematic strand that, though already present in embryonic form in Molière's play, is far more developed in Kleist's version. Kleist took advantage of the elements of the original that are suggestive of a crisis of identity and expanded them radically to create a play whose thematic concerns are very much in keeping with the body of Kleist's own work: the contingency of indi-

THE TRANSLATION AS A DOPPELGÄNGER

vidual identity and experience and the impossibility of certain knowledge of either oneself or the world. If the experience of being doubled, shared by the characters Sosia and Amphitryon in both these plays, immediately raises questions of individuality and originality, the further doubling of these doubles in the translation process gives the chain of copy/original relationships a vertiginous aspect. Kleist's Jupiter is far removed indeed from Molière's Amphitryon. The relationship of German copy to French original is further complicated by Kleist's use of intertexts foreign to Molière's play: a Plautus adaptation by Johann Daniel Falk, and Sophocles' *Oedipus Rex*, for Kleist the ultimate urtext of the crisis of self-identity and knowledge. In his adaptation of a work that presents divine figures wandering about the stage as copies of all-too-mortal originals, Kleist offers us a work that invites reading as an allegory of translation, one in fact that would seem to assert the primacy of the translation over the original text.

BACKGROUND: THE PRE-STORY OF AMPHITRYON

The Amphitryon myth was already subject to various reworkings in classical times. The basic story line is simple: Jupiter (or Zeus) desires the mortal woman Alcmena, who is renowned not only for her beauty but also for her devotion to her husband, Amphitryon. To enjoy her favors, the god transforms himself into a replica of the absent Amphitryon, leading to confusion and eventually confrontation when the real husband returns. Nine months later Alcmena gives birth to twins, the human child Iphicles and the half-god Heracles (Hercules). Of the various (lost) Greek dramatizations of the myth whose existence is recorded, all are tragedies and recount not only Jupiter's visit to Alcmena in the guise of Amphitryon, but also the birth of Heracles. Aeschylus, Euripides, Sophocles, Accius, and Hesiod all wrote dramatic versions of the story, the first two even focusing on Alcmena as protagonist. Hesiod's version turned on what Peter Szondi has described as a "tragic dialectic": before Amphitryon can receive Alcmena's hand in marriage, he must go off to battle to avenge the murder of her brothers; his consequent absence makes her accessible to Jupiter.[2] That the other Greek Amphitryon plays were also written as tragedies is not surprising: Amphitryon and Alcmena are of noble birth and thus are poorly suited to serve as comic figures by classical standards, and a comic prelude to a dignified occasion such as the birth of Heracles would have been equally inappropriate. The one extant Roman version by Plautus, which dates from 200 BC, introduces a comic strand to the play, doubling Amphitryon's replacement by Jupiter with that of his manservant, Sosias, by the lesser god Mercury. But nowhere are the burlesque skits involving Sosias and his double allowed to affect the tone of the tragic scenes which dominate.[3]

By the seventeenth century, however, even aristocrats were considered fair game for writers of comedy, which led to a reframing of the tale. In Peter Szondi's analysis of the Amphitryon myth, the birth of Heracles is tragic, while the night of his conception is comic. Molière's play, which includes only the latter, is framed as a comedy, as is Rotrou's 1636 *Les Sosies*, which was known to both Molière and Kleist. These comedies of manners poke fun at Amphitryon's cuckoldry; the gods are tricksters, Amphitryon has been their dupe. In Molière's version, despite the moments of serious confusion on Amphitryon's part, the play has a happy ending: a scene of divine revelation in which Jupiter identifies himself as Amphitryon's imposter, declares that no serious harm has been done ("Un partage avec Jupiter / N'a rien du tout qui déshonore"[4] [Sharing with Jupiter / In no way dishonors]) and announces the birth of Heracles.

Kleist's adaptation, its subtitle notwithstanding, is a return to a more classical tragic treatment of the story. Like both Plautus's and Molière's plays, Kleist's is split between tragic and comic plot strands involving two parallel sets of characters: the aristocratic and servant couples. But Kleist deviates from Molière in eschewing the final gestures that diffuse the play's tragic development and return the action to the realm of comedy. And his play, unlike that of Plautus, derives the tragic tone of its conclusion not from the triumphal celebration of a hero's birth, but from the final traumatic confrontation between Amphitryon and Jupiter. Generically, Kleist's play can be understood as a tragicomedy, though it differs from twentieth-century tragicomedies like Samuel Beckett's *En attendant Godot* (*Waiting for Godot*) in that Kleist does not so much write scenes that are simultaneously comic and tragic as knit together discrete comic and tragic plot strands. Each tragic scene of Amphitryon's humiliation is echoed by the buffoonery of Sosias's interactions with Mercury and Charis. But the tragic mode dominates his final act, subverting the comic expectations established at the play's outset. By replacing Molière's tidy resolution with a final scene marked by the most profound ambiguity, Kleist signals his distance from Molière in terms that extend from aesthetics to politics to historical context to worldview. His adaptation corrects and improves on its original, resulting in a play that is very much, as Goethe said of it, "das seltsamste Zeichen der Zeit" (the strangest sign of the times).

Yet Kleist's play certainly deserves consideration as a translation of Molière's. For the first two acts of the play, Kleist generally adheres quite closely to Molière's text. Each of the five scenes of his first act corresponds directly to one in Molière's play, and the same is true for the first three scenes of act 2. But Molière's scenes 2.4 and 2.5 are replaced by a completely new 2.4 in Kleist's text, and only parts of Molière's 2.6 and 2.7 survive in Kleist's 2.5 and 2.6. Many of the scenes Kleist retains from Molière's play reveal a willingness on the translator's part to reshape the material as he sees fit. Parts of them are restructured, and speeches are shifted to different contexts, trimmed, expanded, or in some cases replaced outright. Yet other passages show Kleist's skill at capturing the mood and cadence of Molière's individual lines, making it clear that the deviations from the original text are in no way motivated by an inability to reproduce the French lines accurately in German.

The readings of Kleist's translation process to be pursued in the pages that follow are speculative. They cannot be otherwise, since the manuscript of Kleist's translation is lost, and there are no indications of how many drafts the translation went through, whether it was revised extensively (or at all), and, if so, whether these revisions changed the relationship of the translation to the original text. The fact that Kleist adheres much more closely to Molière's French near the beginning of the play suggests that he initially set out to produce a more traditional translation of the play, and only in the course of working on it realized that what he really wanted was to present this material as his own.

Translation as Revision

It would be difficult to construct any sort of catalog of the structural and stylistic similarities and discrepancies between Kleist's and Molière's versions of *Amphitryon* without, at the same time, documenting the shift in thematic focus. On the level of local changes within individual lines, the translation already displays the same shifts in emphasis that Kleist will execute with broader strokes in the new scenes he writes in preparation for his new ending. It is as if he is revising Molière's material to serve the ends he himself has in mind for it. These authorial shifts are evident even in the passages where Kleist follows

Molière's rhetorical patterns the most closely. My examples here are drawn from the scene which displays the highest proportion of translated lines to passages of adaptation: the second act of scene 1, in which Sosias is on his way to announce to Alcmena (in Molière, Alcmène; in Kleist, Alkmene) Amphitryon's imminent return from battle. Sosias is intercepted by Mercury, who proceeds to bully him with both psychological and physical force until Sosias is willing to accept Mercury's claim that it is he, Mercury, who is in fact Amphitryon's manservant Sosias. Through a series of slight changes, Kleist sharpens the characterization of Sosias, making him appear even more timorous, even more distressed than in Molière's scene, and at the same time making Mercury appear as a more threatening force.

Sosias's loquacity, for example, is well served by the longer lines employed by Kleist—lines that disqualify much of his text as service translation in the strictest sense. The French play is written primarily in iambic tetrameter, with some trimeter and pentameter lines. Molière rhymes in irregular patterns, favoring *abab* and *abba* schemes, and often rhyming in units of as many as six lines. Kleist's translation rhymes only occasionally, in what Thomas Mann called "the rhyme of intense feeling" (der Reim im Affekt), emphasizing moments of extreme agitation.[5] Kleist uses iambic pentameter throughout: the blank verse of all his plays except *Die Hermannsschlacht* (*The Battle of Arminius,* which combines pentameter with tetrameter) and the prose passages of *Das Käthchen von Heilbronn* (*Käthchen of Heilbronn*). This is also the meter in the comedy Kleist completed just before beginning work on *Amphitryon, Der zerbrochene Krug* (*The Broken Jug*). The pentameter line allows Kleist to be freer with his comic gestures than he would otherwise have room for. His Sosias is characterized by a mannered wordiness that could not have been accommodated in a tighter line.

> Stellt Euch, wenn Ihr die Güte haben wollt,
> Auf dieser Seite hier [. . .] Pharissa vor
> —Was eine Stadt ist, wie Ihr wissen werdet,
> So groß im Umfang, praeter propter,
> Um nicht zu übertreiben, wenn nicht größer,
> Als Theben.[6]

> Imagine, if you would be so good,

THE TRANSLATION AS A DOPPELGÄNGER

On this side here . . . Pharissa
—which is a city, as you surely know,
As large in size, approximately,
Not to exaggerate, if not larger,
Than Thebes.

Molière's Sosie is likewise given to asides, though his are somewhat more restrained in scope:

Figurez-vous donc que Télèbe,
    Madame, est de ce côté: [. . .]
C'est une ville, en vérité,
Aussi grande quasi que Thèbes.
    (OCM 238–41)

Imagine, then, that Telebos,
    Madame, is on this side: . . .
It is a city, in truth,
Just as large as Thebes.

While the first two lines in both speeches contain the same basic information, the expanded line in German allows for the insertion of the extra phrase "wenn Ihr die Güte haben wollt," a prolixity typical of the German Sosias's speech patterns. The third and fourth lines, too, are heavily augmented. While Molière's Sosie hems and haws a little with the asides "en vérité" and "quasi," Kleist expands the first into a longer phrase, "wie Ihr wissen werdet," and turns the second into the pompous "praeter propter." Each of these phrases can be traced directly back to Molière's French, but Kleist follows each of them with an interpolation not directly connected to anything in the original. Pharissa is, his Sosias says,

So groß im Umfang, [. . .]
Um nicht zu übertreiben, wenn nicht größer,
Als Theben.

This phrase builds on "Aussi grande quasi que Thèbes," but expands on it absurdly by first cautioning against exaggeration and then going on after all to make an even more grandiose claim for the defeated city's size. Kleist's Sosias, then, is even more of a windbag than his French model, perhaps even a parody of Molière's Sosie.

Many of Kleist's revisions of Molière follow a similar pattern. Individual scenes, even speeches, are preserved, but in slightly changed form, and often with new central images.

> Sosie: Cette nuit en longueur me semble sans pareille.
> Il faut, depuis le temps que je suis en chemin,
> Ou que mon maître ait pris le soir pour le matin,
> Ou que trop tard au lit le blond Phébus sommeille,
>   Pour avoir trop pris de son vin.
>   (OCM 271–75)

> Sosie: This night seems to me unparalleled in length.
> Surely during all this time I have been en route
> Either my master has mistaken the evening for the morning
> Or blond Phoebus has been slumbering too long in his bed
>   Because he drank too much wine.

> Sosia: Doch diese Nacht ist von endloser Länge.
> Wenn ich fünf Stunden unterwegs nicht bin,
> Fünf Stunden nach der Sonnenuhr von Theben,
> Will ich stückweise sie vom Turme schießen.
> Entweder hat in Trunkenheit des Siegs
> Mein Herr den Abend für den Morgen angesehn,
> Oder der lockre Phöbus schlummert noch,
> Weil er zu tief ins Fläschchen gestern guckte.
>   (KSe 1:250, 111–18)

> But this night is endlessly long.
> If I haven't been en route for five hours now
> Five hours by the sundial in Thebes,
> I'll shoot it from its tower, piece by piece.
> Either, drunk with victory,

> My master has mistaken the evening for the morning,
> Or else negligent Phoebus is still slumbering
> Because he had one too many last night.

Here, too, Kleist incorporates Molière's lines into an expanded speech. Above all, his revision involves an increase in specificity. While Molière's Sosie speaks of "le temps que je suis en chemin," Kleist assumes that Sosias, tired and aggrieved as he is, would have reckoned out the length of his nocturnal journey, and then provides a concrete image to express Sosias's frustration. This image itself shows that Sosias is not thinking clearly—there is little point in wanting to tell time by a sundial in the middle of the night—which contributes to his overall characterization as a ridiculous figure. The last four lines of the German passage correspond to the last three of the French, with the addition of the phrase "in Trunkenheit des Siegs."

The changes Kleist makes to the text, however, are suggested by elements of the original. Reading the French passage, Kleist must have noted that the words used to personify Phoebus, "Pour avoir trop pris de son vin," resonate as well with Amphitryon's own state of intoxication, suggesting the modification of Molière's line. This association may well have prompted the image "Trunkenheit des Siegs," which assigns this drunkenness in more dignified form—Amphitryon's elation after winning the battle is justified—while attributing a more ridiculous drunkenness to Phoebus with the comic phrase "ins Fläschchen [. . .] guckte" (literally "peered too deep into the bottle"). A similar process of association seems to inform other parts of the translation in this passage. The "blond Phébus" has been transformed into a "lockre Phöbus"—possibly via the word *lockige* suggested by *blond*—and even the notion of shooting the sundial of Thebes from its tower with a rain of arrows may have been suggested by the "archers de Créon" (OCM 257) that appear not many lines earlier in Molière's text and are elided altogether in Kleist's translation.

In any case, alterations of the sort described above can be found throughout even the most faithfully translated passages in the play. When Molière's Mercure calls Sosie "traître" (OCM 315; traitor), Kleist's supplements the epithet "Verräter" with an entire pentameter's worth of imprecation: "Nichtswürdiger Gassentreter, Eckenwächter"

(KSe 1:251, 159; Worthless alley-treader, streetcorner-spy). The French Mercure is hardly polite, but there is little violence in his words. Kleist's Merkur is made to seem angrier and more disdainful, his threat to Sosias more acute. Similarly, where Molière repeats the word *trêve* (respite) as part of an exchange between Mercure and Sosie, Kleist copies the repetition but expands it and adds a level of ambiguity. Mercure has threatened to thrash Sosie anew, and to Sosie's plea, "De grâce, fais trêve à tes coups" (OCM 384–85; I beg you, no more of these blows), Mercure responds, "Fais donc trêve à ton insolence" (384–85; No more of your insolence). In Kleist's version, the passage reads,

> Sosias: Hör auf, mir zuzusetzen.
> Merkur: Eher nicht,
>   Als bis du aufhörst—
> S: Gut, ich höre auf.
>
> (KSe 1:254, 234–35)
>
> Sosias: Stop tormenting me.
> Mercury: Not until
>   You stop—
> S.   All right, I'll stop.

In Kleist's version, Merkur's line seems to suggest something different than it does in the French; one would be tempted to complete it: "Until you stop being Sosias." Thus Sosias's agreement in the following line appears to be an implicit renunciation of his own identity. His speech continues with the assurance that he is now prepared to agree with Merkur in all things—

> recht sollst du haben,
> Und allem, was du aufstellst, sag ich ja
>
> you shall be right,
> And everything you propose I will agree to

—vague enough an assurance not to contradict a strong reading of

Merkur's words.

At other points, Kleist borrows rhetorical structures from Molière, filling them out with his own material, as in the final words Sosias speaks aside before confronting Mercury in 1.2:

> Il est seul, comme moi; je suis fort, j'ai bon maître.
>   Et voilà notre maison.
>
> (OCM 307–8)

> He is alone, like me; I am strong, I have a good master.
>   And here is our house.

> Ich bin allein, er auch; zwei Fäuste habe ich,
> Doch er nicht mehr; und will das Glück nicht wohl mir,
> Bleibt mir ein sichrer Rückzug dort—Marsch also!
>
> (KSe 1:251, 145–47)

> I am alone, he too; two fists I have,
> But he not more; and if luck will not favor me,
> I've safe ground to retreat to there—so forward march!

For the first confrontation between Sosias and his doppelgänger, a construction like "Il est seul, comme moi" is highly appropriate. Kleist copies it in structure, but reverses the point of view. The Sosie who notes that his opponent is alone *before* remarking that he himself shares this weakness is far more self-confident than Kleist's, who first speaks of his own isolation, then reasons that the unknown figure is no better off. Kleist then copies the structure of this sentence a second time, replacing Molière's "je suis fort" with "zwei Fäuste habe ich" (the two fists are yet another doubling) and the phrase's complement, "Doch er nicht mehr." When Molière's Sosie says "Et voilà notre maison," his claim contributes to the strength of his position (he has physical strength, a master, a house). Kleist reinterprets the last bit of Sosie's boasting as something quite different: his Sosias notes that if all else fails he has somewhere to flee.

On the surface, this scene has survived the translation largely intact. Yet the alterations Kleist makes to individual lines combine to produce a result that departs significantly from the concerns of the original: a victimized figure whose dilemma is not merely the stuff of slapstick but one who takes a beating with a real bite to it: Sosias is suffering, as will the play's tragic hero, Amphitryon, not many scenes later, a proper *crise d'identité*.

Since, as has been discussed above, many of the changes Kleist made to the microcosm of Molière's play have a significance that goes beyond the scope of individual passages, the thematic shift thus effected can be traced in more general terms. The use of adjustments on the lexical level, involving what might seem insignificant emendations, is nowhere more clearly demonstrated than in this exchange between Mercury and Sosias:

> Mercure: Qui va là?
> Sosie: Moi.
> M: Qui, moi?
> S: Moi. Courage, Sosie!
>
>   (OCM 309)

> Mercury: Who goes there?
> Sosias: Me.
> M: Who's that, me?
> S: Me. Courage, Sosias!

> Merkur: Halt dort! Wer geht dort?
> Sosias: Ich.
> M: Was für ein Ich?
> S: Meins mit Verlaub. Und meines, denke ich, geht
> Hier unverzollt gleich andern. Mut, Sosias!
>
>   (KSe 1:251, 148–50)

> Mercury: Hold there! Who goes there?
> Sosias: Me.
> M: What sort of me?

THE TRANSLATION AS A DOPPELGÄNGER

S: Mine, with your permission. And mine, I think, can walk
Here unmolested just like others. Courage, Sosias!

The slight shift in Mercury's line of questioning transforms this exchange from a straightforward request for information to a subtle deconstruction of Sosias's sense of self. Molière's query "Qui, moi?" is little more than a surprised reiteration of the initial "Qui va là?" Kleist might have rendered the line verbatim with "Wer, ich?," but instead he writes the conceptually far more complex "Was für ein Ich?" The question suggests that various sorts of answers are possible, that the "Ich" of Sosias might be something other than an autonomous subject, a human being. Sosias's answer, "Meins mit Verlaub," with its use of the possessive form, accepts this line of reasoning. If the "Ich" is something that Sosias *has* (as opposed to something he *is*), then it is an attribute that can be traded, sloughed off, or otherwise lost. His "mit Verlaub" is on the one hand merely a polite gesture, and on the other seems already to be asking Mercury's permission for the identity claim. The willingness of the human characters in the play to let themselves be convinced of the contingency of their own identities and self-understandings is precisely what makes them susceptible to the indignities inflicted on them by their divine visitors.

This susceptibility is particularly pronounced—as it is already to a lesser extent in Molière's play—in the case of Sosias, whose metamorphosis from a figure secure in his own identity to one plagued by the gravest doubts as to who he is at all follows quite a different trajectory in Kleist's scene 1.2 than in Molière's. While Sosie's concessions to Mercure in the context of Molière's scene are largely restricted to verbal play—Sosie appears by turns to be humoring Mercure and to be somewhat dim-witted himself—Kleist's Sosias appears as a figure obligated to confront something he cannot make himself comprehend—that another man is now him.

The scene is shifted in Kleist's rendering from the comic grotesque mode that dominates in the original to an encounter with a more firmly realist basis.[7] This difference can be observed in even the most banal attributes of the scene, for example, the descriptions of the beating Sosias receives at Mercury's hands. Whereas a specific number of blows to be administered—"Mille coups de bâton" (OCM 363; A

59

thousand blows with the stick)—is twice named in Molière's version, Kleist elides both these enumerations and thereby amplifies the sense of threat in the scene. The exaggeration, in the French, of the thousand blows serves a comic function, since it is unlikely that Mercury will literally strike Sosias a thousand times; the threat does not seem real.

Kleist's version of this exchange also picks up on the notion of transformation or metamorphosis suggested in the original and expands it to produce a conceit of considerable thematic relevance. Transformation is obviously an important theme in any work concerned, as is this one, with translation, and indeed it becomes a figure that links several of the play's strands. On the one hand a simple alteration—the assumption of new characteristics—on the other, a more radical sort of change: the exchange of one identity for another, or for none at all, as in the destruction of subjecthood with which Sosias is threatened. In fact, the first appearance of this figure suggests that the process of transformation might well prove fatal: "Ich will dich zu verwandeln suchen" (KSe 1:253, 212; I'll do my best to transform you), Merkur declares (where his French counterpart has offered a thousand blows). The verb *verwandeln* has no direct antecedent in the corresponding lines of Molière's play,[8] though it does correspond to a word that appears at a somewhat later point in the French scene. After a renewed beating of Sosias, Mercury asks him whether he is still Sosias and receives the answer,

> Tes coups n'ont point en moi fait de métamorphose;
> Et tout le changement que je trouve à la chose,
>   C'est d'être Sosie battu.
>
> (OCM 380–82)
>
> Your blows have not produced a metamorphosis in me;
> And the only change I can discern in the matter
>   Is that now I am Sosias the beaten.

The first of these lines is elided in Kleist's texts at the point corresponding to its position in the French. Instead, Merkur's ambiguous offer of transformation ("Ich will dich zu verwandeln suchen") serves as a response to Sosias's protest,

> Weil ich muß Ich, Amphitryons Diener sein,
> Wenn ich auch zehenmal Amphitryon,
> Sein Vetter lieber, oder Schwager wäre.
>
> (KSe 1:253, 209–11)

> Because I must be I, Amphitryon's servant,
> Although I would ten times rather be Amphitryon,
> Or his cousin, or his brother-in-law.

Nor do these lines in which Sosias suggests these other identities he might prefer to his own have any sort of antecedent in the French. Kleist adds them, I would argue, expressly for the purpose of making the central notion of metamorphosis that follows them more resonant. The offer of metamorphosis, then, is highly ironic, since it will turn Sosias not into Amphitryon or one of his aristocratic kinsmen, but merely into a "Sosie battu":

> Dein Stock kann machen, daß ich nicht mehr bin;
> Doch nicht, daß ich nicht *Ich* bin, weil ich bin.
> Der einzge Unterschied ist, daß ich mich
> Sosias jetzo der geschlagne, fühle.
>
> (KSe 1:254, 229–32)

> Your stick can make me cease to be;
> But not cease to be *me,* for I am.
> The only difference is that I now
> Feel myself to be Sosias the beaten one.

Sosias's lines

> Dein Stock kann machen, daß ich nicht mehr bin;
> Doch nicht, daß ich nicht *Ich* bin, weil ich bin

are suggested by phrases Molière uses later in the scene and which Kleist transplants, as it were, incorporating them into this passage. The French Sosie asks Mercure,

CHAPTER 2

> Et peux-tu faire enfin, quand tu serais démon,
> Que je ne sois pas moi? que je ne sois Sosie?
>
> (OCM 414–15)

> And could you bring about, if you were a demon,
> That I not be me? that I not be Sosias?

and later asserts,

> je ne puis m'anéantir pour toi
> [. . .]
> Et puis-je cesser d'être moi?
>
> (OCM 427)

> I cannot disappear for your sake
> . . .
> And can I cease to be me?

Neither of these phrases is translated at the point where it occurs. Nor do they, in their respective contexts, address, as does Kleist's version, the possibility that Sosias might be compelled to become something other than himself. Kleist's Sosias makes a naive claim, and thus sets himself up for challenge as the scene proceeds. Sosias's argument that, short of being killed, he cannot be made to be other than himself, for the simple reason that he exists, is problematic. "Doch nicht, daß ich nicht *Ich* bin, weil ich bin" implies that to be is to be *me*. This is in fact the point of view Kleist's Sosias brings to his encounter with Mercury, and which he is persuaded by Mercury's violence (not to mention Mercury's intimate knowledge of the events of Sosias's life) to relinquish. In Kleist's scene, unlike Molière's, Sosias makes a final request that Mercury tell him what he might be allowed to be:

> Car encor faut-il bien que je sois quelque chose [OCM 512; For I still do have to be something;]
>
> Denn *etwas*, gibst du zu, muß ich doch sein [KSe 1:258, 376, italics in original; For *something*, you'll admit, I do have to be]

THE TRANSLATION AS A DOPPELGÄNGER

This demonstrates a clear shift of perspective, since the lines are in apparent contradiction with Sosias's earlier specification of his own identity as the only one that could possibly pertain to him. His sense of self thus appears to have been radically altered. In Molière's version, the final position is not opposed to any earlier one, since there has been no talk whatever of Sosie's being "metamorphosed" into some other living being, and it is not surprising that the lines

> Ich kann mich nicht vernichten
> Verwandeln nicht, aus meiner Haut nicht fahren,
> Und meine Haut dir um die Schultern hängen
>   (KSe 1:256, 276–78)

> I cannot annihilate myself
> transform myself, leap out of my skin
> And hang my skin about your shoulders

have no antecedent in Molière. Thus, while Molière's play contains certain suggestions of personal identity being put in question, there is no sense, as in Kleist's version, of the violence that must be done to a healthy self to bring it to regard its own identity as mutable. It is the sense of selfhood under attack that raises the thoroughly Kleistian question—not at issue in Molière—of what it means to have an identity at all.

The susceptibility to crises of identity that torments Sosias throughout the play also extends in Kleist's version—as it does not in Molière's—both to Amphitryon (as will be discussed in the next section of this chapter) and to the divine impostor Jupiter. Jupiter's distress has its source in Alcmena's unwillingness to acknowledge inconsistencies in her husband's identity. It is this circumstance in part that provides the basis for Hans Robert Jauß's evaluation of the play's achievement: that it recreates for the characters the plight of Hegels's unhappy consciousness, which does not find self-consciousness through solitary activity but rather through its relationship with some other subject.[9] The clearest exposition of this dynamic comes in the first scene in which Jupiter appears (KSe 1.4). We see him attempting to convince Alcmena, to whom he has just made love in the guise of her husband, that she should keep separate in her mind lover and husband, not allowing her passionate feelings for the one to be derived from her duty to the other. He confuses her, since, as she says, it is precisely the fact that her lover is also her husband that allows her to receive him into her bed. Her refusal to accept this dichotomy of character produces in Jupiter an uncertainty comparable to that experienced by Sosias on encountering his own double. Jupiter's crisis, however, is not one of identity with the other (Sosias's inability to distinguish himself from Mercury) but of non-identity with self (the role of Amphitryon seems to fit him all too well.) Though he has taken great pains to appear in every way to be none other than Alcmena's husband, he is gravely troubled by the fact that she seems to have fallen for the ruse, that is, that she has been unable to distinguish the love-making of the god from that of his mortal counterpart. This problem is introduced much more explicitly in Kleist's text than in Molière's. The scene in both versions hinges on Alcmena's assertion of the simple identity between husband and lover (mari/époux, amant):

> C'est de ce nom [époux] pourtant que l'ardeur qui me brûle
> Tient le droit de paraître au jour
>   (OCM 577–78)

> It is from this name [spouse], however, that the passion burning inside me
> Derives the right to show itself.

Jupiter has just said that he wishes to see her affections uncolored by her sense of duty,

> Qu'à votre seule ardeur, qu'à ma seule personne,
> Je dusse les faveurs que je reçois de vous,
> Et que la qualité que j'ai de votre époux
>   Ne fût point ce qui me les donne.
>   (OCM 573–76)

> That solely to your passion, solely to my person
> I owe the favors I receive from you,

And that my quality of being your spouse
Is not that which grants me them.

Jupiter's desire is not, however, stated here in terms of direct oppositions, as in Kleist's reinterpretation of the passage. He inserts several lines on the subject of conjugal duties, reminding Alcmena that a husband has a legal right to his wife's sexual favors and can, if necessary, take her to court for withholding them. Thus he wants to be reassured that the affection shown him by Alcmena is unrelated to this legal "Förmlichkeit":

> Wie leicht verscheuchst du diese kleinen Zweifel?
> So öffne mir dein Innres denn, und sprich,
> Ob den Gemahl du heut, dem du verlobt bist,
> Ob den Geliebten du empfangen hast?
>
> (KSe 1:261, 454–57)

> How easily can you drive out these little doubts?
> Then open your interior/inner self to me and say
> Was it was the husband, to whom you are promised,
> Or the lover whom you received today?

That Jupiter's question is a request for the most intimate sort of information—a confession of sexual feelings—is acknowledged in the phrase "öffne mir dein Inneres," a highly ironic request in view of the fact that it is the "Inneres" of Jupiter himself that is in question here. His disguise is skin deep, and if Alcmena has been unable to see beneath its surface, his legitimacy as a god will be put in question. The crucial opposition between *Gemahl* and *Geliebter*—the words are more clearly marked as a fundamental pair by their alliteration—is reiterated in Alcmena's response, but only to be denied:

> Geliebter und Gemahl! Was sprichst du da?
> Ist es dies heilige Verhältnis nicht,
> Das mich allein, dich zu empfahn, berechtigt?
>
> (KSe 1:261, 458–60)

CHAPTER 2

> Lover and husband! What are you saying?
> Is it not this holy relationship alone
> That permits me to receive you?

Where Molière's Alcmène speaks only the label, the legal category ("ce nom") in its unproblematic self-identity, Kleist's Alcmena specifies the duality she refuses to acknowledge. Thus the "heilige Verhältnis" she speaks of is ambiguous: it might signify the marriage bond itself or, on the other hand, the relationship (identity?) between lover and spouse.

The lover/spouse opposition that Kleist develops in this scene has its source in Molière's text, but in the original this theme appears somewhat later in the conversation between Jupiter and Alcmène, and in less explicit form. Only after Alcmène has made her statement about the name legitimating her desire does Jupiter articulate the double nature of his role:

> En moi, belle et charmante Alcmène,
> Vous voyez un mari, vous voyez un amant,
> Mais l'amant seul me touche, à parler franchement,
> Et je sens, près de vous, que le mari le gêne.
>
> (OCM 589–92)

> In me, lovely and charming Alcmena,
> You see a husband, and you see a lover,
> But only the lover pertains to me, to speak frankly,
> And I feel, close to you, that the husband is an impediment.

Yet Jupiter describes his position with regard to the antinomy as neutral. Both "amant" and "mari," as he describes it, are aspects of the same figure—opposed, yes, but not able to exclude one another. He describes himself as affected ("me touche") only by the category of lover, who finds the husband in him a nuisance—but both co-exist within him. This is a far cry from Jupiter's instruction in Kleist's version:

> Entwöhne,
> Geliebte, von dem Gatten dich,

Und unterscheide zwischen mir und ihm

(KSe 1:261, 467–69)

Wean yourself,
Beloved, from your husband,
And make a distinction between myself and him.

And when Molière's Jupiter requests of Alcmène,

quand vous verrez l'époux,
Songez à l'amant, je vous prie

(OCM 618–19)

when you see your husband,
Dream of your lover, I beg you

Kleist places on his lips a far more direct statement:

Versprich, sag ich, daß du an mich willst denken,
Wenn einst Amphitryon zurückekehrt—?

(KSe 1:262, 499–500)

Promise, I say, that you will think of me,
When one day Amphitryon returns—?

This conversation between Jupiter and Alcmena occupies 92 lines in Molière's French, and 102 in Kleist's German. The first 90 lines of the translation correspond roughly to the same number of lines in the original. To these Kleist adds a dozen lines that cause the scene to end on quite a different note. In Molière's version, Jupiter is unsuccessful in his attempt to make Alcmena acknowledge his non-identity with her husband. Kleist's Jupiter, however, is able to prompt what is not clearly a negative response to his question "Schien diese Nacht dir kürzer als die andern?" (Did not this night seem to you shorter than the others?): Alcmena replies with an "Ach!" that prefigures the famous last line of the play (KSe 1:262, 506–7). Jupiter's enthusiasm at this moderate success causes him to blow his own cover with the promise to see to it that in the future nights will last no longer than they should—but Alcmena fails to notice the slip.

Szondi registers surprise that the typically Kleistian motif of the spouse/lover duality should have its roots directly in Molière, with whose sensibility such a theme is not obviously in keeping. But in Molière, he notes, the motif is an attribute of the comedy of manners with its tradition of the ridiculous cuckold: "in the figure of the lover, society as a whole is avenging itself, in a sense, on the husband, who deprived it of the woman by marrying her." In Kleist's play, on the other hand, "the distinction between lover and husband forms the basis for the underlying scheme [tieferen Vorgang] of the work as a whole." It is the source of "what we can separate out from the outward comedy of errors [Verwechslungskomödie] and call the inner comedy of errors." Szondi is certainly right to note that the motifs adapted from Molière's play are made by Kleist to serve quite a different thematic constellation. While both Molière and Kleist introduce the figure of the divided subject in this scene, I would claim that the two halves of the split self converge in Molière and diverge in Kleist. There need be no great separation between the husband and the lover in Jupiter's request,

> quand vous verrez l'époux,
> Songez à l'amant, je vous prie
>   (OCM 618–19)

> when you see your husband,
> Dream of your lover, I beg you

The husband is the public aspect of the figure of whom the lover is the private aspect, and the two halves are auspiciously united in the person of the man who enjoys the love of the woman legally bound to him. Kleist's

> Ob den Gemahl [. . .]
> Ob den Geliebten du empfangen hast?

> Was it was the husband . . .
> Or the lover whom you received today?

makes judicious use of the past tense to emphasize the intractability of the either/or dualism—exactly one of these two figures has enjoyed Alcmena's favors, and each excludes the other. Since there is so much more at stake for Kleist's Jupiter than for Molière's, Alcmena's refusal to acknowledge his identity as separate from Amphitryon's takes on a weight in the German that it lacked in its original form.

These are concerns that can no longer be attributed to the seventeenth-century comedy of manners, though Kleist draws, as I have shown, the building blocks for his thematic construction from the lines of Molière's play. Having considered Kleist's adaptation as a translation, I will now examine his *Amphitryon* in its role as an adaptation, that is, in terms of its position within the body of Kleist's literary production.

The Translation as an Original Work

The most obvious marker of the discrepancy between translation and adaptation in Kleist's *Amphitryon* is the role of the play's single important female figure, Alcmena. Her character disappears from the stage after act 2 of Molière's play and no longer influences the development of the play's climax in which the identity of Amphitryon's doppelgänger is revealed. This makes sense for a comedy of manners; having presumably slept with both the mortal and the divine doubles, Alcmena is the holder of dangerous knowledge—she knows these doubles in the double sense of the term. As a potentially subversive figure, a disrupter of the smoothly functioning male-dominated social sphere, she must be swept into the wings. Any drama in which Alcmena is the central figure—as she is in the lost plays by Aeschylus and Euripides—would have to be at least in part tragic: the gods trick her, and from *her* point of view this tale of cuckoldry is deadly earnest. Kleist, unlike Molière, brings Alcmena back on stage in the final act and, moreover, vests her with the authority to rule on the proper identity of husband and imposter. She is to bear witness on the basis of her experience. The fact that the witness she bears is in fact false witness—after she has been declared by Amphitryon himself a reliable arbiter, she identifies Jupiter as her husband—serves only further to undermine the social and epistemological certainty of the world Molière's play inhabits.

Kleist's Alkmene, then, is admitted to a select sisterhood of strong female characters in Kleist's work whose dilemmas are thematically crucial in their respective texts. These women's stories are marked by certain basic similarities, as are the characters themselves. Like Penthesilea, Käthchen of Heilbronn, and Thusnelda of *Die Hermannsschlacht*, Alkmene is a character whose heart has been toyed with. Like the others, she is induced to love, then has her love put in question. Penthesilea's frustration turns her love to madness, while Thusnelda acts out her desire and rage vicariously, causing her would-be lover to be locked up with a starved she-bear. Alkmene's frustration, on the other hand, takes a more complex and inward-turned form that allies her, even more than with these other women, with the title character of *The Marquise of O . . .*, who is led to doubt her own senses and sanity by events that are incomprehensible to her despite being intimately linked to her own "Inneres," her insides or interior, in other words, her sexuality.

Like the Marquise, who is bewildered by her own advancing pregnancy since she has no memory of having slept with any man since the death of her husband years before, Alkmene is unwilling to disregard the evidence of her senses, even after she realizes that her senses have most certainly failed her. When the initial on the diadem that Jupiter (as Amphitryon) has brought her turns mysteriously overnight from an *A* to a *J*, she decides she must have misread it at first. And when Jupiter, still in Amphitryon's guise, tells her,

> Es war kein Sterblicher, der dir erschienen,
> Zeus selbst, der Donnergott, hat dich besucht
>
> (KSe 1:287, 1335–36)
>
> It was no mortal man who appeared to you,
> Zeus himself, the god of thunder, visited you!

she scolds him for the sacrilege, and fails to notice even when he speaks out of character (i.e. as himself, the god), apparently angry at her recalcitrance,

> Laß solch ein Wort nicht, Unbesonnene,

Aus deinem Mund mich wieder hören
(KSe 1:287, 1345–46)

Let me not, o foolish one,
Hear such a word from your mouth again

In response, she says only—in an irony lost on her but not the god—"Verlorner Mensch!" (Lost man!)

For Alcmena, the boundary between the mortal and the divine is fluid. When Jupiter eventually convinces her to entertain the notion that she has in fact been visited by Jupiter, the god, it is only in the context of a defense of her fidelity. The argument emphasizes the intentionality of her love for her husband: by definition, anyone who approaches her and is not rebuffed, even a god, can be only Amphitryon himself. Jupiter also (and still as Amphitryon) reproaches Alcmena for envisioning the mortal image of her husband when she prays to the god at his altar. "Ich brauche Züge nun, um ihn zu denken" (KSe 1:291, 1457; I need features to imagine him), she says. Not only has the god, the divine copy, been devalued; his very existence in Alcmena's mind is shown to be contingent on a mortal form, the earthly original. The god is instrumentalized, and Alcmena is the agent of this instrumentalization: for all her piety, she denies the god's identity in his very presence, creating in effect a crisis of divine identity comparable to that which Sosias and Amphitryon have been made to suffer. These considerations play a role only in Kleist's play; none of the lines discussed above appear in any form in Molière's version.

In fact, Kleist's version emphasizes the constitutive force of Alcmena's perceptions by introducing a subtext of image-making in which the status of model and copy is by no means clearly hierarchical. It is precisely Alcmena's predisposition to confuse mortal and divine, to imagine Jupiter in the image of her husband as she kneels at the altar and to be overwhelmed by the living image of her husband, "Dem Leben treu, ins Göttliche verzeichnet" (true to life, inscribed on the divine) that causes her to think the divine imposter is more truly her husband than the true mortal himself. In the end, she prefers the image. When she scolds Amphitryon as a trickster after making her choice in the final scene, she denigrates his build ("Solch einen feilen Bau gemeiner Knechte" [KSe 1:317, 2249–50; Such a base figure, that of a lowly servant]) and contrasts it to Jupiter's "Prachtwuchs dieser königlichen Glieder" (1:317, 2249–50; The noble build of these royal limbs). Her great love for her husband has idolized him, made his image divine, while at the same time it has served to render mortal her notion of the god. The boundaries between original and copy have been blurred. The mortal original, made more glorious in its copied form, has supplanted the original itself; yet at the same time the divine source of the copy has been compromised, shown to be contingent on the mortal sphere. Jupiter himself offers an explanation for this riddle: as god, he *is* in fact everything, including Amphitryon himself:

> Argatiphontidas und Photidas,
> Die Kadmusburg und Griechenland,
> Das Licht, der Äther, und das Flüssige,
> Das was da war, was ist, und was sein wird.
>
> (KSe 1:318, 2297–2300)
>
> Argatiphontidas and Photidas,
> Mount Cadmus and all of Greece,
> The light, the aether, and the wet,
> That which was, which is, and which will be.

Jupiter declares himself to be all people, all places, all elements, and all times. Thus there is no conflict between his claim to be Amphitryon and Amphitryon's own statement in which he declares himself to be

> Des unerschütterlich erfaßten Glaubens,
> Daß er Amphitryon ihr ist
>
> (KSe 1:318, 2289–90)
>
> of the unshakably held belief
> That he is Amphitryon to her

In *Amphitryon*, logic and belief eventually serve as the means for producing an acute self-denial comparable to that accomplished in Sosias's case by means of fear and pain—animal conditioning. And only after this self-denial, after Amphitryon has declared himself convinced by Alcmena's acknowledgment of Jupiter-as-Amphitryon, does the god concede Amphitryon's identity. Jupiter, Amphitryon declares, is Amphitryon to Alcmena. Since he has acknowledged Alcmena to be infallibly faithful and honest, an arbiter of truth, he cannot dismiss her judgment. This moment is the climax of the play's escalating uncertainties. Kleist places Amphitryon in the position of doubting the evidence of his own senses that tell him he is Amphitryon, and by so doing uses him to illustrate the Fichtean crisis (often referred to as the "Kant-Krise") of which Kleist wrote to Wilhelmine von Zenge in 1801:

> Wenn alle Menschen statt der Augen grüne Gläser hätten, so würden sie urteilen müssen, die Gegenstände, welche sie dadurch erblicken, *sind* grün—und nie würden sie entscheiden können, ob ihr Auge ihnen die Dinge zeigt, wie sie sind, oder ob es nicht etwas zu ihnen hinzutut, was nicht ihnen, sondern dem Auge gehört. (KSe 2:634)

> If all men had green glass instead of eyes, they would have to judge that the objects they behold through them *are* green—and they would never be able to decide whether their eye was showing them the things as they are, or whether something was not being added to them that belonged not to the things but to the eye.

This is a crisis of authenticity of experience: we can never know what effect the process and mechanism of our own perception has on the apparent content of this perception. Thus, for Kleist, we unreliably construct an image of the world around us, since we can never have access to the world itself except through our senses, no matter what sophisticated machinery we devise to aid our perception. The most extreme form of this contingency involves our constructions of our own identities. When Amphitryon declares himself prepared to swear "Daß er [Jupiter] Amphitryon ihr ist" (KSe 1:318, 2290; That he is Amphitryon to her), he is acknowledging that Alcmena, the voice of truth itself—

> O ihrer Worte jedes ist wahrhaftig,
> Zehnfach geläutert Gold ist nicht so wahr
>
> (KSe 1:317, 2281–82)

CHAPTER 2

> O each one of her words is truthful,
> Gold purified ten times is not so pure

—has denied this identity to him. This is the breakdown of the "we-identity" described in Jauß's dialectical reading of the play.[10] In the absence of individual referential certainty, the corroboration of a trusted other offers the only hope of stable reference, even in matters of personal identity. And so the disruption of such a mutually referential dyad (through, for example, the introduction of a counterfeit member) is violent enough to produce a radical decentering, a fall from grace.

Kleist's most important theoretical text, "On the Marionette Theater" ("Über das Marionettentheater") deals in large part with questions of originality and authenticity. Here, they are framed in terms of grace: that enjoyed by the marionettes because their motions are free of human intention, that lost by a young man the moment he becomes conscious of his own physical beauty, and that of a fencing bear whose ability to parry any blow comes from instinct, not skill. All three of the parables that make up Kleist's essay juxtapose original, graceful action (that governed, say, by the laws of gravity, the laws of nature) with self-conscious action (governed by human thought), which is devoid of grace.

Grace resides most enduringly, Kleist tells us, either in the complete absence of human consciousness, or in an infinite consciousness: "in the puppet [Gliedermann] or in the god" (KSe 2:345). Synonymous with human consciousness is the term *Reflexion*: "We see that to the extent that, in the organic world, reflection [Reflexion] becomes darker and weaker, grace [Grazie] becomes more radiant and dominates" (2:345). Reflection is the malaise that affects the youth in the middle story in two different ways. He loses his grace when he begins to reflect on it, but the moment of this loss is marked by his noticing his own reflection in a large mirror. Though Kleist does not use the word *reflection* (or any synonym) directly to describe this mirror image, the connection is clear: the young man has begun to see himself as an image, an appealing other, and thus forfeits the unreflected grace he formerly enjoyed.

In Kleist's "Catechism for the Germans" ("Katechismus der Deutschen") written one year before, in 1809, reflection appears in direct contrast to feeling and action. The Germans, the lesson goes, have been overwhelmed by their own "understanding" (Verstand):

> they reflected [reflektierten] when they ought to be feeling or acting, and thought they were able to handle everything using their wits, and no longer put any store in the old, mysterious power of the heart. (KSe 2:356)

Here the ability to feel and act autonomously is analogous to originality with regard to the reflected mirror image—and indeed these two categories are for Kleist intimately related. The grace implied in "Catechism" is a political grace, enjoyed in the spirit of German nationalism. In his vehemently anti-Napoleon political writings of the years following his 1807 imprisonment at French hands, Kleist calls for spontaneous, decisive action, rather than hesitant, reflective deliberation. The loss of grace is not only an aesthetic failing but a moral one as well.

This situation is complicated somewhat in the case of Amphitryon. He loses his grace (self-assurance, marital happiness) upon being reflected by a double who copies his features perfectly. Having seen himself reflected causes him to reconsider his own identity in terms that permit beliefs such as "Daß er Amphitryon ihr ist" (That he is Amphitryon to her). Yet there is a different subject-object (and original-copy) relationship at work here. The ephebe, by recognizing in himself a copy of the statue, has perceived himself as not original. Amphitryon, confronted with Jupiter in his own guise, perceives himself as an original that has been copied by means of some devilish trick. He would by no means consider himself a reflection of his own double—the double is clearly, for him, the usurper, "Verräter" (KSe 1:304, 1865), at least initially. At the climax of the final scene, however, when Alcmena declares Jupiter to be the real Amphitryon, he is forced to concede that the copy is by definition authentic, an original (since to Alcmena it *is* Amphitryon). Yet, whether or not he sees himself as original or copy, the effect on his self-understanding is the same: he must now gauge himself against this other Amphitryon, whose conduct both Alcmena and Sosias clearly prefer. Jupiter's Amphitryon is more suave, courtly and even-tempered: he does not threaten to beat Sosias when aggrieved—a character trait present in Kleist's play but not in Molière's. In fact, this situation will last even after the departure of Jupiter: Amphitryon knows his behavior will henceforth be measured against that of his divine doppelgänger, robbing him forever of the possibility of truly spontaneous action. He has fallen from grace at the hand of a god, who has forced on him a debilitating self-consciousness.

But if being copied has its dangers, so, too, must being a copy. The divine status of the imitator complicates the usual hierarchy between copy and original. Jupiter, in transforming himself into Amphitryon, has stooped, as it were; he is slumming. Thus it causes him distress when Alcmena—whose perfect probity Jupiter, too, acknowledges—falls for his ruse. Jupiter is not a perfect copy—he is too perfect. Yet in this case the ultraperfection of the copy serves ironically to glorify the original: Jupiter's *Gastspiel* as Amphitryon only increases Alcmena's esteem for her husband. Thus Jupiter's status as character is essentially contradictory: it is clearly within his power to become perfectly Amphitryon, yet to do so is to lose his power as a god. He, the omnipotent copy, must relinquish power to become a copy. Thus when he falls out of character (for instance, when he becomes angry with Alcmena for chiding him about sacrilege), these moments are experienced as disruptions and certainly not as graceful. By chafing against the role he is playing, Jupiter forfeits grace. This is particularly ironic since, as a god, he fulfills one of the two conditions Kleist posits for true grace: in the end, even his infinite consciousness fails him.

While the story of Amphitryon certainly lends itself to considerations of the relationship between power, originality, and grace, these are not important concerns in Molière's play. In fact, Kleist's *Amphitryon* has more in common thematically with the rest of Kleist's work than with the model on which it was based. In this sense, it is a copy that asserts its own autonomy vis-à-vis its original.

Intertexts in the Adaptation

Yet another discrepancy in Kleist's adaptation of Molière's play comes from his use of intertexts that lack a direct relation to Molière's original. This is certainly a way for Kleist to assert his (authorial) autonomy from the original text, an act of defiance on his part as a translator that makes him seem as overqualified for his role as Jupiter is in the constraints of the mortal.

Oedipus Rex

One important intertext of Kleist's *Amphitryon* is shared with *Der zerbrochene Krug*, the play Kleist wrote directly before it: *Oedipus Rex*. The Amphitryon of myth is a famous general who resides in Thebes, the location of the Oedipus saga, whose chronology seems to predate Amphitryon's tale by no more than a generation. The "pre-story" that gives rise to the "tragic dialectic" discussed by Szondi[11]—Alcmena's hand being contingent on Amphitryon's revenging her brother's murder—is excluded from Plautus's retelling, and so the war being fought throughout the play, between the Thebans and the Teleboans, is the only indication of historical context, if an indefinite one, as the play contains no indication of why this war is being fought. But the king of Thebes at this time, in the oldest known Greek versions of the myth, is Creon, brother-in-law and successor to Oedipus; and Tiresias, the blind seer of Thebes, is mentioned as having been the one to identify Amphitryon's impersonator as Jupiter. (This information is included in Hederich's *Gründliches Lexicon mythologicum*, which Kleist is known to have used as a source for *Penthesilea*, and which he may well have consulted when working on *Amphitryon* as well.[12])

A strong thematic link joins the two story complexes. Oedipus, in order to free Thebes from the gods' curse, goes in search of Laius's murderer, unaware that the man he seeks is none other than himself. Amphitryon, too, faces a crisis of self-identity, but in converse relation to that of Oedipus. Each case opposes the protagonist to a supposed stranger who shares various traits in common with him and has transgressed in some way against the community. Oedipus's story is tragic because the transgressive stranger is Oedipus himself; Amphitryon's because he is cast out as an interloper from his own home.

Kleist links the Amphitryon story to the Oedipus myth in ways that deviate significantly from those employed by Plautus and even by Molière. Kleist's Amphitryon allies himself with Laius (as well as Hamlet's father, for that matter) when he laments, on being refused entry to his own house,

> Begraben bin ich schon, und meine Witwe
> Schon einem andern Ehgemahl verbunden
>
>   (KSe 1:301, 1781–82)
>
> I am already buried, and my widow
> Already joined to another husband

And while Molière explicitly mentions Creon as the king of Thebes, in

Sosias's initial monologue (OCM 257), Kleist not only elides this mention, but transforms the opposing army: where Molière speaks of the attack on Teleboa carried out against the general Pterelas, Kleist has Amphitryon's Thebans marching against the Athenians outside Pharissa and triumphing over the Athenian leader, Labdacus. Historically this makes little sense: there is no record of a war between Thebes and Athens, and the only variant of the Amphitryon legend that involves Athenians in any way posits them as allies. Cephalos of Athens, the story goes, came to Amphitryon's aid in battling a powerful fox that had been threatening the countryside and whose death Creon had made the condition for allowing Amphitryon to lead a Theban army against the Teleboans to fulfill his marriage contract with Alcmena.[13] And Labdacus is not Athenian at all, but Theban, the father of Laius and grandfather of Oedipus.

What, then, are we to make of Kleist's juggling of these various myths? His reference to Labdacus—which involves a generation shift, since Amphitryon and Creon are contemporaries in the original myth—would seem to emphasize the relationship between the Oedipus saga and Amphitryon's story. Generation shifts are already problematic in the Oedipus legend, as Creon is revealed to be not only Oedipus's brother-in-law, but his uncle as well, that is, a full generation older than Oedipus.

The link between these two tales also suggests a reading of the Amphitryon myth that goes against the grain of the plot information offered in the play itself. There is a sense in which Jupiter-as-Amphitryon is in fact identical to Amphitryon himself. The god himself suggests such an interpretation in the final scene when he declares himself to be all things, all people, all places, all times. His conversation with Alcmena in 2.4, in which he urges her to keep Amphitryon the lover and Amphitryon the husband separate in her mind, can be seen merely as soliciting Alcmena's acknowledgment of the innate multiplicity of human character, a view of personality that is implied at other points in Kleist's work as well. Thus Kleist is fascinated by complex characters like the Marquise, who in her waking mind has no knowledge of having conceived a child; Penthesilea, whose loyalty to the statutes of the Amazon state eventually induces her to destroy the man she loves along with herself; or Prince Friedrich von Homburg, whose personality unites the absent-minded dreamer with the man of duty so principled he is prepared to condemn himself to death.

THE TRANSLATION AS A DOPPELGÄNGER

Oedipus replaces his father, becomes him in a manner of speaking, when he marries his father's wife and takes over his throne. Jupiter, as the father of all men, is also Amphitryon's father; he is even addressed as such when Amphitryon requests the gift of a son: "Nein, Vater Zeus, zufrieden bin ich nicht!" (KSe 1:319, 2330; No, Father Zeus, I am not satisfied!) By calling Jupiter a father in the moment of requesting that he himself become a father, Amphitryon is expressing his desire to assume the god's role. Jupiter himself usurped Amphitryon's role when he came down to earth to sleep with Alcmena (the converse of the Oedipus story: the father desires the son's wife), but since Jupiter, given his divine status, is always already Amphitryon, is it not presumptuous of the son to insist on his own identity?

> Was du, in mir, dir selbst getan, wird dir
> Bei mir, dem, was ich ewig bin, nicht schaden
>
> (KSe 1:319, 2321–22)
>
> What you, in me, did to yourself will not
> Harm you by me, by what I eternally am,

says father to son in what are no doubt the most complexly infolded lines of the entire play. "Was du, in mir, dir selbst getan" would seem to speak of potential harm Amphitryon has inflicted upon himself by offending the god, but it might just as easily mean "that which I, Jupiter, did to you when I was you." This harm, whatever its cause, will not, Jupiter reassures Amphitryon, harm "dir / Bei mir, dem, was ich ewig bin." These lines, too, are highly ambiguous. The "dem, was ich ewig bin" can most easily be understood as appositive to "mir": the authority by which Amphitryon is freed from harm is Jupiter himself, his eternal nature. Yet the phrase might also stand as parallel to "dir": positing Jupiter as the authority by which Amphitryon will have been exempted from causing harm to the eternal nature of the god. This is self-evident (in the words of Hölderlin's Creon, "Gott regt kein Mensch an, dieses weiß ich"[14]; No man can press God to action, this I know). But regardless of which reading of these lines one chooses to privilege, they are remarkable for the density with which they entwine the two figures: Jupiter is Amphitryon, and Amphitryon, in spite of himself, is Jupiter.

Falk's *Amphitruon*

An odder influence on the text of Kleist's play is the work of Johann Daniel Falk (1768–1826), a writer and acquaintance of Kleist. Falk published his own Amphitryon drama in the spring of 1804: *Amphitruon*, a free adaptation of Plautus.[15] Traces of Falk's text in Kleist's—on the quite concrete level of individual lines—complicate the relationship between Kleist's and Molière's texts, and raise a set of more overtly political issues. If Falk's pronounced hatred of the French, and in particular Napoleon, left its mark in his work, a similar thread can be discerned in the text of Kleist's play. Ironically, the implied political critique of turn-of-the-nineteenth-century France contributes to the subversion of Molière's French text.[16]

Falk, a more productive than talented writer, was best known for his comic writings and the almanac he published: *Taschenbuch für Freunde des Scherzes und der Satire* (*Journal for Aficionados of Humor and Satire*), of which seven volumes appeared between 1797 and 1803. He also, however, nurtured the plan of giving new life to the German stage with the help of antique influences. Kleist is assumed to have met Falk through Christoph Martin Wieland, at whose house at Oßmannsstedt Kleist was a guest for Christmas 1802 and the first two months of 1803. Both Kleist and Falk spent the early summer in Dresden, and were spotted together by Fouqué at the Dresdener Galerie. Kleist at the time was working on *Der zerbrochene Krug*—inspired by a literary wager made with Heinrich Zschokke and Wieland's son Ludwig[17]—and thus was clearly interested, like Falk, in possibilities for adapting antique story lines to a contemporary German setting. (The inclusion of the Sophocles motifs in *Der zerbrochene Krug* had been Kleist's own addition to the task set him by young Wieland and Zschokke.)

Falk's *Amphitruon* has been deservedly forgotten. As a play, it is of indifferent quality, full of overlong, underdramatic scenes marginal to the principal actions and themes. Falk seems to have been particularly pleased with his crowd scenes—he preprinted some of them in the 1803 *Taschenbuch*—but they were in fact not particularly interesting exemplars of a genre that was not to be perfected in German for another three decades, by Büchner and Grabbe. Falk revised his initial blank verse draft into a complex of more irregularly metered lines that often fall into pairs of rhymed couplets, but there is nothing about his language use that can be expected to have made much of an impression on even the young Kleist.

Kleist scholar Helmut Sembdner surmises that Kleist and Falk exchanged ideas "in a joint workshop of trial and experiment" and that Kleist was familiar with even the early drafts of Falk's adaptation.[18] That Kleist was capable of finding inspiration in conversations with literary figures far less talented than himself can easily be confirmed by examining the coy and mediocre little village tale entitled "Der zerbrochene Krug" that Heinrich Zschokke eventually wrote to fulfill his part of the three friends' literary wager.

But the Amphitryon myth was being talked about in other circles as well. August Christian Borheck's translation of Plautus's *Amphitryon* appeared in 1803, and when Kleist spoke about the material with Falk, this no doubt fanned the flames of what was already a kindled interest. In fact, Molière's version of the play may well have come up in Kleist's literary conversations with Zschokke, who only a few years later published a six-volume translation, *Molières Lustspiele und Possen* (*Molière's Comedies and Farces*, 1805–6). And Falk himself, though working primarily from Plautus's text, was, as Sembdner has pointed out, clearly familiar with Molière's play as well, which he used at points as a source of material much as Kleist seems to have used Falk's own play.

Evidence of these borrowings can be found throughout Kleist's text. In Sosias's initial monologue, for example, certain lines in Kleist's version follow those of Falk more closely than they do Molière's. The lines,

Mais enfin, dans l'obscurité,
Je vois notre maison, et ma frayeur s'évade
 (OCM 188–89)

But finally, in the darkness,
I see our house and my fright subsides

become in Kleist's rendering, "Doch sieh! Da zeigt sich, denk ich, unser Haus!" (Kse 1:247, 29; But look! There, I think, our house appears!). The same line appears in Falk's text as "Doch sieh! das ist ja da wohl unser Haus?" (But look! that is indeed surely our house?).[19] Kleist improves the weak center of Falk's line ("ja da wohl") by, first, replacing *ist* with *zeigt sich*, which adds not only a needed syllable but also an appropriate sense of uncertainty: the house *appears* in the darkness (as a sign, *Zeichen*) before Sosias's weary eyes, a less firm claim than that it *is* there. The *denk ich* functions similarly, adding syllables that contribute to the line's non-assertion of secure knowledge. It is highly unlikely that Kleist could have come up with a line so much like Falk's by pure chance (nor that Falk—had he been in a position to adopt lines from Kleist's text—would have managed to make the line so much worse in the process of editing it.)

Similarly, Kleist's "Doch wär es gut, wenn du die Rolle übtest?" (KSe 1:248, 45; But wouldn't it be good if you practiced the role?) is related to the lines of Falk's play that immediately follow the one discussed above:

> Nun wird's wohl gut seyn, wenn ich vor der Thüre
> Erst meine Roll' ein wenig durchprobiere!
> (FBA 573–74)

> Now it will surely be good if I first practice
> My role a bit in front of the door!

The thought that occupies two lines in Falk is compressed by Kleist into one with the inessential elements edited out ("wohl," "vor der Türe," "Erst," "ein wenig"). Molière's line, on the other hand, bears less resemblance to Kleist's "translation" of it:

> Pour jouer mon rôle sans peine,
> Je le veux un peu repasser
> (OCM 200–201)

> So as to play my role without difficulty,
> I'll practice it a little

Kleist was clearly glancing through (if not carefully combing) Falk's lines in search of material that would be useful to him, and perhaps also to help in making the transition, in this case, from Molière's trimeter to a blank verse line. A similar borrowing appears in Kleist's 3.5, where Molière's lines

> Ciel! quel est ce prodige?
> Quoi? deux Amphitryons ici nous sont produits!
>> (OCM 1617–18)

> Heavens! what is this prodigy?
> What? two Amphitryons have been produced here!

appear as "Was seh ich? Himmel! Zwei Amphitryonen" (KSe 1:303, 1840; What do I see? Heavens! Two Amphitryons), a line copied from Falk's 5.4:

> Was seh ich, Himmel? Zwei Amphitruonen,
> In Einem Haus und unter Einem Dach?
>> (FBA 2850–51)

> What do I see, heavens? Two Amphitryons,
> In one house and under one roof?

The slight shift of *Himmel* from apostrophized object to exclamation is fitting.

Falk's play also served Kleist as a source of individual words for use in different contexts. Kleist's translation of Sosie's

> Où puis-je rencontrer quelque clarté fidèle,
> Pour démêler ce que je voi?
>> (OCM 490–91)

> Where can I find some trusty light,
> To sort out what I am seeing?

to "—Wie find ich nun aus diesem Labyrinth?—" (KSe 1:258, 348; How will I find my way out of this labyrinth now?) is influenced by words spoken by Falk's Sosias in a different context: "Ich bitte dich nur: gieb mir Licht in diesem Labyrinth!" (FBA 1126; I ask you only: give me light in this labyrinth!). Kleist corrects Falk's line, which seems to be implying it is the lack of light that makes it difficult to exit a labyrinth.

Kleist may have found Falk's play a source of major plot items as well. The final confrontation scenes in Falk are played out, as in Kleist but not Molière, in front of the assembled populace, and Alcmena is put in the position of choosing between the two Amphitryons. Why would Kleist, in creating a version of Molière's play that was at least in large part a translation, have incorporated scenic elements and even individual lines from another author's play, one that Kleist himself surely cannot have considered to be of particularly high quality? Certainly he would have been capable of recasting the third act in his own terms, and of writing his own lines to replace those of Molière that he modified. If anything, adding Falk as a source text increased the amount of labor the play cost him. I read his use of Falk's text as an act of defiance vis-à-vis Molière. It is evident that Kleist harbored no feelings of reverence toward Molière's play, and by diluting it with snippets of Falk as well as his own rethinking of various passages and scenes, he was diffusing any aura that might have surrounded Molière's text in its function as an original.

A further consideration for Kleist's interest in Falk's play is political. Kleist's anti-French sentiments were to be spectacularly demonstrated, after his 1807 imprisonment in Fort Joux, in his agitatory poems and pamphlets, as well as in the drama *Die Hermannsschlacht,* which he intended as a call to arms against Napoleon's occupying army. Yet his opinion of Napoleon's expansionist politics were already fairly established at least by early 1802.[20] Falk held similar views, and his *Amphitruon* is presented in decisively anti-French terms. His foreword begins with a thinly veiled attack on both Molière and Rotrou in the remark that "while there are a hundred points of overlap between the Germans and this impassioned [*gemüthvoll,* "rich in feeling"] Greek, scarcely one and a half can be found between him and the Frenchmen who are scrambling after wit, flashy effects and punchlines" (FBA 24). The French dramatists are shallow, taken with cheap humorous effects, while the German writers resemble the Greeks a hundred times over. It is clear that Falk in no way sees himself as following in Molière's footsteps, even if he does occasionally borrow a scene or a turn of phrase from his play. And particular moments near the beginning of Falk's version invite us to read his invading gods as specifically French—indeed, his Jupiter might even be a stand-in for Napoleon. Responding to the prayers of his supplicants, who in part have asked for favors which

Jupiter feels lie outside his jurisdiction, Falk's god explains,

> Der Wind gehört
> In die Gerichtsbarkeit von Aeolus;
> Schickt sie zu dem! Es bleibt auf altem Fuß,
> Und jegliche Supplik gelang'
> An ihr bestimmt Departement!
>   (FBA 101–5)

> The wind belongs
> To Aeolus's jurisdiction;
> Send them to him! Let things remain as they are,
> Let every petition reach
> Its destined department!

The petty bureaucracy Jupiter invokes while passing the buck is a clear parody of the departments established in France after the Revolution.

Kleist's *Hermansschlacht* presents the Roman army being fought back by Hermann's troops in the year 9 AD as a cipher for Napoleon's occupation of Germany. *Amphitryon,* too, is the story of an invasion, by a force claiming a higher degree of civilization than the German mortals whose homes it enters. The invader's ostensible cultural superiority is certainly at issue—and questioned—in *Die Hermannschlacht,* in which the envoy Ventidius manages to touch the heart of Hermann's queen Thusnelda with his courtly mincing. When she reports the Roman's apparent infatuation to her husband, Hermann scoffs at the thought that the man is capable of love:

> Nein, sprich, im Ernst, das glaubst du?
> So, was ein Deutscher lieben nennt,
> Mit Ehrfurcht und mit Sehnsucht, wie ich dich?
>   (KSe 1:557, 666–68)

No, say, in all seriousness, do you believe this?
That which a German means by love,
With awe and yearning, as I love you?

Romans and French alike, on this view, are constitutionally incapable of the German virtue of feeling (that which, in the "Katechismus der Deutschen," Kleist chides the Germans for having forgotten).

Kleist's Jupiter, as he appears in the final act of *Amphitryon,* displays a megalomania worthy of Napoleon himself, particularly when he demands Amphitryon's unconditional capitulation:

> Er selber dort soll meines Hauses Adel,
> Und daß ich Herr in Theben, anerkennen.
> Vor mir in Staub, das Antlitz soll er senken.
> Mein soll er Thebens reiche Felder alle,
> Mein alle Herden, die die Triften decken,
> Mein auch dies Haus, mein die Gebieterin,
> Die still in seinen Räumen waltet, nennen.
>
> (KSe 1:306, 1903–9)
>
> He himself shall acknowledge the nobility of my house,
> And that I am the lord in Thebes.
> Before me in the dust he shall bend his head.
> Mine he shall call all the rich fields of Thebes,
> Mine all the herds that cover the pastures,
> Mine, too, this house, mine its lady,
> Who silently rules in its rooms.

Thus, while Kleist need not have associated Molière himself with the French presence in Germany in 1803, his play certainly invites comparison between the divine invaders and their contemporary counterparts, and in this respect, too, his project resembles that of Falk.

Translation as Translation

Amphitryon is Kleist's only important work of translation, yet a leitmotif of translation, adaptation, transplantation, and other sorts of cultural shifts appears throughout his literary production. His first completed play, *Die Familie Schroffenstein*—a work in part derivative of *Romeo and Juliet*—was first written under the title *Die Familie Ghonorez* and set in Spain. Similarly, *Die Marquise von O . . .* is subtitled, "Nach einer wahren Begebenheit, deren Schauplatz vom Norden nach dem Süden verlegt" ("After a true occurrence whose setting has been shifted from the North to the South"). *Der zerbrochene Krug* retells *Oedipus Rex*, with the clubfooted village judge, Adam, trying a crime of which he himself is guilty. *Penthesilea* is an adaptation of a myth with which Kleist took liberties every bit as great as in the last act of *Amphitryon* (in the original myth, Penthesilea is killed by Achilles, and not vice versa). *Die Hermannsschlacht* transforms an episode of German history from the year 9 AD into an allegory of Napoleon's occupation of Germany. Even the nationalistic text "Catechism for the Germans" is subtitled "adapted from the Spanish for young and old" and is in fact based on a Spanish document that appeared in German translation the same month Kleist wrote his version. This list would make Kleist appear to be a sort of literary magpie, borrowing here and there from any text that glitters; yet it was also his practice, in adapting these texts, to alter them dramatically, making them very much his own. If there are no new stories, only new retellings, Kleist was an exemplary reteller, and to that extent certainly an heir to the early Romantic assimilatory impulse for which every past literature was also a future one. (In Antoine Berman's formulation, "Romanticism does not know any past that is not also future."[21])

Kleist's *Amphitryon,* with its pervasive doublings, draws particular attention to its own status as a translation. Sosias and Amphitryon each have their copies, their stand-ins, who imitate their originals in matters of form, appearance, diction, and style, while at the same time differing fundamentally from them: their medium is the divine, not the mortal. (These doublings become vertiginous when one considers the play being performed on stage, with the actor portraying a god portraying a man.) This aspect of the play applies to every version of the Amphitryon myth ever written, but it is particularly pronounced in Kleist's treatment. While there is some consideration even in Molière of the similarities between the "real" and "false" characters (Sosie: "Je vois qu'il a de moi taille, mine, action" [OCM 473; I see that he has my size, look, gestures]; Jupiter: "L'oeil ne peut entre nous faire de différence" [1673; The eye cannot distinguish between us]), only in Kleist are there discussions of the discrepancies. Kleist adds an entire scene in which Alcmena relates to her maidservant Charis her disorientation at finding her husband both the same and so different. She confesses,

> Daß ich ihn schöner niemals fand, als heut.
> Ich hätte für sein Bild ihn halten können,

CHAPTER 2

> Für sein Gemälde, sieh, von Künstlerhand,
> Dem Leben treu, ins Göttliche verzeichnet.
>
> (KSe 1:283, 1188–91)
>
> That I never found him more handsome than today.
> I could have taken him for his picture,
> For his portrait, you see, by an artist's hand
> Inscribed on the divine, true to life.

Alcmena uses metaphors from the visual arts to describe the transformation of her husband, but the "ins Göttliche verzeichnet" refers also to the new signs (*Zeichen*, words) in which Amphitryon has manifested himself to her. The "ver" of *verzeichnen* names the displacement that affects the Marquise of O as well (*verlegt*, transplanted).

Jupiter intentionally seeks interchangeability with Amphitryon, the key to Alcmena's bedchamber. At the same time, he chafes against his role, and in the end transcends it, dissatisfied to be mistaken for his mortal model outright. Something similar can be said of Kleist's copy of Molière: in an ironic twist on Goethe's third epoch of translation, Kleist's play appears designed to stand *in the place of* Molière's, to represent it to an audience for whom, perhaps, the seventeenth century appears as far distant as the French soldiers who have not yet arrived to occupy their towns and countryside. The subtitle of Kleist's play (*Ein Lustspiel nach Molière; A Comedy After Molière*) is a challenge. He is asking the reader to compare his version with Molière's original and appreciate the difference: his play is as much a critique as a copy. Like Jupiter, he puts a spin on the doppelgänger's role. He wants his mortal audience to admire his literary facility, just as Jupiter wants *his* to admire his lovemaking.

In the case of Jupiter, the irony is double-edged. Kleist's Jupiter, by seeking confirmation of his superiority (also his masculinity) when he appears before Alcmena's arbitrating gaze, proves himself a more perfect copy than is becoming to him (this desire being all too human).[22] Unlike Molière's Jupiter, he insists on being chosen by Alcmena before consenting to reveal his identity. Jupiter, acknowledged, acknowledges Amphitryon: the copy insists on being deemed an original in its own right before granting the original's originality. In fact, only the existence of the copy makes originality an issue, just as an original text is original only with respect to its copy, its translation. In a sense, it owes its legitimacy as original to its ability to serve as the basis of that which copies it. Thus Jupiter's declaration "Wohlan! Du bist Amphitryon" (KSe 1:318, 2289–91; Very well! You are Amphitryon), just after Amphitryon, defeated, has declared himself

> Des unerschütterlich erfaßten Glaubens,
> Daß er Amphitryon ihr ist
>
> of the unshakably held belief
> That he is Amphitryon to her

has more than a merely discursive function: it is a constitutive utterance. Or, in terms of Jauß's reading, if the play is about the possibility of naming a "you," then Amphitryon's subjecthood, his originality originates in the moment when the god says "you are you."

Meanwhile, by rewriting Molière's comedy as a tragicomedy in the guise of a translation, Kleist does to Molière what Mercury does to Sosia: presents a stronger, more sharp-witted, and complex copy that does not so much pay tribute to as usurp the position of its original. Kleist's "Lustspiel nach Molière" leaves its modern reader little room for a return to the original. Molière's Sosie—the role, we should remember, Molière himself played at the drama's premiere—has been replaced by a Sosias who not only excels in the wittiness that had been considered the strong suit of Molière's figure (the rhetorical polish that Thomas Mann admired), but also augments this banter with a depth of expression that is very much of Kleist's age. The tenuous nature of personal identity, the contingency of experience, the abandonment of mankind by the gods both literally and figuratively, the fall from grace that was so important a turn-of-the-nineteenth-century trope—these lines of thematic development account for the "swerve" (in Harold Bloom's terminology) Molière's play is compelled to describe in Kleist's hands.

Kleist, by the manner of his translation, declared the original woefully inadequate to serve the needs of his time. His translation is a form of "clinamen" or "misprision proper" (Bloom): it contains a "corrective movement . . . which implies that the precursor poem [or play] went accurately up to a certain point, but then should have swerved precisely in the direction that the new poem moves."[23] The fact that the relation between precursor and predecessor is as direct as translation only raises the stakes of the misprision—Kleist is offering not only to change his relation to the original but to supplant the original entirely.

Kleist's translation, then, offers itself as an allegory of translation. Like the invading gods in the Amphitryon myth, his text copies the form of an original that becomes an original only by virtue of being copied. And like the divine masqueraders, his text is a metacopy that both reproduces its original and repudiates the original's failings, claiming for itself a new status as both copy *and* original. Like Jupiter—who wishes to show simultaneously that he can *be*, perfectly, Amphitryon, and that he is made of fancier stuff—Kleist's translation by turns parades its own service-translation perfection and transcends it in a stunning display of unmistakably authorial prowess, one worthy of at least a literary divinity.

The relationship between mortals and the gods also plays a crucial part in Sophocles' Theban plays and Hölderlin's translations of them. And here, too, the pursuit of service-translation perfection will be seen to have a theological component. But for Hölderlin, as will become clear in the following chapter, this troubled relationship can make it dangerous to speak as a poet, and even more so to translate.

3
Hölderlin as Translator: The Perils of Interpretation

The fact that the great poet Friedrich Hölderlin was also a translator might have escaped late-twentieth-century notice if not for a few sentences near the end of Walter Benjamin's seminal essay "The Task of the Translator." Singling out Hölderlin's translations for praise, Benjamin pronounces them "Urbilder ihrer Form" (archetypes of their form) and describes them in terms he otherwise reserves only for that holiest of holy texts, the interlinear translation of the Bible. Hölderlin is the ultimate foreignizing translator, one whose devotion to the letter eventually caused him to leave the realm of service translation far behind him. Paradoxically, it is the impassioned pursuit of fidelity that, in the end, makes his translations so idiosyncratic. The extreme literalness of his renderings of Pindar and Sophocles—which made them attractive to Benjamin—has been much remarked on. Most recently, Charlie Louth's *Hölderlin and the Dynamics of Translation* (1998) traces the themes of encounter, transition, and transformation in Hölderlin's work as a whole and specifically with reference to his translations of Pindar's victory odes; and Rainer Nägele's *Echoes of Translation: Reading between Texts* (1997) reflects on Hölderlin's translations in a series of linked essays on the eros of intertextuality. The notorious syntactical complexity of much of Hölderlin's own poetry, which is generally acknowledged to have derived from his fascination with

Greek language and verse forms, invites comparison with the language of his translations, in which he clearly favored a word-for-word approach.[1] This is particularly true of Hölderlin's Pindar translations, but—as I will argue—somewhat less so in his translations of Sophocles, which, unlike the Pindar translations, were to see publication in Hölderlin's lifetime; *Oedipus der Tyrann* and *Antigonä* appeared in print in 1804 under the title *Die Trauerspiele des Sophokles* (*The Tragedy Plays of Sophocles*).

In Hölderlin's poetological writings, too, the notion of translation plays a key role. The "Allgemeiner Grund" ("General Basis") that immediately precedes the theoretical essay "Der Grund zum Empedokles" ("The Basis for Empedokles," 1799), for example, uses translation as a model to describe the process of literary composition:

> Die Empfindung drückt sich nicht mehr unmittelbar aus, es ist nicht mehr der Dichter und seine eigene Erfahrung, was erscheint, wenn schon jedes Gedicht, so auch das tragische aus poëtischem Leben und Wirklichkeit aus des Dichters eigener Welt und Seele hervorgegangen seyn muß, weil es sonst überall die rechte Wahrheit fehlt, und überhaupt nichts verstanden und belebt werden kann, *wenn wir nicht das eigene Gemüth und die eigene Erfahrung in einen fremden analogischen Stoff übertragen können.*[2]

> Feeling is no longer immediately expressed, it is no longer the poet and his own experience that appears, although every poem, including tragic poems, is necessarily a product of the poetic life and reality of the poet's own world and soul, since otherwise real truth is everywhere lacking and nothing at all can be comprehended and given life *if we cannot translate our own minds and our own experience into foreign, analogous material.*

Every process of writing, then, requires the translation of the poet's subjectivity: "er trägt sie in fremde Personalität, in fremde Objektivität über" (HKn 1:867; he translates them into foreign personality, foreign objectivity). What Hölderlin calls the *Totalempfindung* (total feeling)—"der Geist, das Göttliche, wie es der Dichter in seiner Welt empfand" (867; spirit, the divine, as the poet felt it in his world)—is both fragile and ephemeral in nature and can best be safeguarded in the containing text ("wie in einem Gefäße"; 867, as in a container) which, as analogy, is most distant from the "wahren zeitlichen und sinnlichen Beziehungen" of "des Dichters eigenem Gemüth und eigener Welt" (866–67; the true temporal and sensual relations of the poet's own mind and his own world).

Thus every successful act of writing—each one whose product displays "die rechte Wahrheit" (real truth)—involves a process of translation, in the same sense of the term Novalis uses when he writes "Am Ende ist alle Poesie Übersetzen"[3] (In the end, all poetry is translation). And since the *Totalempfindung* survives most fully in the analogy between elements most distant from one another, the ability of the "analogische[r] Stoff" to convey "das Göttliche, wie es der Dichter in seiner Welt empfand" corresponds to the distance separating the poet's original subjectivity from the objectivity that is its translation. The scope of the translation process determines the richness of the text.

Hölderlin's work on the drafts of *Empedokles* coincided with his revisions of his translations of Sophocles' Theban plays, and it is quite clear that the two projects were complementary as explorations of the relation between Hellenic and Hesperian culture. Yet it is not possible to derive a clear assertion of Hölderlin's beliefs about translation from the poetological texts that accompany his work on *Empedokles*. In fact it would seem that, at least on the surface, his approach to translation (of which he never gave any consistent account) was diametrically opposed to his theory of original composition during this period. Rather than seeking to preserve the *Totalempfindung* expressed in an original text by recasting it in a form distant but analogous to that of the original, Hölderlin as translator devoted himself to a meticulous reconstruction of the original form in all its details, with a relentless precision that went far beyond that of even the late Voß.

This heavily service-oriented ideal, however, is something Hölderlin arrived at only gradually. His earliest known translation—the opening of Homer's *Iliad* (1788)—is highly sense-oriented with little attention paid to preserving the formal characteristics of the original. Only in his Pindar translations (1800) did Hölderlin come to develop that pronounced literalness which became his hallmark as a translator and which he was to put to more controlled use, three years later, in his renderings of Sophocles' choruses. This literalness—in the sense of verbatim, word-for-word translation that mimics the syntax of the original—

is so extreme that it sometimes gives the impression that Hölderlin was attempting to transplant these texts whole into his own language, rewriting the Greek poems with German words. Friedrich Beissner speaks of a "hinhörendes Verfahrensart" by which Hölderlin "in der inhaltlichen Beziehung der Worte zueinander, der am Anfang oder gegen Ende des Satzes oder Verses stehenden, der benachbarten oder getrennteren, einen formenden Rhythmus spürt"[4] (a modus operandi based on listening by which he perceives a formative rhythm in the interaction of the meanings of the words that stand at the beginning or near the end of a sentence or line, whether in immediate proximity or with some separation). This notion of formative rhythm—syntax understood as the crucial link between formal and thematic considerations—is very much in keeping with the readings I will be offering of Hölderlin's translations of both Sophocles and Pindar.

The question of literalness in translation and its thematic implications is raised by Hölderlin in his discussion of *Oedipus* ("Anmerkungen zum Oedipus"; "Notes to Oedipus"), in which interpretative translation, which allows itself a certain freedom with regard to the source text, appears as a correlate of Oedipus's sin of presumptuous interpretation. The fear of what Hölderlin calls *nefas* (sacrilege, hubris, disgrace), and hence an anxiety about deviating from the original text, makes literalness in translation imperative. Yet this position is reversed, or at least appears to be, in Hölderlin's difficult "Anmerkungen zur Antigonä" ("Notes to Antigone"). Here he speaks of the translator's duty to recast references to the gods and the mythological tales concerning them in terms of concepts more readily graspable by contemporary readers—which implies a departure from literal translation.

There is, then, an essential tension running throughout Hölderlin's work on translation between the most rigorous literalness (syntactical as well as semantic) and the will to adapt, adopt, and assimilate foreign works in a new form. Yet in fact, as I will argue, this apparently paradoxical position leads Hölderlin, in the end, not to an aporia but to a crossroads, a synthesis of languages that allows him to import elements of Greek into his own native German and proves a key component of his project to bring the Greek culture of antiquity to nineteenth-century Germany. Translation, moreover, was not simply a means to this end; the manner of Hölderlin's translation made the process inseparable from the end itself.

This chapter will trace the status of Hölderlin's literalness—when does the authorial give way to the foreignizing?—throughout his development as a translator and consider to what extent the apparent paradoxes surrounding it can be reconciled into a consistent position on the task of the translator. I will briefly discuss Hölderlin's formation as a translator before outlining the theoretical positions implied in his work on Sophocles' plays and, finally, will turn to the most difficult of his translations, Pindar's victory songs and the Sophoclean choruses.

Hölderlin's Background as a Translator

Situating Hölderlin historically and theoretically within the context of turn-of-the-nineteenth-century translation is no simpler than the task of contextualizing his poems. It is not known how attentive he was to the work of other translators,[5] particularly as he had access to Classical texts in their original languages. He had begun his studies of Greek as well as Latin (and as David Constantine surmises, probably Hebrew as well)[6] while a pupil at the *Klosterschule* in Nürtingen, which he attended until the age of fourteen. In 1785 his schoolwork at the *Klosterschule Denkendorf* included composing poems in Latin, and he certainly read widely in both Latin and Greek at the *Stift* in Tübingen.

We do know, though, that Hölderlin was acquainted with Voß's translations by 1799 at the latest. In his essay "Über die verschiedenen Arten, zu dichten" ("On the Different Methods of Poetic Composition"), conceived as a contribution to his own literary journal *Iduna* which never advanced beyond the planning stage, he quotes from Voß's translation of *The Iliad*. The essay anticipates Hölderlin's theory of the "Wechsel der Töne" (alternation of tones) that would be worked out in more detail some years later. Here he writes that *The Iliad* exemplifies the "natural tone" of the epic work, whose purpose is to communicate the "individuality" of the main character, in this case Achilles. Immediately after quoting the translation, he comments, "Der ausführliche, stetige, wirklichwahre Ton fällt in die Augen" (The extensive, constant, genuinely true tone is striking); though he is speaking of the Greek original, he clearly finds this tone well conveyed in Voß's rendering. The translator is identified only in a footnote:

> Ich brauche wohl wenigen zu sagen, daß diß Vossische Übersetzung ist, und denen, die sie noch nicht kennen, gestehe ich, daß auch ich erst seit kurzem damit bekannter geworden bin. (HKn 2:69)

CHAPTER 3

> Most readers will not need to be told that this is a Vossian translation, and for the benefit of those who do not yet know it, I confess that I, too, have only recently become more familiar with it.

The formulation is oddly coy. Hölderlin has only recently become "more familiar" with this 1793 translation, a circumstance he explicitly confesses only to those readers who do not yet know Voß's work. Quite possibly he looked into it for the first time during his work on this essay for *Iduna*, wishing to spare himself the labor of translating the lines of Homer he was quoting. He was certainly well aware of the difficulties involved in such a task: he had already tried his hand at translating Homer a decade earlier (1788), at the age of eighteen, producing a prose version of the first book of *The Iliad* and a bit over half of the second, in all the equivalent of over a thousand lines of Greek verse. This project had been undertaken the summer before Hölderlin moved from Maulbronn to Tübingen to enter the *Stift* and may well have been an exercise connected with his studies of the Greek text. On the other hand, this was only seven years after the appearance of Voß's *Odüssee* (1781), which had been widely celebrated, and the absence of a German *Iliad* capable of meeting the same standards might have aroused the ambitions of the young enthusiast. True, there were already numerous prose translations available in German, but Hölderlin in his version also experiments with the verse form: there are a number of hexameter lines embedded in the prose of his translation, such as: "Also betete er, ihn erhörte Phoebus Apollo, stieg von den Spizen des Himmels mit zürnendem Herzen herunter" (HKn 2:120; Thus did he pray, and Phoebus Apollo heard him, descended from the peaks of the heavens with furious heart).[7] More generally, too, one can note a definite favoring of the trochee throughout the translation. Many of its sentences that cannot be resolved into hexameter lines can be scanned with a clear trochaic (in part dactylic) emphasis: "**Wer** aber **un**ter den **Gött**ern **brach**te die **bee**de in einen **Ha**der zusam**men**?" (HKn 2:119; But who among the gods brought these two into a quarrel with each other). It is quite possible that Hölderlin, translating these passages, was not only furthering his studies of the Greek but also experimenting with the possibility of producing a translation entirely in verse.

The verse form is certainly the focus of Hölderlin's translation of an excerpt from Lucan's *Pharsalia* two years later. It is not known how much of this long Latin poem he translated; his version survives in a fair copy, but the extant pages of the manuscript contain only the first 587 lines. There is clear evidence that Hölderlin polished and repolished these hexameters, and the result is translation in a quite modern sense: a solid attempt to render both the form (trochaic hexameter) and the sense of the poem's individual lines.

But by the time we next see Hölderlin return to translation, a full decade later in 1800, he has abandoned this mode in favor of the literalness of his mature period, which appeared at once in its most extreme form in his Pindar translations and was modified somewhat in his work on Sophocles. It is a matter of dispute whether Hölderlin's translations of Pindar's victory songs in 1800 were ever intended for publication or were merely written down and revised in the course of Hölderlin's private study of Pindar's work.[8] In the case of the Sophocles translations no such doubt is possible: *Oedipus der Tyrann* and *Antigonä* appeared in print in 1804 under the title *Die Trauerspiele des Sophokles*. Hölderlin's decision to translate these plays for publication may well have reflected the wish to contribute something to the German stage after having found himself unable to bring the *Empedokles* project to completion.[9] My discussion of his mature period as a translator will focus first on these plays, and only later on Pindar, since the theoretical commentaries he wrote to accompany the Sophocles translations offer the most useful points of reference we have for the discussion of these texts. It is also in these notes that Hölderlin first begins to thematize the translation process as a form of interpretation and mediation.

Hölderlin's Oedipus as Interpreter

Sophocles' *Oedipus Tyrannos* tells the story of one man's attempt to interpret a divine voice. This theme is particularly emphasized in Hölderlin's version of the play, in which the interpretation of a crucial passage serves as the basis for the reading Hölderlin presents in his commentary, "Notes to Oedipus." The impetus for the play's tragic development, he writes, lies in the conversation between Creon and Oedipus in which the oracle's fateful declaration is announced.

> Die *Verständlichkeit* des Ganzen beruhet vorzüglich darauf, daß man die Scene ins Auge faßt, wo Oedipus den Orakelspruch *zu unendlich deutet,* zum *nefas* versucht wird (HKn 2:311, Hölderlin's emphases).

The *comprehensibility* of the whole is based primarily on one's observing the scene where Oedipus *interprets* the oracle's pronouncement *too infinitely,* is tempted to commit *nefas.*

Hölderlin goes on to describe Oedipus's error of interpretation: Apollo's command as reported by Creon—

Man soll des Landes Schmach, auf diesem Grund genährt,
Verfolgen, nicht Unheilbares ernähren

We must hunt down the shame our country's ground
Has nourished, not nurture the incurable

—ought, he writes, to have been understood to mean, "Richtet, allgemein, ein streng und rein Gericht, haltet gute bürgerliche Ordnung" (HKn 2:311; Uphold, in general, a rigorous and pure court, maintain good order in the citizenry.[10] But Oedipus "gehet ins *besondere*" (goes into the *particular,* Hölderlin's emphasis) with his question, "Und welchem Mann bedeutet er [Apollo] dies Schicksaal?" (HKn 2:311; Which is the man he means who had this fate?; OeK 224). Hölderlin considers the factor of "particularity" to have been introduced willfully by Oedipus himself. The overly specific (particular) interpretation, in Hölderlin's view, is "too infinite," in that Oedipus has substituted for the oracle's general statement one of the many subcategories into which it could presumably—through interpretation—be divided. His error is not simply to have asked how the land should purify itself, but to have presupposed, in the form of his question, that this purification must inevitably involve the punishment of a guilty individual.

As several readers of the "Anmerkungen zum Oedipus" have already noted,[11] Oedipus's supposed misprision follows from Hölderlin's own skewed translation of the Greek term *miasma* (stain or defilement) in the oracle's pronouncement with the far more general *Schmach* (disgrace). There is an important distinction between *disgrace,* an abstract moral state, and the more concrete *defilement.* It is far easier for the more general disgrace or *Schmach* to be attributed to a collective body such as the city of Thebes. *Miasma,* which might have been rendered by a term like *Befleckung* (staining), suggests rather the particular act of a particular man and can pertain to the collective body only by association. As Bernard Knox writes, glossing the term *miasma* in his notes on Sophocles' play, "The blood of the murdered man is thought of as something which pollutes not only the killer but all those who come in contact with him."[12] A city, therefore, can be defiled, but it is difficult to imagine how it could itself be the defiler, and thus the term *miasma* already suggests that the city's malaise has its roots in a quite specific act of wrongdoing on the part of an agent distinct from the city itself. Hölderlin, then, in translating *miasma* as *Schmach* makes the concept more general, only to have his Oedipus make it specific.

The textual material most likely to undermine Hölderlin's reading of this passage is, as Fred Lönker notes, elided in the "Anmerkungen zum Oedipus." In his reiteration of the scene, Hölderlin omits Creon's statement (relating the oracle's pronouncement) to which Oedipus's question "Und welchem Mann?" is in fact the response:

Verbannen sollen, oder Mord mit Mord
Ausrichten wir, solch Blut reg' auf die Stadt[13]

Banish, or with a murder answer murder
Is what we must. Such blood excites the town
   (OeK 225)

Creon's mention of banishment and murder clearly points to a particular misdeed that is to be avenged. Moreover, Hölderlin's translation "Verbannen sollen [. . .] wir" softens the specificity of the Greek *andrelatountas* in that line, which refers explicitly to the driving out of one particular man.[14]

The words *particular* and *infinite* thus appear as synonyms in Hölderlin's commentary. Oedipus's "infinite" interpretation goes beyond the finite abstraction of the oracle's pronouncement to introduce what is, in Hölderlin's view, untoward particularity. The infinite is reserved for the gods, and Oedipus's presumption brings on disaster. It is only Oedipus's question "Und welchem Mann bedeutet er diß Schicksaal?" that, in Hölderlin's reading, links the oracle's pronouncement to the death of Laius, making inevitable the rest of the play's tragic development. This view would seem to imply that Oedipus

CHAPTER 3

ought to have contented himself with ordaining a series of purification rituals for the city instead and might then never have had the ill fortune to learn his own identity.

By "going into the particular," Oedipus has, in Hölderlin's view, transgressed. The word *nefas* (Latin for crime or wrong) denotes a violation of *fas* (divine law), which is opposed to *jus* and *lex* (the laws of man). It is surely not irrelevant to Hölderlin that the *fas* of *nefas*, which comes from *fari* (to speak), is thus related to *fatum* (a prophetic declaration, oracle, fate). The *nefas* to whose temptation Oedipus succumbs is to "interpret the statement of the oracle too infinitely." His speech is priestly, *priesterlich*, his sin the hubris of having presumed to give a strong interpretation of the oracle. The offense, *ne-fas*, negates the divine word; it is a trespass, a visit to the forbidden territory beyond the law. Yet this sin comes about through Hölderlin's rendering of these lines: such a reading would not have suggested itself on the basis of the Greek text alone. This, then, is unquestionably an authorial intervention on Hölderlin's part.

Hölderlin's understanding of Oedipus as presumptuous predated his work on the Sophocles translation. Already in 1800, in a passage from Pindar's second Olympian ode, he emphasizes the sacrosanct nature of the oracle. Pindar writes that fate has sent men both suffering and joy since the moment of the fateful patricide:

> Seitdem getödtet hat den Laios der verhängnißvolle Sohn,
> Zusammentreffend, und jenes in
> Pytho geheiligte Urwort vollendet
>   (HKn 2:189, 70–72)

> Since Laius was killed by the fateful son,
> Coming together, and fulfilled
> that original word sanctified in Pytho

This *Urwort* in Hölderlin's translation—palaiphaton (prophecy) in the Greek—lends support to Hölderlin's own condemnation of Oedipus's conduct: the *Urwort* is not just the origin of all that follows it, but also, as original, somehow inviolate (*geheiligt*). Oedipus's reading of this original word is at the same time sacrilege and completion. The Urwort is *vollendet* (sanctified) by him, through his interpretative action.

Clearly any oracle that calls for some action requires human agency for completion—man is to respond to the god's dictates—yet it is also clear that the Urwort is not, in Hölderlin's view, fulfilled in the positive sense by Oedipus's intervention. This completion, then, is ironic: it is precisely by seeking to avoid the fulfillment of the prophecy, by fleeing what he thought to be the city of his birth, that Oedipus first puts himself in a position to become an agent of the fate he so fears. The Urwort also invokes the translation theme. The divine word is an original text, and its "completion," valid or not, is a translation.

Viewed as an interpreter of the divine word, Oedipus has much in common with the figure of the poet that appears in many of Hölderlin's major poems. The poet mediates between the gods and man, providing a service to the gods who cannot themselves perceive their own glory:

> Denn weil
> Die Seeligsten nichts fühlen von selbst,
> Muß wohl, wenn solches zu sagen
> Erlaubt ist, in der Götter Nahmen
> Teilnehmend fühlen ein Andrer,
> Den brauchen sie;
>
> ("Der Rhein," HKn 1:345)
>
> For since
> The most blessed ones themselves feel nothing,
> Some other one must, if it is permitted
> To say so, feel in the gods' name,
> Taking their part,
> They need him;

The poet's services are needed, yet in his mediating function he is always at risk of going too far, committing the *nefas* of considering himself more at one with the gods than with man, attempting to usurp too much power like that exuberant young demigod of a river, the Rhein. All such hubris will be punished like that of Prometheus, to whom the river is compared. Thus the very gesture of asserting the poet's role must be accompanied by a gesture of humility ("wenn solches zu sagen / Erlaubt ist").

The poet serves mankind as well through this mediation, providing a source of lasting things ("Was bleibet aber, stiften die Dichter," "Andenken"; But poets establish what remains, "Commemoration") that endure even in dark times marked by distance from the gods. This is why an answer can be found, in "Brod und Wein" ("Bread and Wine") to the narrator's disheartened admission that he does not know "wozu Dichter in dürftiger Zeit" (HKn 1:378; to what end [we have] poets in difficult times):

> Aber sie sind, sagst du, wie des Weingotts heilige Priester,
> Welche von Lande zu Land zogen in heiliger Nacht
> (HKn 1:380)

> But they are, you say, like the wine god's sacred priests, who journeyed from land to land in the sacred night.

The poets in their mediating roles are like priests disseminating the divine word. And, like priests, they interpret it:

> der Vater aber liebt,
> Der über allem waltet,
> Am meisten, daß gepfleget werde
> Der veste Buchstab, und bestehendes gut
> Gedeutet.
> ("Patmos," HKn 1:453)

> but the father,
> Who rules over everything, loves
> Above all that the solid letter
> Be cultivated and that which exists
> Interpreted well.

If "der veste Buchstab" is all that is left to us in this "dürftiger Zeit," then everything depends on the poet's ability to sustain and interpret the divine word, on the moment of inspiration that strikes the soul of the poet,

> Daß schnellbetroffen sie [die Seele], Unendlichem
> Bekannt seit langer Zeit, von Erinnerung
> Erbebt, und ihr [der Seele], von heilgem Stral entzündet,
> Die Frucht in Liebe geboren, der Götter und Menschen Werk
> Der Gesang, damit er beiden zeuge, glükt.
>
> ("Wie wenn am Feiertage," HKn 1:263)
>
> So that [the soul], quickly struck, long accustomed
> To the infinite, trembles with memory
> And that its song—kindled by the sacred rays,
> The fruit born in love, the work of gods and man—succeeds,
> So as to bear witness to both.

The two actions described in this passage are parallel: the soul of the poet is seized with trembling (*erbebt*) and the song "succeeds" (*glükt*), comes successfully into existence to fulfill its role of bearing witness to both gods and men ("damit er beiden zeuge") of the completed mediation. But the memory that causes the poet's soul to tremble can only be that of the "Unendlichem" to which it has been familiar "seit langer Zeit," the infinite nature of the gods themselves—comprising the sum total of all specificity—that upon which Oedipus encroaches at the moment of his fatal *nefas*, when he interprets the oracle's message too infinitely, in terms reserved for the divine absolute, out of reach of mortal man. This "*zu* unendlich" marks a zone of dangerous transgression, the desire for divine power or knowledge that can seize those who occupy an intermediate position between man and the gods—priests, poets, kings, and demigods. For Oedipus to be able to achieve an "infinite" interpretation, he would have to be a god himself. His "too infinite" interpretation is merely error.

Hölderlin's poet is a medium for the divine word. His Oedipus, the man who solved the Sphinx's riddle, appears to be one as well. Yet his reception of the oracle's message—what ought to be a moment of perfect mediation and understanding—fails, and this failure is greatly emphasized in Hölderlin's translation of the play. Does this failure of mediation, caused by a desire for too perfect mediation, refer as well to the position of the translator? The poet himself engages in a form of translation, giving earthly form to a divine message, as does Oedipus the king, who takes the oracle as basis for a decree. But the moment of successful mediation, that lightning-flash of inspiration in which "Der Gesang [. . .] glükt," is not itself reproducible. It can produce lasting things, but the process of inspiration is itself momentary, dependent on the happy confluence of circumstances that gave rise to it. To pretend, in translating, to have recaptured the poet's original divine spark of inspiration would be to risk sacrilege, *nefas*. This may explain why Hölderlin, in translating, was at such pains to reproduce the containing form of the original text, particularly as he perceived his age as one in which poets may be too feeble to accomplish such containment:

>   Denn nicht immer vermag ein schwaches Gefäß sie zu fassen,
>   Nur zu Zeiten erträgt göttliche Fülle der Mensch
>   ("Brod und Wein," HKn 1:378)

>   For a weak container cannot always hold it—only sometimes
>   can divine fullness be borne by man ("Bread and Wine")

The only hope is to reconstruct the *Gefäß* (container) itself in the expectation that some shimmer of its divine content will spontaneously follow; this strategy characterizes Hölderlin's peculiar brand of relentlessly foreignizing translation that drives service translation into the realm of the authorial. In terms of their form, these translations represent an outright refusal to translate.

The Translation of *Oedipus*

If the translator is not himself to be guilty of the presumption Hölderlin criticizes in Oedipus, he must adhere as closely as possible to the letter of the original text, not allowing himself to indulge in inadmissible interpretation. Hölderlin's respect for the *Gefäß* of Sophocles' play is evident throughout his translation. In fact it was precisely the flexibility of his syntax, which goes far beyond standard German usage to approach that of the Greek, that caused his translation to be so vehemently rejected by his contemporaries. Heinrich Voß the younger was hardly alone in his opinion when he wrote to his friend B. R. Abeken: "Was sagst Du zu Hölderlins Sophokles? Ist der Mensch rasend oder stellt er sich nur so, und ist sein Sophokles eine versteckte Satire auf schlechte Uebersetzer?" (HKn 3:432; What do you think of Hölderlin's Sophocles? Is the man insane, or is he only pretending to be, and is his Sophocles secretly a satire of bad translators?) But while Hölderlin's translation gives the impression it was produced by copying the Greek word for word, there is rarely an exact syntactical correspondence between his lines and those of the original.

> O König Apollon! trift er nemlich hier ein,
> Mag glänzend er mit Rettersauge kommen.
>
> (HKn 2:253, 79–80)

> O King Apollo! Surely if he has come
> He may appear eyes shining with salvation.
>
> (OeK 225)

The second of these lines in the original Greek, *soteri baie lampros hosper ommati*, (literally,with-saving may-he-come brilliant even-as with-eye) displays a quite different syntactical structure than does Hölderlin's German. The two halves of the "saving eye" that frame the line in Greek (a crucial image given the play's thematic emphasis on vision and its lack) are not only brought into immediate juxtaposition but joined in a compound noun. The eye is now the object of the preposition *with*, linked more directly to the *he* than in the Greek, where it forms part of the simile "shining *like* his eyes." Yet the context of the line preserves the image without the translation of *hosper*: something as glorious as a *Rettersauge* is certain to shine of its own accord, and the change does not significantly alter the sense of the line as a whole. In fact, the arrangement of words in Hölderlin's line is such that the two syllables on which the primary emphasis falls are *glänz-* and *Rett-;* particularly given the similarity of their vowel sounds, the words *glänzend* and Retter stand out as dominant and linked. Thus the most semantically important elements in the line are also those most strongly emphasized by syntax and meter.

The language of Hölderlin's text is thus in fact a sort of hybrid. It gives the impression of imitating the syntax of the Greek lines without literally doing so. The imitation at work here is much larger in scale: Hölderlin is copying not individual lines but the structure of the Greek language itself with its complete syntactical freedom. This language is neither specifically German nor Greek. In fact, it is an excellent example of the sort of language Friedrich Schleiermacher was to call for, a decade later, in his lecture on translation: language "zu einer fremden Ähnlichkeit hinübergebogen"[15] (bent to a foreign likeness). Hölderlin's German approaches the Greek, imitating its structures and cadences, much as the translation as a whole approaches its original.

In approximating Sophocles' text, Hölderlin's translation also emphasizes particular thematic elements, making certain details appear more prominently than in the original. This tendency can be observed, for example, in the passage in which Oedipus recounts the original prophecy that caused him to flee Corinth:

> Gar wohl. Es sagt' einst Loxias mir nemlich,
> Ich müsse mit der Mutter mich vermischen,
> Entreißen mit der Hand sein Blut dem Vater.
> Deßwegen bin ich lange von Korinth
> Und weit hinweg geflohn, mit Glük, doch ist
> Es lieblich auch, zu schaun der Eltern Augen.
>   (HKn 2:288, 1018–23)

> Quite well. For Loxias once said to me
> That I would have to mix myself with my mother,
> With my hand rip out my father's blood.
> Therefore I long ago fled Corinth
> And went far away, sucessfully, yet
> It is also sweet to gaze upon one's parents' eyes.

The massive alliteration of "Ich *m*üsse *m*it der *M*utter *m*ich ver*m*ischen" reproduces a pattern similar to that of the Greek line: *khrenai migenai metri tei 'mautou*. The fact that *müssen* and *Mutter* happen to fit this pattern in German may have encouraged Hölderlin to use the euphemistic "mich vermischen"; but the very vagueness of the word serves to heighten the sense of horror surrounding the taboo circumstance that is being evaded (as it is in Jocasta's retelling of the prophecy made upon her son's birth: she recounts only that the child was predicted to kill his own father). The word *vermischen*, as used here, resonates with the sense it holds elsewhere in Hölderlin's work—an association with ignorance, the absence of clarity, and distance from the gods:

Bei Nacht, wenn alles gemischt
Ist ordnungslos

("Der Rhein," HKn 1:348)

At night, when everything is mixed,
without order

("The Rhine")

In "Entreißen mit der Hand sein Blut dem Vater," Hölderlin alters the order of the line's elements (*patroion haima, khersi tais emais helein*; paternal blood, with-hands these my to-take). His line is made more violent than the original not only by the powerful verb but also by means of the separation of "paternal blood" into "his blood, the father." *Blood* precedes *father*; it appears first as disembodied element before being attached to a person (from whom, when he is named, it has already been torn). The verb *entreißen* also serves to literalize strangely the hands of the "tais [. . .] helein." Blood, being liquid, can be spilled or even shed but not ripped or wrenched from a body, which would require it to be grasped. The presence of the hands in the line, though their function in the Greek is clearly synechdochal (in the sense of the English phrase: "he died at his son's hands"), emphasizes the strong physical component (*reißen*) of the verb, resisting a figurative reading. The resulting grotesque image serves aptly as a measure of the speaker's horror and effectively contrasts with the quieter tones that end this speech:

doch ist
Es lieblich auch, zu schaun der Eltern Augen.

Here, the assonance of the words *auch, schauen, and Augen* joins with the placement of *Augen* in the strong final position, not only to emphasize the word (which is embedded in the middle of its line in the Greek) but also to give a harmonious sound to Oedipus's nostalgic thought, sharpening the irony of the line (seeing Jocasta dead one act later will cause him to put out his own eyes).

Hölderlin's emphasis, on the level of individual lines, of thematically crucial elements contributes to his slight sharpening of the case against Oedipus. In Sophocles' play, Oedipus is guilty without personal fault, cursed by the gods, his crime foretold at birth in a world in which all individual agency is denied him. Attempts to outwit the gods—to nullify a prophecy, for instance, by abandoning a child to the elements—are bound to fail. Yet Hölderlin insists that the responsibility for Oedipus's crime must rest with Oedipus himself, as is clear from his presentation of the oracle scene in his notes on the play. And the *nefas* Hölderlin finds in Oedipus's actions enters his translation at other points as well. In the scene in which Oedipus confronts Tiresias, he scolds the seer for not having been able to free the city of the Sphinx's curse:

> Doch ich, der ungelehrte Oedipus,
> Da ich dazu gekommen, schwaigte sie [die Sängerin/sphinx],
> Mit dem Verstand es treffend, nicht gelehrt
> Von Vögeln.
>
> (HKn 2:265, 401–4)

> But I, untutored Oedipus,
> When I came to her she fell silent,
> Hitting it by *nous*, not taught
> By birds.
>
> (OeK 233)

Not only is Oedipus insolent to the blind seer (in both Greek and German) but (in German only) he appropriates for his understanding (*Verstand*) a word that is properly speaking an attribute of Apollo: the gerund *treffend*. This word appears in the first major chorus at the end of act 1: "Phöbus fernhin treffend" (HKn 2:256, 167; far-striking Phoebus; *phoibon ekabolon*). This is the same standard attribute (*hekebolou Apollonos*) that accompanies the first mention of the god in the first song of Homer's *Iliad* (which in 1788 Hölderlin translates as *weithinschießend* (wide-shooting). In Johann Heinrich Voß's 1793 *Ilias*, which Hölderlin knew, it is *ferntreffend* (2:119; far-striking).[16] But the link between Oedipus's powers of understanding and the god is made not by Sophocles but by Hölderlin: the Greek original of "Mit dem Verstand es treffend" uses a different verb, *gnomei kuresas*.[17] The German Oedipus also links Creon to Apollo early in the play (that is, before

THE PERILS OF INTERPRETATION

Oedipus becomes suspicious of Creon's motives):

> Denn treffend hat Apollo, treffend du
> Bestimmet diese Rache dem Gestorbnen
>
> (HKn 2:255, 132–33)

> For rightly has Apollo, rightly you have
> Determined the dead man this revenge
>
> (OeK 226)

Here, too, the *treffend* is a different word in Greek (*epaxios gar phoibos, axios de su*). Hölderlin's Oedipus, then, is markedly more presumptuous than that of Sophocles. Jocasta participates in this hubristic *nefas* to a somewhat more modest extent when she offers to show Oedipus "ein treffend Zeichen" (HKn 2:277, 729; a fitting sign; *semeia . . . suntoma*) that no mortal man can possess the skills of clairvoyance. And Oedipus's father Laius is said in Greek to have set out the morning he was killed to consult the oracle (2:255, 113; *theoros . . . hos apestale*), whereas in Hölderlin's German, he goes to look upon God: "Gott anzuschauen, gieng er aus, so hieß es" (OeK 226; He left to look at God, they say).[18] All these characters may have been condemned by the gods, but they seem also, at least in part, to have brought their ill-fortune upon themselves.

The translation of Oedipus, then, asks to be read in light of a crucial paradox. While Hölderlin emphasizes the characters' hubris and thus the dangers of interpretation, he himself, as translator, indulges in strong acts of interpretation, the apparent literalness of his work notwithstanding. If Oedipus is guilty of the crime of hubris, it seems that Hölderlin himself is all the more so—and such transgressions, as he himself tells us, provoke the fury of the gods. It would seem that the humility of the mediator ("wenn solches zu sagen erlaubt ist") is difficult to sustain. The foreignizing translator aspiring to work fully in a service mode becomes an author in his own right, one who stands in opposition to the author of the original work. These ideas about the relation between interpretation and transgression are further complicated in Hölderlin's translation of and commentary to Sophocles' *Antigone*, in which he introduces a new set of terms for discussing translation as a form of interpretation.

CHAPTER 3

ANTIGONE

While Hölderlin's translation of *Oedipus* emphasizes the dangers of overly specific, "particular" interpretation, the focus of his *Antigone* is on generality.[19] The word *allgemein* (general) and its cognates appear at a number of crucial points in the translation, for example, when Antigone admonishes her sister Ismene who, after refusing to help Antigone bury their brother, declares herself willing to share Antigone's guilt and death sentence. Antigone's admonition to her sister, "Stirb du nicht allgemein" (HKn 2:338, 568; Do not die generally) seems to imply that Antigone's fate is a general one, pertaining to the community as a whole. Since the defilement of *miasma* affects not only the one who has offended the gods but all those who come in contact with him, individual fate is also communal fate. The word translated as *allgemein* has a Greek basis (*koinos*) in common with other phrases Hölderlin sometimes renders as *gemeinsam* (communally), such as the "gemeinsamen Todes" (2:324, 152; *koinou thanatou*) shared by the brothers Eteocles and Polynices, as well as the first word of the play, Antigone's address to Ismene, "Gemeinsamschwesterliches!" (2:319, 1; fellow-sisterly-one; *koinon autadelphon*). The same term occurs when Creon reproaches Tiresias for making overly general claims: "Was sagst du dieses Allgemeine?" (2:356, 1090; Why do you say this general thing?; *pagkoinon*) And near the end of the play, Creon imagines he hears his dead son saying to him,

> Geschlachtet an dem Boden liege
> Des Weibs Theil über allgemeinem Zerfalle
>   (HKn 2:366, 1349)
>
> Slaughtered on the ground lies
> the woman's part/fate above general disintegration.

This final *allgemein* in the last scene of the play is Hölderlin's addition, a reading of the lines

> sphagion ep' olethroi,
> gunaikeion amphikeisthai moron.

By this alteration the line is made to refer not just to Creon's wife, who has killed herself, but to the *polis* itself, which has been thrown into chaos by Creon's attempt to uphold its statutes.

The notion of generality is invoked by Hölderlin in his notes on the play to describe the lines the chorus speaks at the beginning of act 4, just before Antigone is lead away to her death. They are to be understood, he writes, "als reinste Allgemeinheit und als eigentlichster Gesichtspunct, wo das Ganze angefaßt werden muß" (HKn 2:372; as purest generality and as the most actual point of view, where the whole must be grasped). He goes on to explain that this chorus presents the "höchste Unpartheilichkeit" (highest impartiality) of the two "Karaktere" motivating Antigone and Creon such that neither one is stronger than the other:

> Einmal das, was den Antitheos karakterisirt, wo einer, in Gottes Sinne, wie *gegen Gott* sich verhält, und den Geist des Höchsten geszlos erkennt. Dann die fromme Furcht vor dem Schiksaal, hiermit das Ehren Gottes, als eines geseszten. (HKn 2:372–73)

> First that which characterizes the *antitheos* where one, acting according to God, comports himself as if *against God* and recognizes the spirit of the highest outside of law. Then the pious fear of fate, that is, honoring God as a fixed entity.

The choral passage he is describing relates the stories of Danaë, Lycurgus, and Cleopatra, wife of the Thracian king Phineus, in each of which the will of the gods is shown to be unaffected by mortals' attempts to flout it. By writing of this passage in terms of "Unpartheilichkeit," Hölderlin suggests that mortals' subordination to fate affects equally those who, like Creon, honor the letter of religious law and others who, like Antigone (the antitheos), are filled with the spirit of the gods but violate specific laws. The "reinste Allgemeinheit" reduces these figures to the essential structural relationship governing the hierarchy in each of these particular cases ("parteilich" because of individual motivation) between mortal and divine will.

The second decisive feature of Hölderlin's translation of *Antigone* is "demonstrable presentation," a term he uses to describe his treatment of the gods in the play. Frequently he elides their names, replacing them with the principles with which they are associated, and not only when this is customary, as in the case of Dike (Justice). Nike appears as *Sieg* (Victory), Ares as *Schlachtgeist* (Battle Spirit), Eros as *Geist der Liebe* or *Friedensgeist* (Spirit of Love or Peace Spirit), Aphrodite as *die göttliche Schönheit* (Divine Beauty), Bacchus as *Freudengott* (God of Pleasure), and Zeus as *der Erde Herr, Gott, Vater der Erde,* or *Vater der Zeit* (Lord of Earth, God, Father of Earth, or Father of Time). Even Semele, as Beissner has discussed,[20] appears in the chorus that begins act 5 as "Wasser, welche Kadmos geliebt" (HKn 2:359, 1162; Water Cadmos loved). In his notes on *Antigone*, Hölderlin comments on this practice, citing as an example the lines he has rendered as

> Sie zählete dem Vater der Zeit
> Die Stundenschläge, die goldnen
>   (HKn 2:353, 987–88)
>
> She counted for the Father of Time
> the strikings of the hour, the golden ones

rather than the more literal alternative, "verwaltete dem Zeus das goldenströmende Werden" (administered for Zeus the golden-streaming becoming). The version Hölderlin gives as literal is itself a warping of Sophocles' *gonas khrusorrutous,* which means not "golden-streaming becoming" but "offspring flowing with the gold" and refers to the golden rain through which Danaë was impregnated by Zeus. In any case, the transformation based on Hölderlin's reading "goldenströmende Werden" is necessary, he writes, "Um es unserer Vorstellungsart mehr zu nähern. [. . .] Wir müssen die Mythe nemlich überall *beweisbarer* darstellen" (HKn 2:372, Hölderlin's emphasis; So as to approximate it more closely to our mode of representation. . . . We must present the myth *more demonstrably* everywhere).

If the essence of the god is thus defined as one of the attributes with which he is associated—that is, if he is understood above all as the personification of a characteristic or natural force, a specific instance or instantiation of it—then the "demonstrable" (beweisbare) presentation of a god can be said to describe him in quite particular, concrete terms,

THE PERILS OF INTERPRETATION

as is also the case in the interpretation of "das goldenströmende Werden" as "Stundenschläge, die goldnen." At the same time, by supplanting the proper name assigned to a god in a particular culture and a particular mythology, the demonstrable presentation names him as a function that transcends linguistic boundaries, and thus generalizes him.[21] The (untranslatable, immutable) proper name is replaced by a mode of representation that *demonstrates* the god's nature, his essence; it points to him as an instance of a general force or element. "Demonstrable presentation," then, is a way of naming a thing in terms of the structural relationship that defines its "generality."

The demonstrable presentation of the myth relates as well to what, in his much-cited letter to Casimir Ulrich Böhlendorff of 4 December 1801, Hölderlin calls the "Junonische Nüchternheit" (Junonean sobriety) or "Klarheit der Darstellung" (clarity of presentation) he associates with Hesperian poets, as opposed to their Hellenic forebears whose native element is "das Feuer vom Himmel" (HKn 2:912; the fire from heaven) or "das heilige Pathos" (2:912; sacred pathos). This illustrative or intellectualizing relationship to the gods—their nature is to be demonstrated—is a departure from the instinctive closeness to the gods Hölderlin attributes to the poets of antiquity. Demonstration, with the poet assuming an active (descriptive) role in the process of mediation, is the opposite of inspiration, which casts the poet as passive medium. The shift from inspiration to demonstration—each one of them part of a culturally determined "mode of representation"—is an instance of the "vaterländische Umkehr" (patriotic turn) that Hölderlin describes in the "Anmerkungen zur Antigonä" as "die Umkehr aller Vorstellungsarten und Formen" (2:375; the reversal of all modes of representation and forms). Even the poet most profoundly steeped in the mode of representation belonging to another culture, another age, must turn to a set of forms befitting his own age, his own culture.

The "vaterländische Umkehr" has been described, in a set of complementary readings offered by Wilhelm Michel, Beda Allemann, and Peter Szondi, in terms of a path of development that leads, in Allemann's words, "aus dem Nationellen in das Antinationelle, um ins Eigne zurückzukehren"[22] (from the national into the anti-national, in order to return to what is its own). While Greeks and Hesperians each have their own natural (inborn, native) mode of expression, it is precisely the opposite category in which they are best able to gain mastery.

113

CHAPTER 3

It is more difficult for them to come to master those skills that are theirs by default, their own birthright. Eric Santner has described this process as a crucial part of a master narrative running throughout Hölderlin's work. "One has to leave home and alienate oneself from its immediacy in order to appropriate, with a certain detachment, one's own legacy. One returns home 'sentimentally.'"[23] This means, for the Hesperian (or, in particular, German) poet, first emulating the characteristics of the Greek model in order, then, from this position of enriched cultural experience, to return to the realm of the German. The national affiliation that was formerly naive in the Schillerian sense, and thus not available for mastery by the poet, is now sentimental: the poet strives to master his native mode of presentation as deliberately as if it were foreign to him. The turn is a return home, to a home that is itself created, constituted by the turn toward it.

This binary model of opposed cultural characteristics—which lends itself to a reading in Hegelian terms of the constitution and enrichment of consciousness through its differentiation from an Other—has been further developed by Andrzej Warminski. He notes that the relationship between Greeks and Hesperians in Hölderlin's description is, even as a chiastic reversal, by no means symmetrical.[24] While Greek nature is Hesperian culture, and Hesperian nature is Greek culture, it is not true that Hesperian culture per se is *Greek* nature: "the fire from heaven," Hölderlin tells us, is the element of "Oriental" culture—which in *Empedokles* is identified as that of the Egyptians and associated with Empedokles' erstwhile mentor Manes.[25] Even the Hesperian poet who has labored to achieve mastery of "the fire from heaven" will never occupy the position of the Greek who has inherited this trait from an even older culture. There is no symmetry in this system of interlinked tropes, and for the Hesperians, no direct form of inheritance.

The Hesperian poet who presents the older culture's gods "more demonstrably," in terms of their allegorical functions, is shifting his objective from an attempt to identify with the Greek poet's inspiration ("the ecstatic" or "warmth") to "sobriety" and "precision," the features associated with his own (Hesperian) nature. This is a trope in the form of a translation. The poet who translates enters into the sphere of the foreign text—through a trope, an as-if, by which he imagines himself in the position of its author—then transports what he can of this text back into the sphere of his own language and culture. The poet who translates a Greek text is performing the *vaterländische Umkehr*. If the Greek text is part of the same cultural sphere in which Hesperia's nature has its origins, its translation in terms of the "more demonstrable presentation" serves to bring it closer ("Um es unserer Vorstellungsart mehr zu nähern") to a Hesperian mode of presentation. The god reduced to his allegorical function can be transported between cultural spheres. If "Zeus" belongs to the ancient Greeks, the "Father of Time" can be Greek, Hesperian, or perhaps even Egyptian.

Even so, this *vaterländische Umkehr*, Hölderlin writes, can never be complete: "Eine gänzliche Umkehr in diesen [Vorstellungsarten und Formen] ist aber, so wie überhaupt gänzliche Umkehr, ohne allen Halt, dem Menschen, als erkennendem Wesen unerlaubt" (HKn 2:375; A complete turn in these [modes of representation and forms], however, like all complete turns, without hold, is forbidden to man as a cognizant being). The possibility of a complete reversal is excluded. Although the word *unerlaubt* would seem to suggest that the *Umkehr* has been forbidden man by some divine power, the emphasis placed on "dem Menschen, als *erkennendem* Wesen" points to man's own cognitive faculty as the disallowing force. The *Umkehr* is not a departure from the Greek for the sake of the German, but rather a turn back to German from within the perspective of Greek culture. Hölderlin, then, is advocating, in Peter Szondi's words, not "die Abwendung vom Fremden und den Weg ins Eigene [...], sondern die harmonische Entgegensetzung beider als dichterischer Mittel"[26] (not turning away from the foreign and taking the path into that which is one's own . . . , but rather juxtaposing the two harmoniously as poetic means of expression).

It would be reasonable to suppose that Hölderlin developed the theory of the "more demonstrable presentation" in connection with his translation of *Antigone* precisely because the play itself presents a clash of sensibilities, the worldviews represented by Creon and Antigone. Hölderlin himself equates the narrative of the *vaterländische Umkehr* with the plot of *Antigone:*

> Die Art des Hergangs in der Antigonä ist die bei einem Aufruhr, wo es, so fern es vaterländische Sache ist, darauf ankommt, daß jedes, als von unendlicher Umkehr ergriffen und erschüttert, in unendlicher Form sich fühlt, in der es erschüttert ist. Denn vaterländische Umkehr ist die Umkehr

aller Vorstellungsarten und Formen. (HKn 2:375)

> The manner of proceeding in *Antigone* is like in an uprising in which, as long as something patriotic is at stake, it is a matter of each thing—as if it were being seized and shaken by infinite reversal—feeling itself in the infinite form in which it is being shaken. For patriotic reversal is the reversal of all modes of representation and forms.

This plot or "Hergang," as Hölderlin goes on to explain, is the shift of emphasis from Creon, the king of Thebes, to Antigone, who is the daughter of Oedipus and niece of Creon. Both figures claim divine law as the basis for their mutually exclusive positions: Creon orders that Antigone's brother Polynices, a traitor to the state, be denied the honor of burial, while Antigone insists that it offends the gods to let one's own flesh and blood go unburied. Hölderlin characterizes these two figures according to their relation to the gods: Antigone is identified as one who "in Gottes Sinne, wie *gegen* Gott sich verhält, und den Geist des Höchsten gesezlos erkennt" (HKn 2:372–73; acting according to God, comports herself as if against God and recognizes the spirit of the highest outside of law). Creon is identified with "die fromme Furcht vor dem Schiksaal, hiermit das Ehren Gottes, als eines gesetzten" (373; the pious fear of fate, that is, honoring God as a given). Each of these two positions entails respect for the divinity (necessity), but they differ formally, in the mode of representation of the god. In the play, Creon's initial conviction that he is right to punish Antigone for her lawlessness gives way to sympathy for her position. Hölderlin describes these two standpoints as equal in strength: they are "gleich gegen einander abgewogen und nur der Zeit nach verschieden, so daß das eine vorzüglich *darum verlieret, weil es anfängt,* das andere *gewinnet, weil es nachfolgt*" (373; equally weighed against each other and differing only in time, so that the one *loses primarily because it begins,* and the other *wins because it follows after*).

If the shift in emphasis from the letter to the spirit of divine law (from "die fromme Furcht vor dem Schicksaal" to "in Gottes Sinne, wie *gegen* Gott") is, as Hölderlin writes, a form of *vaterländische Umkehr* then the figures of Creon and Antigone are each standing in for a particular "mode of representation." By describing the transition between their mutually contradictory positions as resembling an uprising (*Aufruhr*), Hölderlin equates the process of the *Umkehr* itself—one set of national characteristics being adopted after another set has dominated—with the political action of the play, the public protest that follows when Creon's sentencing of Antigone to death becomes known. If the adoption of a new "mode of representation" in aesthetic matters is comparable to a political uprising, so then is the translation that transforms existing material from one "mode of representation" to another. Antigone, whose reverence for the gods takes a form that is in violation of the dominant "mode of representation" at the time when she takes action, is—like the translator writing of the gods in terms that will allow them to be transported between cultural contexts—attempting to mediate between old and new forms of reverence, representation of the gods.

Hölderlin, writing "Wir müssen die Mythe nemlich überall beweisbarer darstellen," is mindful of the fact that Sophocles' play was itself a presentation of an older myth, not a tale set in Sophocles' own age. The Greek text of *Antigone* presents the myth in accordance with the *vaterländische Vorstellungen* that apply to Sophocles; and Hölderlin, with his "more demonstrable" version, is presumably translating in accordance with his own. The most obvious result of this transformation is to downplay the sense of man's lives as ruled by a panoply of individual gods, as was characteristic of antiquity: the tale of Danaë was already a myth to Sophocles, but the gods he wrote of were still perceived as far more real presences in fifth century BC Athens than they were in Germany at the turn of the nineteenth century.

At the same time, the *vaterländische Umkehr* that prompts Hölderlin to translate Ares as spirit of battle and Aphrodite as the divine beauty, substituting allegorical function for personifying name, has a precedent in Sophocles' age, as can be seen, for example, in his treatment of Dike, a lesser deity, one of the Horai, who stands for Justice. She appears only once in Sophocles' play as a bodied figure, "xunoikos ton kato theon dike" (FrA 15:308, see note 2; HKn 2:334, 468); for the most part her appearances are abstract, as in "all' ouk easei touto g' he dike s'" (FrA 15:318; HKn 2:338, 559).[27] Her function suits her legend, according to which she "used to live among men in the Golden Age, retired to the mountains in the Silver Age, and finally, during the wickedness of the Bronze Age, fled to heaven."[28] Her story in turn echoes the withdrawal of the gods described by Hölderlin in "Brod und Wein"—

CHAPTER 3

Zwar leben die Götter
Aber über dem Haupt droben in anderer Welt
(HKn 1:378)

To be sure, the gods are alive
but they are above our heads in a different world

—a withdrawal that mixes its theologies to present Jesus Christ as existing in the same continuum as the polytheistic Greek deities.

A translation that replaces the names of the divine figures with their attributes so as to accord with the mode of presentation customary in the translator's age is certainly making free with the original; and the fact that this is the only aspect of the translation explicitly discussed by Hölderlin in his notes to *Antigone* would suggest that this tendency is indicative of Hölderlin's translation practice in general. This view would, at the very least, contradict the reading of Hölderlin's *Oedipus* translation as put forth in the second and third sections of this chapter. And it is not, in fact, a position consistently adhered to in the translation itself. In *Antigone,* the names of the gods are used at certain crucial junctures for effect, as when Antigone most explicitly confronts Creon's law with the divine law she herself claims to be representing. Creon asks: "Was wagtest du, ein solch Gesez zu brechen?" She responds: "Darum. *Mein* Zevs berichtete mirs nicht" (HKn 2:334, 466–67; How did you dare to break such a law?; For this reason. *My* Zeus did not tell it to me).

At the same time, Hölderlin's understanding of the "more demonstrable presentation" in practice is somewhat broader than one might expect. A more general application for this principle is suggested in his reading of an exchange between Creon and his son Haemon:

KREON.
Wenn meinem Uranfang' ich treu beistehe, lüg ich?
HÄMON.
Das bist du nicht, hältst *du nicht heilig Gottes Nahmen.*

statt: trittst du der Götter Ehre. Es war wohl nöthig, hier den heiligen Ausdruk zu ändern, da er in der Mitte bedeutend ist, als Ernst und selbständiges Wort, an dem sich alles

Übrige objectiviret und verklärt. (HKn 2:371; Hölderlin's italics)

CREON.
If I faithfully stand by my original beginnings, do I lie?
HAEMON.
That is not you if you *do not hold sacred the name of God.*

instead of: you trample the gods' honor. It was no doubt necessary to change the sacred expression here, since it is meaningful in the middle, as earnestness and autonomous word, upon which all the rest is objectified and transfigured.

Hölderlin's explanation "da er in der Mitte bedeutend ist" refers to the structure of the Greek line in question: "ou gar sebeis, timas ge tas theon paton," the second half of which could have been translated "trittst du der Götter Ehre."[29] The Greek word for *honor, timas,* comes near the middle of the line, making it "in der Mitte bedeutend," all the more so as this dialogue between Creon and Haemon comes in act 3, near the middle of the play, and can be said to illustrate its conflict most clearly, since Haemon, in his double role as Creon's son and Antigone's betrothed, is the character with the most powerfully divided loyalties. The verbatim translation would have *Ehre* as its final word, leaving the line with an "empty" center. Hölderlin's translation fills the line's center with "hältst du nicht heilig," and replaces *honor* with *holy,* as the "Ernst und selbständiges Wort." The translation emphasizes the line's importance by linking it to one of the last lines spoken by the chorus at the end of the play to encapsulate Creon's dilemma:

Man muß, was Himmlischer ist, nicht
Entheiligen
(HKn 2:368, 1399)

One may not defile what belongs to the divine ones.

Entheiligen, aseptein, is not related to *timas* as is *heilig;* the link is Hölderlin's.

CHAPTER 3

The translation of these lines and their explanation involves a paradox. Hölderlin writes of the "heilige[r] Ausdruk" (sacred expression) in the context of the alteration of this expression, which would seem to jeopardize its holiness. At the same time, he translates the line in question as "hältst du nicht heilig Gottes Nahmen." How is preserving the sanctity of a god's name compatible with changing it? Hölderlin's observation that the line is "in der Mitte bedeutend" (meaningful in the middle) implies that it is in the structure or function of the line itself that he locates its holiness, as if the sentence were a vessel whose shape must be preserved to allow it to contain its portion of divinity. It is perhaps by the same token that he justifies translations such as "Schlachtgeist" or "die göttliche Schönheit," which do not literally preserve "Gottes Nahmen," but nevertheless communicate something of the elided names' holiness. This reading is supported by the rest of Hölderlin's explanation:

> Wohl die Art, wie in der Mitte sich die Zeit wendet, ist nicht wohl veränderlich, so auch nicht wohl, wie ein Karakter der kategorischen Zeit kategorisch folget, und wie es vom griechischen zum hesperischen gehet, hingegen der heilige Nahmen, unter welchem das Höchste gefühlt wird oder geschiehet. (HKn 2:371)

> No doubt the manner in which time shifts in the middle is not changeable, and thus also not the way a character categorically follows categorical time, and the way it goes from the Greek to the Hesperian—different from the sacred name under which the highest is felt or takes place.

What is immutable here is the pattern or structure, the shift of times, whether it be from Greek to Hesperian or from Creon's conflict with Antigone to his acceptance of her position. What is at the core of the line under discussion, the structure of the keeping-sacred, remains the same, while the "holy name" that signifies this sacred undergoes change. Creon, it should be remembered, represents for Hölderlin the adherence to the letter of divine law, honoring the gods by man-made rules, while Antigone is lawless in her worship. The rules change, but the worship itself is constant.

Hölderlin's literalism in translation, then, is in theory a structural one. He will replace individual elements in accordance with the modes of presentation appropriate to his age, but the form of the work is to be preserved. In his translation practice, this is not always the case. The change from "honor" to "keep sacred," which aligns this passage in the dialogue between Creon and Haemon with the last speech of the chorus that ends the play, is in fact a formal change, altering the relation between its parts, and there are many more of these.

Yet many passages in the translation *are* marked by a striking adherence to the letter of the Greek text. Perhaps the most famous example is Ismene's line "Was ist's, du scheinst ein rothes Wort zu färben?" (HKn 2:319, 21; What is this? You appear to be dyeing a red word). It has already been pointed out that this line is a mistranslation, based on Hölderlin's confusion of *kalkhainous*' (red with fury) and the verb *kalkhaino* (to dye purple, or search for the purple-fish). What is striking about the line in German is Hölderlin's willingness to adhere to the literal phrase rather than taking refuge in a metaphor that would have offered a rationalization for the image. This resistance to metaphor, if it may be so called, can be traced back to the same impulse that prompts Hölderlin to replace the names of the Greek deities, which have become metaphorical signifiers for their attributes or functions, with their particular characteristics. Just as the gods are literalized, reduced to their specific functional elements, so too is the specificity of the image, the dyed red word, given legitimacy in Hölderlin's translation. The phrase that is "in der Mitte bedeutend," the god that has an allegorical signification—both, like the red word, become privileged signifiers, that which Hölderlin as translator considers it his duty to preserve.

The heavy emphasis placed on the signifier in these translations is fitting. Both *Oedipus* and *Antigone* can be read as thematizing crises of signification. When Oedipus asks,

> wo findet man
> Die zeichenlose Spur der alten Schuld?
>   (HKn 2:254, 107–8)

Where can one find the sign-less trace of the old guilt?

with Hölderlin's word *zeichenlos* (sign-less) standing in for the far less emblematic *dustekmarton* (difficult to conjecture), it is because he cannot understand these signs, cannot read the trace of his own history. In *Antigone*, with both Creon and Antigone struggling to defend their own readings of the gods' will, even the animal sacrifices Tiresias uses as the basis for his prophecies fail to yield up their meaning, appearing as "zeichenlos[e] Orgien" (HKn 2:355, 1051; *asemon orgion*). If the holy can be figured in various forms, only the absence of sign, of form can preclude its presence. One confronted with the "zeichenlos" has been abandoned by the gods.

The characters in these two plays, then, are faced with the challenge of recognizing the signs as signs and interpreting them. Yet, as has been discussed above, this project has its hazards—hazards greatly emphasized in Hölderlin's translation. Hölderlin's Creon reproaches Antigone, who claims she has the support of her fellow citizens, with having performed an illegitimate act of interpretation: "Schämst du dich nicht, die ungefragt zu deuten?" (HKn 2:336, 531; Are you not ashamed to interpret them unbidden?); in the Greek, on the other hand, he merely scolds her for daring, unlike the other citizens, to speak her mind.[30] Oedipus, too, as reported in *Antigone*, causes his own downfall by his desire to know himself. In the first scene of the play, Ismene remembers him as having died, "verhaßt und ruhmlos untergegangen," not after wrongs he himself brought to light, as indicated in the Greek (pros autophoron), but "Nach selbstverschuldeten Verirrungen" (2:321, 52–53; Hated and perished without fame . . . after self-incurred errings). And the chorus speaks words that link Antigone to her dead father—

>   Dich hat verderbt
>   Das zornige Selbsterkennen
>   (HKn 2:350, 905–6)
>
>   You were ruined
>   by angry self-recognition

—where the Greek speaks only of her passionate resolve.[31] If interpretation has its dangers, the price of recognition is destruction.

Hölderlin's Creon suffers from the absence of a fixed point of reference, direct access to divine law. Oedipus, too, in his attempts to interpret the divine messages that have been given him, is struggling against the odds: he lacks inspiration. Both of them are confronted with a world that appears radically out of joint. Hölderlin's translation, at its most difficult, places the reader in a similar position: that of finding herself faced with a tangle of signs so chaotic as to give the impression of being *zeichenlos* (signless). In these translations, Walter Benjamin has written, "stürzt der Sinn von Abgrund zu Abgrund, bis er droht in bodenlosen Sprachtiefen sich zu verlieren"[32] (meaning plunges from abyss to abyss until it threatens to become lost in the bottomless depths of language). Though Benjamin does not say so, he is surely thinking in particular of Hölderlin's translations of the choruses that separate the acts of Sophocles' play. Here, in contrast to the body of the play, Hölderlin does for the most part follow the syntax of the Greek lines, and the result is highly disorienting. He tends to adhere in the choruses to the word-order of the Greek even when this produces an all-but-opaque German text:

> Aber drinn die grauen
> Fraun und die Mütter
> Das Ufer des Altars, anderswoher
> Andre die grausamen Mühn
> Abbüßend umseufzen,
> Und der Päan glänzt und die seufzende Stimme
> Mitwohnend.
>   (HKn 2:257, 188–93)[33]

> But within, the gray
> Women and the mothers
> The banks of the altar, from elsewhere
> Others the cruel efforts
> Do penance surround with sighs,
> And the paean gleams and the sighing voice
> Cohabiting.

This mode of translation bears far less relationship to that followed by Hölderlin in the rest of the Sophocles translation than it does to his translations, done several years previously, of a number of Pindar's victory odes. Pindar's poems are known, even now, for their extreme difficulty, the dense hypotactic compaction of their syntax; because of this even the most literal sense of many of their lines remains subject to debate. Hölderlin's translations of seventeen of the Olympian and Pythian odes reflect this density of language, so much so that the literal sense of his lines often seems on the point of breaking down altogether. Since it is in these translations that Hölderlin developed the technique he was later to apply to the choruses of the two Sophocles plays, I will preface my discussion of the choruses with a brief examination of Hölderlin's Pindar.

Pindar

It is generally thought that Hölderlin's Pindar translations were probably not intended for publication. As David Constantine has argued, Hölderlin was concerned less with producing a viable translation than with taking Pindar's poems apart at the seams in an attempt to "arrive at poetic language, at his own poetic vernacular, in a mechanical and calculated way."[34] This involved producing word-for-word versions of each line, regardless of the difficulty thus introduced into the German text. There is a paradox inherent in such a project. Hölderlin, as we know from his essays on poetics, was profoundly interested in the metrical structures used by Greek writers. A verbatim translation, however, with each word in a line replaced by a close German equivalent, will clearly correspond to its original metrically only in the rarest instances and by chance, undermining the search for a "mechanical and calculated way" (if Constantine is right) of producing poetic effects. Yet Hölderlin may also have been interested in correspondences on a grander scale. His "Lehre vom Wechsel der Töne" is concerned not with individual metrical units but the larger units of lines and phrases and the changes in tone produced by their juxtaposition. Such patterns in Pindar clearly interested him, and his verbatim translations were a useful approach to their study in German.

The Pindar that Hölderlin encountered was even more difficult a poet than the one we know today, in large part because of the division of his stanzas. The colometry, or line division, of Pindar's poems was the subject of much confusion up to and including Hölderlin's time—a confusion that had already begun by the turn of the second century BC. Aristophanes of Byzantium, head of the fabled library at Alexandria, produced a version of the Pindaric odes divided into strophes, antistrophes, and epodes, and within these stanzas into a large number of short lines, or *cola,* sometimes ending in the middle of a word.[35] His line breaks continued to provide the basis for Pindar editions through the turn of the nineteenth century, including the 1798 Heyne edition used by Hölderlin, the first volume of *Pindari Carmina cum Lectionis varietate et Adnotationibus iterum curavit.* It was not until 1821, with the publication of August Boeckh's *Pindari Epiniciorum Interpretation Latina com Commentario Perpetuo,* that Pindar's odes were understood to have been composed not in short metrical units but in "periods" that combined varying numbers of cola and always ending at the end of a word. These periods contain up to thirty syllables (in the first Pythian ode, period length varies from nine to thirty syllables). The relationship between sound and sense, meter and phrase, differs dramatically from that in modern notions of verse structure. Syntax and rhythm remain "two separate systems working together, now diverging, now coinciding, with no regularity governing the interplay between them."[36] It was the faulty division of Pindar's periods into short, often choppy lines—based on the failure to recognize the system by which his odes were organized—that resulted in the perceived irrationality of his verse that influenced many other poets in addition to Hölderlin.

For Hölderlin, Pindar's odes provided a model for lines pared down to a stark minimum of elements. The "harte Fügung" that characterizes them in Norbert von Hellingrath's term—constructions that emphasize each word as a separate signifying element, the resistance to synthetic combination[37]—is an extreme form of parataxis. Pindar's lines in Hölderlin's translation go beyond "die mikrologischen Gestalten reihenden Übergangs" (the micrological figures of sequential transition) described by Theodor Adorno[38]—the juxtapositions that resist conceptualization—to challenge the primacy of syntax in semantic coherence. From the point of view of the German writer, the Greek language with its freedom of syntax was itself inherently paratactic, a property eminently apparent in the short irregular lines associated with Pindar. If, as Adorno writes, "[d]ie paratakische Auflehnung wider die Synthesis hat ihre Grenze an der synthetischen Funktion von Sprache überhaupt"[39] (the paratactical rebellion against synthesis reaches its limit with the synthetic function of language itself), Hölderlin has staked out for the German writer territory that lies outside the border of the German language's syntactical function but remains within that of the Greek. The great achievement of Hölderlin's work on Pindar was that his translation succeeds in reproducing this resistance to synthesis.

CHAPTER 3

The extent to which Hölderlin's German Pindar is indebted to Greek syntax is readily apparent throughout the translation.

> Viele mir unter dem Arme
>   schnelle Pfeile
> Innen im Köcher
> Tönend beisammen sind; durchaus
> Aber das Ausleger
> Bedarf.
>
> (HKn 2:191, 149–54)

> To me many beneath my arm
>   swift arrows
> Inside the quiver
> Are resonantly together; absolutely
> Though that which interpreters
> Requires.

This is the poet's claim that he has many songs in his quiver. The arrow metaphor appears in the first Pythian ode as well, but here Hölderlin translates it more "demonstrably," as *Zaubergesänge* (HKn 2:201, 20; magic songs). These arrows are swift; they reach their audience. Pindar writes that they ring out for the listeners blessed with understanding (*Phonanta sunetoisin*); in Hölderlin's translation, whether by design or oversight,[40] the specification of these particularly receptive listeners is elided, giving additional weight to the claim that follows: "Aber das Ausleger / Bedarf." Pindar's line suggests that the general public needs interpreters to understand his work ("es- / De to man, epmeneon / Chatizei"[41]). Hölderlin's is much broader, whether one reads it as a statement about the reception of the arrows ("dies bedarf aber Ausleger"), or as an existence claim about the need for interpretation in general ("es gibt aber manches, was Ausleger bedarf"). That he considered, and rejected, readings of the line closer to the literal sense of the original is indicated in his manuscript: line 153 first began "Aber das All" (but the all); and this *All* (the generality, meaning listeners in general) was later omitted.[42]

In any case, this passage is massively compressed by German stan-

THE PERILS OF INTERPRETATION

dards, even somewhat more dense—in the sense of lacking connectors—than the Greek model it mimics. While the first four lines are strictly patterned on the syntax of the Greek original, Hölderlin alters the placement of the verb, which makes the effect of the syntactical distortion even more extreme.

> Endon enti pharetras
> Phonanta sunetoisin[43]
>
> (FrA 16:154, 151–52)

The *sind* (enti, are), which in German ought to follow closely after its subject, is postponed by an additional line in Hölderlin's translation, not only emphasizing the syntactical flexibility allowed by the Greek but extending it. His decision cannot be explained by a wish to preserve the length of the lines, as "schnelle Pfeile" and "Innen im Köcher" both differ in syllable count from their Greek equivalents.

As the above example suggests, Hölderlin placed great importance on establishing a correspondence between Pindar's age (and his role as poet within it) and his own situation. As a *professional* poet—Pindar worked for money and on commission—he lent himself well to being taken as exemplary for the *Dichterberuf,* the poet's profession. His work also thematizes the poet's role in a way directly relevant to Hölderlin's concerns. The odes or victory songs were works commissioned to celebrate the winning contenders in athletic competitions, yet the poet shows himself to be a cautious praiser. Most of his praise, in fact, is reserved for the gods. His praise of the high-ranking individuals who commissioned his work is delivered always in the context of retelling divine legends and emphasizing the necessity of accepting the gods' will and fate. The gods, Pindar writes, dole out "two pains for every good"; mortal man is to make the best of this circumstance, cloaking the bad within the good.[44] Thus Pindar notes in the second Olympian ode that while the house of Oedipus was destroyed,

> Übrig geblieben ist aber Thersandros
> dem gefallenen Polynikes
>
> (HKn 2:189, 76–77)

CHAPTER 3

Thersandros, however, remained
to the fallen Polynices.

The survival of Polynices' son Thersandros, grandson of Oedipus, is, after all, grounds for rejoicing—particularly as it is to him that Theron, the chariot race victor who commissioned this ode, traces his ancestry.

Certainly it would be dangerous to protest the gods' will, just as it would be to provoke their jealousy by praising a man too highly: dangerous to the one praised. Pindar's lines about Theron imply that his praiseworthiness is directly linked to the gods' decision to spare the life of his ancestor:

> Woher vom Saamen habend die
> Wurzel, sich schikt
> Daß Agesidamus [Theron][45]
> Lob und Gesang
> und Leier gewinne
>
>   (HKn 2:189, 82–86)
>
> Having the roots of this
> Seed, it is fitting
> That Agesidamus [Theron]
> Win song and praise
> and the lyre.

Hölderlin's vision of the praising poet as himself endangered—his vision, that is, of hubris as *nefas*—appears to be deeply indebted to Pindar's view. That the one is an extension of the other is apparent in Hölderlin's translation of the lines in which Pindar warns that the arrogant—those too susceptible to the pleasures of being praised—will find their punishment after death, for there is someone beneath the earth who "weighs transgressions in this realm of Zeus, / and there is iron compulsion in his word."[46] Hölderlin translates,

> Aber in dieser, in Jupiters Herrschaft
> Die Frevel, auf Erden richtet
> einer, feindlich dem Worte, möchtest du sagen in Noth
>
>   (HKn 2:190, 106–8)

> But beneath this, Jupiter's rule
> The trespass is judged on earth
> By one who is an enemy of the word, in extremis you would say.

This "feindlich dem Worte," based on Hölderlin's reading of the line "dika- / zei tis, echthra logon phrasais anagka"[47] suggests that it is the praising word itself—and by extension the poet—that risks the wrath of the judging force. Hölderlin's version transforms Pindar's more conservative notion of man as subject to fate into a very Hölderlinian view of the dangers of poetic mediation. This is most certainly authorial translation, foreignizing or not: the words of the translations speak Hölderlin's mind.

Thus the Hölderlin who approached *Oedipus* and *Antigone* in 1803 was versed in a form of translation that differed radically from the methods he had employed in his early prose translation of Homer and his metrical version of Pharsallas. That the largely verbatim mode of the Pindar translations was a method of choice, not of necessity, is indicated by the highly controlled language of Hölderlin's two Theban plays. His use of verbatim translation in the choruses is meant to stand out, just as the chorus texts in the original Greek, with their wide variance in form, stand out from their iambic trimeter contexts. In fact, the choruses in Sophocles' Greek are differentiated from the surrounding dialogue text by a number of formal traits. As originally performed, they would have been marked by musical accompaniment and the chorus's dance movements as well as by meter and the dialect that might vary from those of their containing texts. They are characterized as well, as Charles Segal has written, by "a far greater proportion of dense poetical language, gnomic utterances, and mythical paradigms."[48] It stands to reason, then, that Hölderlin's German versions of these passages should stand out from the rest of his translation, and it is here that his authorial stamp is most clearly in evidence.

The Sophoclean Choruses

If the Pindar translations can be seen as an exercise in the use of the German language to achieve the sort of expressiveness available in Greek, the same certainly holds true of the Sophoclean choruses. These translations display a number of stylistic parallels to Hölderlin's own late hymns, particularly in the use of anticipatory adjectives and other means of creating hypotactic structures. The mode of the translations is largely word-for-word reproduction, and deviations tend to be not syntactical but semantic, so that while individual words are subject to interpretation, alteration, or even in some cases outright mistranslation, the structures that contain them generally are not. The result, for the most part, is a combination of semantic coherence and syntax that resists division into semantically complete units.

We often find, then, in Hölderlin's translations of the choruses, passages that are difficult in much the same way as Hölderlin's own poems, whether through an uncertainty of reference in the adjectives and pronouns or through unfamiliar syntactical patterns that seem to withhold words necessary for comprehension until late in a semantic sequence. Hölderlin's parataxis in the sense of individual words resisting synthesis is combined with a pronounced structural hypotaxis. One of the most extreme examples of this, near the end of the first chorus in *Oedipus,* has already been the focus of critical attention:

> Darum o goldene
> Tochter Zevs, gutblikende, sende
> Stärke. Und den Ares, den reißenden, der
> Jezt, ohne den ehernen Schild
> Mir brennend, der verrufne, begegnet,
> Das rükgängige Wesen treibe zurük
> Vom Vaterland, ohne Feuer, entweder ins große
> Bett Amphitrites oder
> In den unwirtlichen Hafen,
> In die Thrazische Welle.
>
> (HKn 2:257–58, 194–203)

> Therefore o golden
> Daughter of Zeus, kindly-glancing one, send
> Strength. And drive back Ares, the tearing one, who
> Now, without the iron shield
> Encounters me, in flames, the disreputable one,
> The backwards creature, drive him back
> From the fatherland, without fire, either into the great

Bed of Amphitrites or
Into the inhospitable harbor,
Into the Thracian waves.

In particular the line "Das rükgängige Wesen treibe zurük" has been subject to discussion,[49] as Hölderlin based his translation on a reading of the Greek no longer held to be accurate. "Ohne Feuer," too, is a misreading of the Greek *apouron* (over the border) as *apuron*. Yet what is striking about this passage is the way Hölderlin incorporates the elements of these lines into a text that combines semantic coherence with a syntax that resists synthesis. The *begegnet* that motivates the *mir* at the beginning of the fifth line is deferred until the end of that line; the appositive phrase "Das rükgängige Wesen" follows three complex lines after its antecedent; and the initial difficulty of identifying the subject of "treibe zurück" complicates the final lines of the passage. Yet its import, once the syntax is untangled, is clear: Athena, the speaker pleads, is to drive Ares, the embodiment of destructive forces, from the country. The fire that Hölderlin has added to the chorus in translation, if inadvertently, only adds to the passage's cohesiveness. It is preceded in an earlier part of the text by the epithet *brennend* and followed by a series of fire-based metaphors for divine power: after Jupiter's "zündend[e] Wetterstrahlen" (HKn 2:258, 206; igniting storm rays), the speaker invokes "den zündenden, ihn, der Artemis Schein" (2:258, 213; Artemis's igniting shine) and Bacchus "Mit der glänzend scheinenden Fakel brennend" (2:258, 218; burning with the gleaming, shining torch). In large part, Hölderlin's translations of the choruses are characterized by extreme syntactical fidelity. The anticipatory adjectives, for example, which frequently appear in the choruses (unlike in Pindar's hymns), are generally preserved in their original positions, e.g., "Zu der glänzenden gekommen, zu Thebe" (2:256, 152; to the gleaming one having come, to Thebes). At points, this foreignizing impulse requires significant contortion of the German syntax:

Sags mir, der goldenen Kind,
Der Hoffnung, du, unsterbliche Sage!
  (HKn 2:256, 159–60)

Tell me, child of the golden

Of hope, you, immortal legend!

The pattern established in "Zu der glänzenden gekommen, zu Thebe" is amplified in the final two lines quoted above, with *der goldenen* anticipating *Hoffnung*, and *Kind* a metaphor preceding its antecedent, *Sage*.[50] Both passages copy the order of the Greek elements,[51] but the *du* in the final line is Hölderlin's interpolation, its purpose to underscore the fragmentation of the syntax: without the *du*, [*d*]*er Hoffnung* would modify *Sage* rather than *Kind*.

At other points, Hölderlin does allow himself liberties with the syntax of the original, and it is above all in these passages that his authorial intent manifests itself.

> Wirst du ein neues, oder, wiederkehrend
> Nach rollenden Stunden, mir vollenden ein Verhängniß?
>> (HKn 2:256, 157–58)

> Will you complete a new [fate or thing] or, returning,
> After rolling hours, complete for me a fate?

> o peritellomenais
> orais palin ezanoseis chreos
>> (FrA 15:94, 158–59)

Wiederkehrend and *rollenden* are switched in position. This change was not, I would argue, made so much to normalize the word order as to preserve the semantic unity of "Nach rollenden Stunden, mir vollenden ein Verhängniß?" The passage is difficult. Having chosen Stunden (hours) rather than *Jahreszeiten* (seasons) as a translation for *orais* (which could mean either), Hölderlin is committed to a figurative reading of the line: the *Verhängnis* imposed by the oracle comes not in the course of the seasons, but with the cycle of hours taken as an index for time in general. At the same time, the adjectival gerund *peritellomenais* is given a curiously physical reading (these hours do not pass, they "roll"), which anticipates the literalized description of Danae in *Antigone* ("Sie zählete dem Vater der Zeit / Die Stundenschläge, die goldnen"; HKn 2:353, 987–88). The *rollenden* also forms an interior off-rhyme with *vollenden*, a rhyme that would be perfect if the words were not stressed on different syllables. The effect is in fact one of rolling or recirculation, while the word *vollenden*—an odd translation of *ezanoseis chreos* (you will impose as a duty)—recalls the version of the Oedipus story contained in Hölderlin's translation of Pindar's second Olympian ode:

> Seitdem getödtet hat den Laios der verhängnißvolle Sohn,
> Zusammentreffend, und jenes in
> Pytho geheiligte Urwort vollendet
>   (HKn 2:189, 70–72)

> Since Laius was killed by the fateful son,
> Coming together, and fulfilled
> that original word sanctified in Pytho

Hölderlin has allowed the constellation of *vollenden* and *Verhängnis*—which certainly reflects his own view of man as subject to the will of the gods—to enter into this chorus, though neither of the two words is literally present.

At points Hölderlin even adds entire phrases not demanded in such form by their contexts. Some of these are phrases whose author is clearly the poet Hölderlin. At the beginning of the second act, for example, the chorus speaks of man's monstrous nature:

> Denn der [Mensch], über die Nacht
> Des Meers, wenn gegen den Winter wehet
> Der Südwind, fähret er aus [. . .]
>   (HKn 2:331, 351–53)

> For man, over the night
> Of the sea, when against the winter
> The south wind blows, he sets sail . . .

The phrase "wenn gegen den Winter wehet / Der Südwind" is a considerable expansion—uncharacteristic for Hölderlin's usual practice in the play—of the Greek phrase *cheimerio noto* (beneath winter winds). It sounds less like Sophocles, even in Hölderlin's translation, than like the

CHAPTER 3

opening of Hölderlin's poem "Andenken." Similarly, the lines

> Und grün Gestad,
> Voll Trauben hängend
>   (HKn 2:360, 1181–82)
>
> And green shores,
> Hung full of grapes

from the chorus at the beginning of act 5 recall the phrasing of "Hälfte des Lebens"; the Greek *polystaphylos* (full of grapes) would not have required the illustrative gerund.

There are passages in which the translation accentuates the syntactical features of the Greek, creating German lines of a shape even less familiar than a verbatim translation would have been.

> Und der Himmlischen erhabene Erde
> Die unverderbliche, unermüdete
> Reibet er auf; mit dem strebenden Pfluge,
> Von Jahr zu Jahr,
> Treibt sein Verkehr er, mit dem Rossegeschlecht'
>   (HKn 2:331, 355–59)
>
> And the subline earth of the divine ones,
> The uncorruptable, untiring [earth]
> He stirs up; with the striving plow,
> From year to year,
> He conducts his business with the race of horses

The first half of this passage follows the Greek text word for word and in sense. But Hölderlin then uses a semi-colon to set off semantically as well as syntactically what ought to have been a continuation of the first thought in the Greek: that man wears away

> the Earth, the immortal, the inexhaustible—
> as his plows go back and forth, year in, year out
> with the breed of stallions turning up the furrows.[52]

By delaying the phrase "mit dem Rossegeschlecht'," which in the original comes one line earlier,[53] Hölderlin weakens the narrative context that links plow and horses in the act of plowing. "Treibt sein Verkehr er" (*poleyon*) both expands the verb signifying man's plowing and widens its suggestive range to include all manner of activity in the process by which man wears away at the earth.[54]

Hölderlin's translation, then, goes beyond the "Greekness" of the Greek text, emphasizing certain points of syntax that enhance the unfamiliarity of the German lines that result. It stands to reason that, as a poet wishing to learn from these foreign structures, he should concentrate his attention on those aspects of the Greek language he intended to put to use. The passages translated in such a way as to emphasize the structural flexibility of the Greek language create the impression that their sense is indeed, as Benjamin describes it, plummeting from abyss to abyss. These abysses separate Hölderlin and the Hesperian world that surrounds him from his dream of a Germany rejuvenated under the influence of Greek culture.

Conclusion

For Hölderlin, the translator is the figure who threads his way between these "bottomless abysses of language." Translators are thus allied to the poet figures, agents of divine mediation, who circulate like priests amid the nocturnal confusion of "Brod und Wein" ("wozu Dichter in dürftiger Zeit?"). The translator whose "more demonstrable presentation" of the ancient texts transports them to within the reach of contemporary "modes of representation" is serving as a link in the tenuous chain that connects the lost world of Greek culture to Hölderlin's own. In this "dürftiger Zeit" of cultural and spiritual impoverishment, the only hope for escape from barbarism lies in somehow rediscovering, indeed recovering, something of the closeness to the gods Hölderlin associates with the Hellenic world. One of the most explicit articulations of this belief comes in the opening to the famous "Scheltbrief" (scolding letter), the penultimate section of his novel *Hyperion,* in which the title character describes his horror at what he experiences on his arrival in Germany:

> So kam ich unter die Deutschen. Ich foderte nicht viel und war gefaßt, noch weniger zu finden. Demüthig kam ich, wie der heimathlose blinde Oedipus zum Thore von Athen, wo

ihn der Götterhain empfieng; und schöne Seelen ihm begegneten—

Wie anders gieng es mir! (HKn 1:754)

And so I came among the Germans. I did not ask for much and was prepared to find even less. Humbly I came, like the homeless blind Oedipus at the gates of Athens, where the grove of the Gods received him; and beautiful souls met him—

The reference is to Sophocles' play *Oedipus at Colonus,* of which Hölderlin translated only a brief fragment—precisely those lines in which Oedipus learns he has reached the holy ground of the Eumenides ("der Götterhain") that is to be his final resting place (HKn 2:377). While Hyperion identifies himself with Oedipus, he makes Odysseus the representative of the few Germans who, like Hölderlin, have not been corrupted by the widespread German barbarism:

Es ist auch herzzerreißend, wenn man eure [German] Dichter, eure Künstler sieht, und alle, die den Genius noch achten, die das Schöne lieben und es pflegen. Die Guten! Sie leben in der Welt, wie Fremdlinge im eigenen Haußge, sie sind so recht, wie der Dulder Ulyß, da er in Bettlersgestalt an seiner Thüre saß, indem die unverschämten Freier im Saale lärmten und fragten, wer hat uns den Landläufer gebracht? (HKn 1:756)

And it is heart-rending when one sees your [German] poets, your artists, and all those who still hold the spirit in esteem, who love and tend the beautiful. The good ones! They are living in the world like strangers in their own homes, they are just like the long-suffering Ulysses sitting in beggar's garb at his own door while the shameless suitors were carousing in the hall and asking: who brought us this vagabond?

These strangers in their own homes can feel at home only when this home itself has become strange, foreign in the most positive sense. The only home—the only language—that might feel native to these artists is a hybrid: a German language so attuned to Greek patterns that it resembles a sort of Greek written with German words. Hölderlin became so successful at this sort of hybrid writing that many of the lines of his translations that seem most likely to correspond to the Greek in the manner of interlinear translation in fact depart syntactically from their originals. In a sense, these texts take service translation to such a radical extreme as to become more authorial than any other work examined in this volume. Their lines exist in a space between languages, in the abyss where, in Benjamin's description, the meaning of the translated text is lost.

Yet Hölderlin was able to apply the same techniques in somewhat more moderate form to produce a Sophocles translation that, though it was rejected by his contemporaries, perhaps need not have been. The twentieth-century fascination with Hölderlin's Sophocles—his *Antigone*, for instance, was reworked by Brecht for the stage and filmed with its text intact by Danièle Huillet and Jean-Marie Straub—suggests that his translations captured something that has made them retain their artistic relevance even as the language of Hölderlin's age becomes increasingly remote. Indeed, it may be precisely the strangeness of their language that has kept them from aging—an idiom not obviously rooted in the early nineteenth century but rather a timeless mode of speech constructed from a synthesis of two languages that seeks to express the Hellenic within the Hesperian, a "mode of representation" that summons up an age when the gods could still be thought of as living presences.

That this alien dialect informs the language of Hölderlin's own poems as well suggests that through his work on the Sophocles and Pindar translations he was in fact preparing himself to become the poet "in dürftiger Zeit": learning the one language that could possibly allow him to mediate the words of the absent gods. It is a task that requires, on the one hand—as we learn from Oedipus—the most circumspect caution, yet also—as we learn from Antigone—the courage to interpret the divine word.

The question of interpretation through translation will play an equally significant role in the following chapter, on Goethe's translations of Diderot. But this time it is not the words of the gods that are at stake, but rather nature itself whose works are to become the subject of artistic representation.

4
The Paradox of the Translator: Goethe and Diderot

The previous two chapters were devoted almost exclusively to the close study of particular works of authorial translation; this final chapter has a different aim. Here, Goethe's translations of works by Denis Diderot will be read as part of an ongoing dialogue on the subject of the artistic imitation of nature. Themselves representations, these translations form part of a theoretical discussion of representation that touches on works produced in various genres, a discussion carried out over the course of several decades. The themes of translation as metaphor for literary inheritance and as index of cultural development served in the previous two chapters as points of reference for my discussion of translation in this period. They are here augmented by a third theme: translation as a mimetic enterprise, as itself a representational work of art. Seen in this light, the notion of authorial translation, as a form of representation that resists at the same time as it represents, will gain an additional level of resonance. This book, then, which began with a historical study of translation in the Age of Goethe, will conclude in a space of theoretical inquiry marked out by Goethe's own translations.

In Diderot, Goethe found both a contemporary and a forebear who was in many ways his likeness in a convex mirror: encyclopedic by predilection, Diderot was spectacularly diverse in his interests, "specializing" over the course of several decades in everything from novels, dramas, and short stories to the visual arts, drama theory, physiology, philosophy, linguistics, society gossip, and *Geistesgeschichte*. Although to Goethe's mind Diderot's efforts were spread not only wide but thin, Goethe became a great admirer of the Frenchman's prose: "Seine Erzählungen, wie klar gedacht, wie tief empfunden, wie körnig, wie kräftig, wie anmutig ausgesprochen!"[1] (His stories, how clearly conceived, how profoundly felt, how substantial, how powerful, how gracefully articulated!) He thought highly enough of two of Diderot's texts to translate them: "Essais sur la peinture" ("Essays on Painting") in 1796, and the novel *Le neveu de Rameau* (*Rameau's Nephew*) in 1804–5. In his translation of the novel, Goethe pays particular homage to the sharp wit and meticulously turned phrases (often with a barb at the end) that characterize Diderot's writing—and emulates them splendidly. Yet his translation of "Essais sur la peinture" reflects the wariness of an initiate reading a supposed dilettante: he augments his translation with a running commentary on Diderot's text, rewriting as much as he replicates.

In the case of the novel, Goethe's translation, *Rameaus Neffe*, was to have even a greater effect on the original text, that of replacing it outright. Goethe's translation of the late Diderot's then-unpublished novel was prepared from a manuscript, one of only several copies in circulation, that had been procured by a friend of Schiller. Schiller had then urged the project on Goethe. The German publisher Göschen had planned to follow the 1805 publication of Goethe's translation with an edition of the French original, but Napoleon's invasion of German territory intervened, and in the many years of anti-French sentiment that followed, the project was forgotten. Meanwhile the original manuscript went astray, and it seemed no other copies were to be found anywhere in France. In 1821, a back-translation from Goethe's text was published by De Saur and Saint-Geniès, who billed it as a "newly discovered" manuscript of Diderot's novel. And when, three years later, a copy of the real manuscript surfaced, it was declared to be a fake and refused publication! Finally the French publisher packed off both versions to Goethe himself, who authenticated the rediscovered text. Even Goethe's copious notes to his edition—a sort of glossary with entries on various persons mentioned in the novel, as well as topics such as "music" and "taste"—were translated into French, though, to Goethe's displeasure, his text was edited and rearranged by his translators.

Goethe's translations of Diderot's texts stand as a record of the encounter between worldviews that were often at odds, particularly where artistic judgment was concerned. These translations are in large part highly authorial in their approach, with Goethe allowing himself numerous interventions. These will be explored here particularly with regard to the question of mimesis, imitation, which played such a pivotal role in late-eighteenth-century discussions of art.[2] It is precisely in terms of the relationship between art and nature, between the work and its model, that Goethe's discomfort with Diderot's thought is most plainly displayed. The traces of this divergence are everywhere apparent, since both Goethe and Diderot invoke forms of mimesis again and again in their writings on art—including, in Goethe's case, the art of translation. To say that a translation stands in an imitative relation to its original is not an ambitious claim,[3] but it will serve as my point of departure for an exploration of how Goethe's comments on translation curiously reflect the discussions of imitating representation that are found not only in Diderot's study of painting, but also in his great essay on the theater, "Le paradoxe sur le comédien" ("The Paradox of the Actor"). In his translation of "Essais sur la peinture," Goethe rejects Diderot's account of the role played by the imitation of nature in the visual arts, but—as will be demonstrated in the pages that follow—his own writings on translation, and to a lesser extent those on painting as well, show him to be heavily indebted to a model of representation very much akin to Diderot's.

GOETHE AS TRANSLATOR AND TRANSLATION THEORIST

While translation was certainly not foremost among the literary genres in which Goethe was active, he translated a number of short texts (poems and fragments) from several modern and classical languages and produced four major translations during the period of Weimar Classicism (around the same time, as Manfred Fuhrmann has recently speculated, as the translation scene in *Faust* is likely to have been written[4]). In addition to the novel and essay by Diderot, Goethe translated two of Voltaire's plays, *Tancred* and *Mahomet*, in 1799 and 1800–1801 for his theater in Weimar and for Iffland's in Berlin, as well as the autobiography of Benvenuto Cellini (1796–97). This is a sufficient body of work to warrant scholarly interest, so it is curious that, two hundred years after the fact, there is still no book-length study published on Goethe as a translator.

In the late twentieth century, Goethe's impact on the field of

CHAPTER 4

literary translation was based largely on his writings on translation theory. His much-cited "Notes on Translation" from the *West-östlicher Divan* (*Western-Eastern Divan*, 1819) were anticipated in 1813 by a passage on translation methods in book 11 (volume 3) of his memoir *Dichtung und Wahrheit* (*Poetry and Truth*). But as Fuhrmann has convincingly argued, Goethe himself rarely translated according to the sorts of principles he was later to espouse in his theoretical writings.[5] His translations of Benvenuto Cellini's autobiography and the two Voltaire plays were produced using quite a free hand—including deletions, insertions, and the rearrangement of text passages—and Goethe himself called his *Mahomet* an adaptation rather than an actual translation. In his translations of Diderot, on the other hand, we see him both at his most faithful and at his freest: his rewriting of Diderot's ideas about painting stands in sharp contrast to the meticulous exactitude with which he follows the cadences of *Le neveu de Rameau*. Diderot's novel was, after all, among all the longer works translated by Goethe, the one separated by the smallest cultural and temporal distance from Goethe's own writings. At the same time, even this relatively faithful translation displays points of divergence from the original text that are by no means coincidental, and the nature of these divergences sheds light on Goethe's role not only as a translator and translation theorist but also as an influential voice in turn-of-the-nineteenth-century discussions of artistic representation.

Goethe's most commonly cited remarks on translation are found in the notes appended to his *West-östlicher Divan*, a collection of poems influenced by—though not directly translated from—several Oriental languages. The book's full working title was *Versammlung deutscher Gedichte mit stetem Bezug auf den "Divan" des persischen Sängers Mahomed Schemseddin Hafis* (*Collection of German Poems with Constant Reference to the "Divan" of the Persian Singer Shams ud-din Mohammed Hafiz*), *divan* being Persian for a collection in general or, in particular, a collection of songs. Goethe had discovered Hafiz's poems in 1814 in the translations of Josef von Hammer, and he also read a number of works on Persian, Arabic, and Turkish literature in English, French, Italian, and Latin as well as German—including various translations. Johann Gottfried Herder had published translations of the Persian poet Saadi, and Goethe certainly knew Saadi's work in the mid-seventeenth-century versions of Adam Olearius.[6] But while Goethe's book was not itself a work of translation, its relationship to the poems of Hafiz and Saadi was more than one of mere "influence." Goethe borrowed from these poems not only themes and motifs, individual lines and sequences, but also, occasionally, literary forms, such as the *ghasal,* a couplet form that alternates final words sharing a single rhyme with repetitions of a single word. In many of the poems he emphasized the continuity between his own work and that of these elective forebears:

Wer sich selbst und andre kennt,
Wird auch hier erkennen:
Orient und Okzident
Sind nicht mehr zu trennen.[7]

He who knows himself and others
Will recognize here as well:
Orient and Occident
Can no longer be divided.

These lines offer an interesting twist of logic in which the declaration we might expect from Goethe—that to know both Occident and Orient is to understand the kinship between ourselves and our Others—is replaced by its converse. It is rather self-knowledge and understanding our relationship to others, these lines insist, that reveal the indivisibility of East and West. The Orient is thus defined not in its own terms but through its relationship to the self, as a paradigmatic Other exemplifying everything we are not. (Goethe's lines implicitly concede something Edward Said would remark of German Orientalism in retrospect—that it was a bookish interest cultivated *from home.*[8]) The self considering its Oriental Other has assimilated it fully, if not invented it outright. Of course, Orientalism of this sort is now quite easy to attack. Goethe's notion of the Orient is transparently, naively Western, and even his concept of *Weltliteratur* seems to imply a world at whose center he resides.[9] At best, one can attempt to recuperate Goethe's position, at least in part, on the basis of his implied acknowledgment of his own Occident-centric subject position, in what Todd Kontje suggests be called "an ironic essentialism" or "transcendental Orientalism."[10]

In his notes on translation in the afterword to the *Divan,* Goethe famously describes—as noted briefly in chapter 1—the history of translation as falling into three stages or "epochs." The first or "simple prosaic" (*schlicht-prosaische*) epoch, in the manner of Luther's Bible translation, paraphrases or reports on the information content of the original in prose, even when the original is in verse. The second or "parodistic" epoch, as exemplified by Christoph Martin Wieland's translations and those of many French translators, respects the foreign origins of the material, but presents it in terms of the translator's own cultural field of reference: verse is translated as verse, but in verse forms with which the translation's readers are already familiar. In the third, and highest, epoch of translation, the translator attempts to make the translation "identical to" the original, that is, to preserve form and style as much as possible. Goethe names the Homer translator Johann Heinrich Voß as the German pioneer of this epoch. This sort of translation, the most extreme form of which is the interlinear version, serves, Goethe argues, to give a more accurate indication of a text's content than even the first, paraphrastic sort. Goethe then goes on to name various of the Orientalist translators whose work provided him with source texts for the *Divan,* and he praises Hammer in particular for the third-epoch fidelity of his translations.

The first two of these epochs of translation are described in slightly different form in *Dichtung und Wahrheit.* Goethe praises the Shakespeare translations of Wieland and Johann Joachim Eschenburg for introducing Shakespeare gently ("auf eine leichte und heitere Weise") to German readers—an introduction, he suggests, that was more effective than a more challenging prosaic translation would have been.

> Ich ehre den Rhythmus wie den Reim, wodurch Poesie erst zur Poesie wird, aber das eigentlich tief und gründlich Wirksame, das wahrhaft Ausbildende und Fördernde ist dasjenige was vom Dichter übrig bleibt, wenn er in Prose übersetzt wird. (MA 16:526)

> I revere both rhythm and rhyme, which are what make poetry poetry in the first place, but that which in fact deeply and thoroughly affects us, that which truly teaches and stimulates, is that part of the poet's work which remains when it has been translated into prose.

THE PARADOX OF THE TRANSLATOR

He goes on to specify that he is speaking primarily of the educational potential of literary texts. Schoolboys, after all, tend to make fun of thoughts expressed in fancy verse—so wouldn't it be better, he asks, to present them with great ideas in their most straightforward form? He cites the example of Luther who, as he says, performed a greater service to religion than he would have had he attempted to reconstruct "die Eigentümlichkeiten des Originals" (MA 16:526; the pecularities of the original) in his Bible translations. For the masses, a clear prose translation is always preferable, while "Jene kritischen Übersetzungen, die mit dem Original wetteifern, dienen eigentlich nur zur Unterhaltung der Gelehrten unter einander" (16:527; Those critical translations that attempt to compete with the original only really serve to entertain academics). So the Goethe of *Dichtung und Wahrheit* had not yet come to believe in the importance of translating the form as well as the content of a text—or at least wasn't yet prepared to formulate such a belief in theoretical terms. His statements about translation in *Dichtung und Wahrheit* can be seen as a retroactive justification of the sort of translation Goethe himself had been practicing a decade earlier. But by the time he completed the *West-östlicher Divan*, his ideas about translation had become more complex, and had also, in the process of their development, moved further away from his own translation praxis.

The newly formulated principles of translation in the *Divan* describe the relationship between original and translation in each epoch in terms of placement and position. "Simple prosaic translation" "macht uns [. . .] mit dem Ausland bekannt" (MA 11.1.2:262; acquaints us with foreign countries); it offers us access not to the foreign word but to the foreign world, with the translator as go-between. The modus operandi in "parodistic translation" is "sich in die Zustände des Auslandes zwar zu versetzen, aber eigentlich nur fremden Sinn sich anzueignen und mit eignem Sinne wieder darzustellen" (11.1.2:262; to place oneself in the foreign context, but only to the end of assimilating foreign sense, which one then renders in one's own terms). So the second-epoch translator goes abroad (literally or figuratively) like the translator of the first epoch, but on a more complex errand. Even in the apparently straightforward substitution of sense of one's own for "foreign sense," the terms become problematically intermingled. Once the translator has set out to appropriate (*sich aneignen*) the foreign sense, this foreign thing becomes something of his own (*eigen*). So, how is the re-presentation of the

CHAPTER 4

material "in one's own terms" to function? The "foreign" has been made "own," yet this "own" is no longer the same as it was before the translator's journey. The terms of Goethe's description reveal the difficulties inherent in translation of this sort, the crucial moment in the encounter with the foreign, since one who encounters a linguistic and cultural Other is immediately situated within a virtual Occident that comes paired with an Orient against which it is defined (much as in the poem from the *Divan* discussed above). This is not a mere play on words, but a genuine expression of the translator's precarious situation. No transmission leaves the transmitter unscathed.

The position of translator and translation in Goethe's third epoch is by far the most difficult, and it is here that, for the first time, Goethe writes of translation as a mimetic undertaking. The translator, he writes, should attempt "die Übersetzung dem Original identisch [zu] machen [. . .], so daß eins nicht *anstatt* des andern, sondern *an der Stelle* des andern gelten solle" (MA 11.1.2:264, italics mine; to make the translation identical to the original so that it can stand not just *instead of* the other but actually *in its place*). This directive involves a tricky distinction between *anstatt* and *an der Stelle*. Semantically the two overlap, but whereas *anstatt* suggests alternatives, *an der Stelle* emphasizes the physical impossibility of having two different things share a single location. A translation that stands anstatt, *instead of,* its original glosses or complements it, while the translation *an der Stelle, in place of,* the original would seem to render its existence superfluous. It is, then, no longer a matter of the translator changing his location; it is the original itself now in danger of being dislocated, in the process of being imitated by a translation that strives to reproduce not only its matter but also its manner. By describing the translation process in terms of placement, imitation, and replacement, Goethe's notes on translation offer a basis for comparison with other accounts of mimetic representation—including those proposed by Diderot.

A quite different model for the translation process is offered in Goethe's preface to his translation of Diderot's "Essais"—the "Geständnis des Übersetzers" ("Translator's Confession"), which begins with an account of a conversation with a stranger. Goethe describes a moment of writer's block in which the writer, although fully immersed in his topic and freed from all external distractions, finds himself unable to begin.

THE PARADOX OF THE TRANSLATOR

> In demselbigen Augenblicke tritt ein Freund, vielleicht ein Fremder, unerwartet herein, wir glauben uns gestört, und von unserm Gegenstande hinweggeführt; aber, unvermutet lenkt sich das Gespräch auf denselben, der Ankömmling läßt entweder gleiche Gesinnungen merken, oder er drückt das Gegenteil unserer Überzeugung aus, vielleicht trägt er etwas nur halb und unvollständig vor, das wir besser zu übersehen glauben, oder erhöht unsere eigne Vorstellung, unser eignes Gefühl, durch tiefere Einsicht, durch Leidenschaft für die Sache. Schnell sind alle Stockungen gehoben, wir lassen uns lebhaft ein, wir vernehmen, wir erwidern. Bald gehen die Meinungen gleichen Schrittes, bald durchkreuzen sie sich, das Gespräch schwankt so lange hin und her, kehrt so lange in sich selbst zurück, bis der Kreis durchlaufen und vollendet ist. Man scheidet endlich von einander, mit dem Gefühl, daß man sich für diesmal nichts weiter zu sagen habe. (MA 7:519)

> At just this moment a friend, perhaps a stranger, unexpectedly enters; we feel we've been disturbed and led away from our object of study; but unpredictably the conversation returns to just this topic, the new arrival either displays a similar viewpoint or expresses the opposite of our convictions, perhaps he describes only halfway, fragmentarily, something we believe we have a better grasp of, or else he enhances our own idea, our own feeling, with his deeper insight, his passion for the subject. Soon all hesitation has vanished, we enter wholeheartedly into the conversation, we listen and respond. Now the opinions keep step with one another, now they find themselves at cross-purposes, the conversation keeps oscillating back and forth, keeps withdrawing back into itself, until the entire circle has been traversed and stands completed. Finally one takes one's leave, with the feeling that, for now, one has nothing left to say to one another.

Goethe tells a story of productive distraction in which the apparent disruption of the writing process in fact proves beneficial, even necessary to writing. Certainly it's been pointed out often enough (by Walter Benjamin and Robert Walser, among others) how "Ziellosigkeit führt zum Ziel" (Aimlessness leads to the aim): how distraction can sometimes prove the most direct route to the writer's goal.[11] On the other hand, what Goethe here describes is a very peculiar sort of distraction. The writer's mind is not being gotten *off* his topic; rather, the topic is being reintroduced to him from a new perspective. I am using these passive locutions consciously, as does Goethe, since in his description of this scene, it is not the speakers in whom the power to direct the conversation is located. Rather, the conversation turns, leads itself to a subject the way a planchette crosses a Ouija board to spell out a message that comes as a surprise to the one whose fingers graze its surface. The friend enters "unexpectedly" (*unerwartet*), the message arrives "unpredictably" (*unvermutet*): with adjectival participles that deny agency to a self that might expect or predict (*erwarten, vermuten*) the way this conversation will develop. This passage, then, is all about the would-be writer surrendering agency in the writing process, or rather—my locution being perhaps insufficiently passive—having it taken away from him. By the time the writer, at the end of this narrative, exclaims triumphantly "Ich komme wieder zu mir selbst!" (MA 7:520; I return to myself), the primacy of this "myself" has been much diminished—the singularity of the "I" having been infected by the "we," the "one," that dominate throughout the passage.[12]

Equally interesting are the terms in which Goethe describes the catalyst of this scholarly production: "At just this moment a friend, perhaps a stranger, suddenly enters." It is a friend who enters, we are told, but in the next breath Goethe notes that this friend may simultaneously be a *Fremder*, a foreigner or stranger. The term *stranger* is used not in opposition to the *friend*; the writer is disturbed not by "a friend *or* a stranger," but rather by a friend who might also happen to be a stranger. This is curious. It stands to reason that this stranger might be considered a friend inasmuch as he liberates the writer from his writer's block—certainly a helpful, friendly action. But the word *friend* precedes this interaction, and it seems to imply a sort of elective kinship regardless of strangerhood, which after all can quickly be remedied by a "Gespräch."

This "Gespräch" is, in German, not literally (etymologically) an exchange. It is a "speaking" detached from subject and context and leads the speaker not into a true partnership with the friendly other who has interrupted him, but rather back into himself. The completed circle of this conversation ("withdrawing back into itself, until the entire circle has been traversed and stands completed") echoes the movement in Goethe's epochs of translation, where the successful completion of the third epoch, the approach to the interlinear version, brings the translator to the point where "finally the entire circle is completed in which the approach of the foreign and the native, the known and the unknown takes place" (MA 11.1.2:265).[13]

In Goethe's writings about translation, then, parallel roles—leading the self back to the self—are played by the foreign author, who serves the writing self as interlocutor, and by the original text, the constraints of whose syntax help the translator find his way back to semantic fidelity, that is, help him be true to his understanding of what the foreign text has to say to him. Both are finally concerned with an enriching of the self: that of the individual writer as well as, on a larger scale, the German literary tradition and the cultural understanding it fosters. This is a vision akin to the national aesthetic education by means of literary translation called for by Friedrich Schleiermacher several years earlier.

Pantomime and Transformation: *Rameaus Neffe*

Among Goethe's longer translations, the one in which the approach to the translation process is most closely related to the methods described in his theoretical writings is that of Diderot's novel *Le neveu de Rameau*. *Le neveu* is a text complicated not only by the labyrinthine history of its transmission, but also by its leitmotif of role-playing, masquerade, and deception of all sorts. An imaginary dialogue between the title character and a "moi" (me) who is suggested by various textual clues to be Diderot himself, the book leaves its reader guessing about many things, not least of them what Diderot wants us to think of the sometimes scandalous views expressed by "lui" (him). Rameau's nephew is a consummate *poseur*, a sort of professional sycophant who ekes out a humble existence by flattering the wealthy, who then invite him to supper. At the moment we meet him, he has just had the misfortune of being expelled from the home of an erstwhile benefactor because, in his words, "ich einmal Menschenverstand hatte, ein einziges Mal in meinem Leben" (MA 7:582; I once displayed common sense, a single time in my life). He proceeds to regale his interlocutor with various tales of getting ahead not so much by "Verstand" as by wiles. We might reasonably assume the Moi of the dialogue, who is addressed as "monsieur le philosophe," to be the proper guardian of reason and of reasonable behavior, particularly as he often voices indignation at Rameau's accounts of the triumph of sloth and underhanded tricks. But here, too, Diderot complicates matters. His Rameau, for example, tells us how he has learned what behavior traits to avoid by studying the plays of Molière—"Also wenn ich den *Geizigen* lese, so sage ich mir, sei geizig, wenn du willst, nimm dich aber in acht, wie ein Geiziger zu reden" (7:615; So when I read *The Miser*, I tell myself: be miserly if it pleases you, but be careful not to sound like a miser). He has learned these things, he says, "systematisch, durch richtigen Blick, eine vernünftige (raisonnable) und wahre Ansicht" (7:615; systematically, by looking at things the right way and having sensible and true views). That the "libertinage" of this bon vivant can be described as the product of civilized and rational reflection—of healthy common sense, as it were—is a conclusion bound to run afoul of Goethe's sense of the moral universe. And if it is the open secret of Diderot's text that there is in fact a great deal of similarity between the two main characters, that they are not so much antagonists as two sides of the same coin, the distinction between them tends to be buttressed in Goethe's translation: he shows us a libertine on the one hand and a thinker on the other, a human parasite and a man fully devoted to the life of the mind. This shift involves a weakening in several passages of the connection suggested by Diderot between rational thought and libertinism, between philosophy and the demimonde.

Goethe's translation announces its intentions already on the first page of *Rameaus Neffe*. While the famous punchline "Mes pensées ce sont mes catins"[14] (My thoughts are my whores) is preserved more or less intact in "Meine Gedanken sind meine Dirnen" (MA 7:569) (the only question being whether *Dirnen* was as unambiguously negative as *catins* in early-nineteenth-century usage[15]), Goethe is at pains to take the edge off the passage and blunts the transformation from fantasy to reality that is crucial to the argument of the book as a whole. Throughout, Goethe's version is more playful than Diderot's, and it lacks the suggestion of potential violence that haunts the original text.

Diderot's text begins with a dream, Goethe's with a state of rational inquiry. "C'est moi qu'on voit toujours seul, rêvant sur le banc d'Argenson" (OCD 5:387; I'm the one who can always be seen alone, dreaming upon Argenson's bench) becomes "Mich sieht man immer allein, nachdenklich auf der Bank d'Argenson" (MA 7:569; I can always be seen alone, thoughtful upon Argenson's bench). Here, as in *Le rêve de d'Alembert,* which Diderot wrote nearly a decade later, the dream state provides the basis for philosophical reflection. The association of ideas then leads the narrator to consider the prostitutes "mit unverschämtem Wesen, lachendem Gesicht, lebhaften Augen, stumpfer Nase" (7:569; with impudent airs, laughing faces, lively eyes and pug noses), fickly followed about by young libertines near the bench where he sits dreaming. If ideas are like prostitutes, then their scrutiny is of questionable worth, though, as we learn in *Le rêve de d'Alembert,* prostitution is not without its social value. Diderot's prostitutes are invoked as if merely to provide a simile for the way in which our dreamer tags along behind his own thoughts—but then these metaphorical maids of ill repute are paid such significant descriptive attention that they enter the text as characters in their own right. But while in Diderot the mind enters this deplorable state with very little slippage—"J'abandonne mon esprit à tout son libertinage" (OCD 5:387; I abandon my mind to all its libertinage)—Goethe's narrator consciously entrusts (*überlasse*) his mind merely to its *Leichtfertigkeit*—a word which certainly has connotations of immoral conduct but which is also much broader in its meaning (thoughtlessness, easy-go-lucky behavior), providing a moral buffer zone. In fact, while the dream state can be seen to provide a site for such slippage throughout the dialogue, Goethe is careful to weed the literal translation of the word *rêver* out of his text altogether. Sometimes he renders it *denken,* sometimes *nachdenken,* sometimes *sinnen*— but the word *träumen* does not appear anywhere in his translation of the novel (MA 7:569, 593, 616, 647, 651). One might speculate as to whether the heavy use given the word in Schlegel's *Lucinde* (1799), Novalis's *Heinrich von Ofterdingen* (published posthumously in 1802), and other such aggressively Romantic works had spoiled his taste for it.[16]

Diderot's text is characterized by an essential ambiguity, such as appears even in the initial description of Rameau: "eine Zusammensetzung von Hochsinn und Niederträchtigkeit, von Menschenverstand und Unsinn; die Begriffe vom Ehrbaren und Unehrbaren müssen ganz wunderbar in seinem Kopf durcheinander gehn" (MA 7:569; a mixture of the high-minded and the base, of common sense and idiocy; the notions of the honorable and the dishonorable appear to be curiously intermingled in his head). For the most part, Goethe's translation, which has been understandably celebrated for its elegance, wit, and fidelity, preserves this feature of Diderot's text. But the slight shifts in emphasis that can be observed throughout have the effect of taking the edge off Diderot's intention, of taming the text.

Most of the points at which Goethe's translation deviates from the original are minor misreadings, either on his part or on the part of the copier of the manuscript from which he worked.[17] For *variété* (variety), he misreads *vérité* (*Wahrheit*, MA 7:617; truth); for *tronc* (trunk), *trône* (*Thron*, 7:578; throne); for *manteau* (coat), *menton* (*Kinn*, 7:652; chin); and for *meut* (moves), *meurt* (*stirbt*, 7:588; dies). None of these slips are particularly telling. There are passages in which he mistranslates words or phrases inconsequently—perhaps because the original contained expressions unfamiliar to him. For example, the phrase "je glanais un peu là-dessus" (OCD 5:448; I made a bit extra on it) becomes "doch nicht gern" (MA 7:620; but not gladly); the verb *fagoter* (rig out) becomes *schnüren* (7:643; bundle); "sans que je m'en formalise" (OCD 5:401; without my taking offense) becomes "ohne daß es mir auffällt" (MA 7:582; without my noticing); a *grison* (OCD 5:479; a gray-coated lackey) becomes a *Kuppler* (MA 7:648; procurer); and so on. His translation contains a number of figures of speech that have been translated literally into German, such as "Heu in den Stiefeln haben" (MA 7:590), a slight mistranslation of "avoir du foin dans vos bottes," that is, to have hay in one's bale, to be well off (the word *botte* can mean either bale or boot). Certain specifically musicological terms give him trouble: he translates "une quinte superflue" (OCD 5:411; augmented fifth) as "mit überflüssigen Quinten" (MA 7:589; with superfluous fifths), and replaces the specific word *triton* (OCD 5:411) with *Dissonanzen* (MA 7:589). And there are several points where details of local color are deleted, such as "Ihr wißt, ich bin unwissend, töricht, närrisch, unverschämt, gaunerisch, gefräßig" (MA 7:581; You know that I am ignorant, idiotic, foolish, impertinent, gluttonous) for "Vous savez que je suis un ignorant, un sot, un fou, un impertinent, un paresseux, ce que nos Bourguignons appellent un fieffé truand, un escroc, un gourmand" (OCD 5:400; You know that I am ignorant, an idiot, a fool, lazy, that which our Burgundians call an out-and-out tramp, a crook, a glutton). This latter exclusion is curious in the work of one whose translation theory will eventually plead for a form of translation that aims to become identical with the original text.

Goethe's *Rameaus Neffe* is also marked by the outright omission of a significant number of words, phrases, even sentences; for the most part, this appears to be the result of oversight rather than editorial intent. Occasionally, though, these omissions and changes appear to have been undertaken intentionally. Usually a moral motive can be traced, although at times Goethe seems to have had other justifications in mind. Various minor changes have the effect of reducing the terminology specific to music theory or popular science. Other interventions require more specific interpretation.

In particular, a number of these changes involve vocabulary associated with Diderot's materialism. It stands to reason that his Rameau, who is practically a proto-Brechtian in his repeated assertions that the only valid reason for exerting oneself is to get some food between one's teeth, should be a materialist as well. Among other things, Rameau speaks of determinism based on physical phenomena, such as in the passage in which he is discussing his love for his son and his possibly fruitless hope that the son will escape inheriting his father's bad traits—a discussion framed in terms of the "molécule paternelle" or "molécule premier" (OCD 5:469; paternal or primary molecule). The word *molécule*, which entered the French language in the late seventeenth century,[18] was only beginning to see widespread use in the 1760s, when Diderot wrote *Le neveu de Rameau;* but *Molekül* certainly existed in German by the time Goethe's translation appeared in 1805.[19] Nonetheless, Goethe turns the molecule into a fiber—a concept current in German as well as French at least since Albrecht von Haller—translating the word variously as *Faser, Erbfaser, Grundfaser,* and *Urfaser* (MA 7:639). He uses the same word to translate *fibre* when it appears in a later passage (OCD 5:477). The result of the change is to remove the character of Rameau from the cutting edge of eighteenth-century scientific discourse. He no longer sounds like someone who's been reading the *Encyclopédie*. It also sacrifices the humor that comes from the juxtaposition of the scientific term and the quotidian context: Rameau speculates what will happen "si la molécule voulait qu'il [the son] fût un vaurien come son pére" (OCD 5:469; if the molecule were to decide that he shall become a good-for-nothing like his father). The tendency to eliminate scientific-sounding words appears also in Goethe's treatment of the phrase "épicycle de Mercure" in Rameau's exhortation,

Perchez-vous sur l'épicycle de Mercure et de là distribuez, si cela vous convient, et à l'imitation de Réaumur, lui, la classe des mouches en couturières, arpenteuses, faucheuses, vous, l'espèce des hommes, en hommes menuisiers, charpentiers, coureurs, danseurs, chanteurs, c'est votre affaire. (OCD 5:481)

Perch yourself upon the epicycle of Mercury, and from there, if you please, in imitation of Réaumur as he divides the class of flies into tailors, surveyors and harvesters, sort humankind into cabinetmakers, carpenters, runners, dancers, singers, it's your business.

Goethe translates, somewhat vaguely, "Stellt Euch auf eine Planetenbahn" (MA 7:650; Place yourself upon a planetary orbit). This change might have been seen as inconsequential if the original phrase hadn't been a reference to Montaigne, as the dialogue's Moi points out a few lines later: "Et vous voilà aussi, pour me servir de votre expression, ou de celle de Montaigne, *perché sur l'épicycle de Mercure* et considérant les différentes pantomimes de l'espèce humaine" (OCD 5:482; And there you are, to use your own expression, or rather that of Montaigne, perched upon the epicycle of Mercury considering the various pantomimes of the human species). The reference is to Montaigne's essay "On Presumption" (*Essais* II, 17), in which he attacks speculative philosophers who view everything from too great a distance and with too little clarity.[20] Goethe elides both the mention of Montaigne's name and the reiteration of the quote, instead turning the Moi's accusation into a question: "So versteigt Ihr Euch doch auch in höhere Regionen und betrachtet von da herab die verschiedenen Pantomimen der Menschengattung?" (MA 7:651; So you, too, presume to ascend to higher regions and from there look down upon the various pantomimes of the human species?). If Diderot's characters exist in a world circumscribed by molecules on the one hand and epicycles on the other, Goethe's move on a more conventionally terrestrial plane.

There are other key words in Diderot's text that undergo significant transformation in Goethe's translation. One is *honnête*, a word that appears dozens of times in *Neveu*, often with ironic intent—particularly given Rameau's introduction as one for whom "les notions de l'honnête et du déshonnête soient bien étrangement brouillées dans sa tête" (OCD 5:388; the notions of the honest and the dishonest—or proper and improper—have become curiously intermingled in his head). Goethe tends to translate the word as *ehrlich*, but for over half its appearances, it shows up in other forms: *brav, ehrbar, ehrenvoll, ordentlich, rechtlich,* and *rechtschaffen,* or else is omitted altogether.[21] Admittedly, *honnête* is a common word in French, used in various contexts to various effects,[22] but as Diderot employs the word, it is so relativized, put so ironically into question, that its loss is in fact a loss.

Goethe made a number of small cuts in Diderot's text in the name of propriety.[23] While the elided passages display various sorts of vulgarity, the offending lines most often contain sexual references. Diderot's Rameau comments "j'aime à voir une jolie femme [. . .], à sentir sous ma main la fermeté et la rondeur de sa gorge" (OCD 5:425–6; I love to look at a beautiful woman . . . , to feel beneath my hand the firmness and roundness of her bust); Goethe's character says he "mag auch ein zierliches Weib besitzen,[24] sie umfassen" (MA 7:600; I also like to possess a lovely woman, to embrace her)—with no mention of round bosoms. Goethe writes that an otherwise repressed woman is overwhelmed at night "von gewaltsam verführerischen Bildern" (MA 7:603; by violently seductive images), where Diderot specifically mentions at this point two contemporary works of erotica with which she has become obsessed.[25] Goethe cleans up Diderot's description of Rameau's wife—"des tétons, des jambes de cerf, des cuisses et des fesses à modeler" (OCD 5:486; tits, legs like a deer, thighs and buttocks fit to be modelled in clay); it becomes "Brust, Rehfüßchen und Schenkel, und alles zum Modellieren" (MA 7:654; breast, the feet of a deer and thighs, and all of it fit to be modelled in clay). And he completely elides one story, noting "Hier erzählt Rameau von seinen Wohltätern ein skandalöses Märchen, das zugleich lächerlich und infamierend ist, und seine Mißreden erreichen ihren Gipfel" (MA 7:623–24; Here Rameau relates a scandalous tale involving his benefactors that is at once ridiculous and libelous, and his improper speech reaches its pinnacle); the censored scene describes a man crying for help as he suffocates beneath the weight of his corpulent mistress.[26]

While it is not particularly surprising that Goethe found these passages unsuitable for popular consumption, it is nonetheless undeniable that a fascination with the bawdy is crucial in defining the title character's "libertinage" and that the German text thus winds up distinctly paler than the original. In fact, Diderot's use of the sexual grotesque is strategic. The last episode mentioned above (the fat woman crushing her mate) is the penultimate step in a series of stories of escalating cruelty and violence that culminate in the tale of a scoundrel, identified here only as the "renegade of Avignon" (*renegade* meaning one who rejects Catholicism), who invests many months into gaining the confidence of a wealthy Jew. This accomplished, he tricks his victim into preparing to flee town—and sending away all his worldly goods—by claiming that both of them have been denounced to the Spanish Inquisition. The renegade himself then denounces the Jew to the Inquisition and flees with his fortune. Rameau tells this tale with a sort of appreciative glee, well captured by Goethe in his translation of the story's punchline:

> Aber das Erhabene seiner Bosheit zeigt sich erst darin, daß er selbst seinen Freund, den Israeliten, angegeben hatte, daß die Inquisition diesen bei seinem Erwachen in Empfang nahm und nach einigen Tagen ein Lustfeuerchen mit ihm anstellte, und so war der Renegat ruhiger Besitzer des Vermögens dieses verfluchten Abkömmlings derer, die unsern Herrn gekreuzigt haben.
> *Ich.* Ich weiß nicht, wovor ich mich mehr entsetzen soll, vor der Verruchtheit des Renegaten oder vor dem Ton, mit dem Ihr davon sprecht.
> *Er.* Das ist, was ich Euch sagte. Die Schrecklichkeit der Handlung hebt Euch über die Verachtung weg. [. . .] Ihr solltet einsehen, wie hoch ich in meiner Kunst stehe. (MA 7:627)

> But the sublimeness of his wickedness became apparent only once he had denounced his friend, the Israelite, and the Inquisition came for him one morning, and, a few days later, made a lovely little bonfire out of him, and so now the renegade was the carefree owner of the fortune of this accursed descendent of the ones who crucified our Lord.
> (Moi.) I don't know which should horrify me more: the renegade's infamy or the tone in which you speak of it.
> (Lui.) That's what I was saying. The horrificness of the deed raises you above your contempt. . . . You'll have to appreciate how well-versed I am in my art.

It is precisely this "sublimeness of the wicked" that names Diderot's privileging the grotesque in its capacity to induce aesthetic pleasure. The misdeed of the wicked renegade, it seems, is being celebrated as a sort of virtuoso performance in its own right. Diderot underscores this point with the ironic epithet "beau feu de joie" (OCD 5:456; nicely translated by Goethe as *Lustfeuerchen,* MA 7:627; lovely little bonfire), with which Rameau reports the victim's death at the stake, and with his apparent adoption ("the ones who crucified our Lord") of the point of view of the Inquisition tribunal itself.

Goethe adds a curious twist to the tale by identifying the plot's victim initially not simply as a Jew (as does Diderot), but as "eine[n] heimlich[en] Juden" (MA 7:625). This "secret" or "clandestine" Jew, as becomes clear in the course of the story, is assimilated, passing as a gentile precisely so as to avoid the fate that, in the end, befalls him. Perhaps Goethe wants only to be certain his audience realizes that this story is set during the Inquisition (which is stated outright only later) and that among the victims of its religious intolerance were Jews. Still, the information that the Jew's identity is clandestine appears only a half-dozen sentences into Diderot's story, when the renegade has gained his supposed benefactor's confidence to the point of being informed that the latter cannot eat pork. The word *secret/clandestine* appears in Diderot's version only later, when we are told that "Die Prozedur des Tribunals ist heimlich" (7:626; The procedure of the tribunal is clandestine). No doubt unwittingly, Goethe has established a rather dubious connection between the workings of the Inquisition and the private life of this hapless Jew. Since secrecy can easily be construed as morally deplorable, a way of carrying out harmful acts with impunity, then the very secrecy of the Jew's identity can be said to imply a fundamental culpability that might serve to justify his eventual execution. This added layer of complexity in an already rather complex passage is an unhelpful intervention.

Diderot's Rameau, in telling his story from the perspective of one well pleased with its outcome, is an actor, and the hero/villain of his tale is one as well. In the middle of the story when the renegade comes to announce to the Jew the imminent arrest of both of them, he does so as the walking caricature of distress: "mit zerstörter Miene, gebrochener Stimme, totenbleichem Gesicht, an allen Gliedern zitternd" (MA 7:626; with a ravaged expression, his voice broken, his face pale as a corpse, his limbs shaking). The Jew, Rameau says, ought to have seen through him and sent him packing at that moment because "der Renegat in seiner Verstellung das Maß überschritten hatte" (7:626; the renegade had gone too far in his masquerade): he overacted. Here a real deception is afoot, but Diderot's character describes the renegade's failing in artistic (theatrical) terms. The renegade is lucky in that his ruse succeeds where his artistry does not (the Jew, in other words, is too easily duped), but in any case his failing is easily described: he has violated the rules of mimetic representation. Thus it is only apparently a non-sequitur when this episode is followed by a discussion (initiated with almost no transition) of the role of mimesis in music, the art in which one would least expect to see it given much of a role.

Two of the words that prove especially problematic in Goethe's translation are *ligne* and *modèle*, which appear repeatedly in Rameau's long monologue on the subject of imitation in music. For Rameau, music can reach the highest pinnacle of artistry only when it achieves what we might call the *ductus* of natural speech, natural expressions of passion or anger, natural laments.

> Man muß die Deklamation wie eine Linie ansehen und den Gesang wie eine andre Linie, die sich um die erste herschlängelt. Je mehr diese Deklamation, Muster des Gesangs, stark und wahr ist, an je mehr Punkten der Gesang, der sich ihr gleichstellt, sie durchschneidet, desto wahrer, desto schöner wird er sein. (MA 7:629)

> One must imagine declamation as a line and the singing as a second line that twines about the first one. The more this declamation, which is the model for the song, is strong and true, and the more points of intersection there are between this singing, which is emulating the declamation, and the declamation itself, the truer, the more beautiful the song will be.

In other words, an effective musical lament will not necessarily contain the same words in the same order as a real spoken lament uttered in the world, but will parallel it in its modulations of intensity, of emotion, of vocal depth. The declamation is the "Muster" or "modèle" for the song—and this "pattern," as we will see elsewhere in Diderot, holds for all art in relation to its source in nature. The relation is not linear, but it is one of line.

This argument is carried out over the next several pages with respect to various contemporary composers, but in Goethe's translation the vocabulary does not remain constant. At one point he inappropriately translates *ligne* as *Reihe*: "Der tierische Schrei der Leidenschaft hat die Reihe zu bezeichnen, die uns frommt" (MA 7:636; The animal cry of passion should define the *series* suitable for us), and the word *modèle* appears variously as *Muster, Vorbild,* and *Unterlage* (7:636–37). In the last of these, the context provides solid justification for the variation in terms, but at the same time the shift in vocabulary obscures the fact that Diderot (through Rameau) is making the case for a relationship to sounds found in nature (or in spontaneous human utterance) that holds for all musical expression. Goethe also gives various translations for the word *sublime* (*erhaben,* 7:627; *vortrefflich,* 7:629; *sublim,* 7:630). This is either carelessness or simple misjudgment in the second and third cases, as the third appears in a sentence clearly referring back to the second in a discussion of music. On the other hand, one can see why Goethe might have wished to vary the word so as to avoid suggesting a link between the aesthetic experience of music and the phrase "the sublimeness of his wickedness" which introduces the punchline to the tale of the renegade (7:627).

In short, these major and minor adjustments in Goethe's translation of *Neveu,* clearly authorial interventions in what is largely a work of service translation, have the effect of weakening the links Diderot establishes not only between intellectual endeavor and various less dignified spheres of activity—concupiscence, inebriation, and treachery—but also, if to a lesser degree, between the sorts of representation at work in the visual arts and in music. As we will see, this disagreement as to the extent to which the various arts overlap with respect to the imitation of nature is crucial in understanding Goethe's response to Diderot. It appears in more extreme form in Goethe's translation of Diderot's essay on painting.

Beautiful Imitation: "Versuch über die Malerei"

Diderot's "Essais sur la peinture" was first translated into German not by Goethe, but by C. F. Cramer in 1796. Cramer published all seven of the essay's chapters (Goethe included only the first two) in what was announced as the first installment of an edition of Diderot's collected

CHAPTER 4

works. This edition, as it turns out, got only as far as volume 2: *Die Nonne* (*The Nun*, 1797), and at one point its publisher, Hartknoch in Riga, tried to persuade Herder to contribute translations as well. Goethe must have known of Cramer's translation, which was advertised in the September 1796 issue of the journal *Der allgemeine Litterarische Anzeiger*, but already in early August of that year he had written to an acquaintance, the Swiss painter Heinrich Meyer, of his intention to translate the "Essais." There is nothing to suggest that Goethe saw Cramer's translation before completing his own.[27]

Goethe's translation of the first two chapters of Diderot's "Essais sur la peinture" is as much a critique and correction of Diderot's views as it is a translation. Goethe uses the text to mark his difference from Diderot on such topics as the relationship between art and nature and the training of young artists. His method remains constant throughout: he translates a few lines at a time of Diderot's essay, following them with his own, usually much longer, commentary on the same topic. He even goes so far as to reproach Diderot for his faulty views, referring to him at one point as his opponent (*Gegner*, MA 7:525). In the first chapter, on drawing, Goethe objects above all to Diderot's conflation of nature and art in his description of beautiful forms and their study. Where Diderot writes that the student of art should learn from nature, particularly in portraiture (rather than learning to represent the human figure from the academic exercise of drawing artificially posed models under a teacher's supervision), Goethe protests that the beauty of art is far removed from that of nature, insisting on a strict division between rules in art (the conventions established over many years by the artists of a nation) and the laws of nature (eternal and immutable, but not necessarily the source of beauty).

The translation begins with a dispute about natural beauty: Goethe corrects Diderot's claim "La nature ne fait rien d'incorrect" (OCD 10: 461; Nature makes nothing that is incorrect) to read "Die Natur macht nichts inkonsequentes" (MA 7:521; Nature makes nothing that is inconsistent). Diderot is arguing for a basic rightness in the ways of nature, even when they involve physical disfigurement, and eventually he will equate this correctness with beauty. He describes, for example, a woman who lost her eyesight in childhood: her lids have sunken back into their sockets, and the rest of her face has shifted slightly to take this change into account. This shift is, for Diderot, beautiful; for Goethe, it is not. As Goethe writes in an aphorism, "Die

Kunst soll das Penible nicht vorstellen" (MA 17:905, *Maximen und Reflexionen*; Art should not display the embarrassing). Goethe makes slight adjustments to Diderot's premises so as to prevent the conclusion that all things in nature are beautiful. He transforms the claim "de tous les êtres qui existent, il n'y en a pas un qui ne soit comme il doit être" (OCD 10:461; of all the creatures that exist, there is not one that is not as it should be) into "unter allen organischen Naturen, die wir kennen, ist keine, die nicht wäre, wie sie sein kann" (MA 7:521; of all the organic natures [beings] known to us, there is not one that is not as it can be). The translation of *êtres* as *Naturen* (though Goethe translates the word as *Wesen* in the rest of the essay) confuses matters somewhat, since it is nature that is at stake in the first place. And while, for Diderot, nature is never incorrect—everything is as it is by necessity, and necessity is necessarily right and fitting—Goethe replaces "wie es sein soll" with "wie es sein kann," resulting in a claim that is all but tautological, hardly a claim at all.

Goethe takes issue, above all, with Diderot's conception of the work of art in its relation to nature. Diderot's essay was clearly composed (as Goethe acknowledges in his prefatory note) as a reaction against a school of mannered, academic painters in France who created a sort of stylized art that paid little attention to verisimilitude. Much of the first "chapter" of his essay consists of a diatribe against the, in his view, excessive academic training of young painters, who spend years in art schools drawing from models and studying anatomy. These models, Diderot argues, are not natural; even though they are human beings, they are posed by the professors in various unnatural positions that represent only obliquely real actions in the real world:

> Qu'ont de commun l'homme qui tire de l'eau dans le puits de votre cour et celui qui n'ayant pas le même fardeu à tirer, simule gauchement cette action, avec ses deux bras en haut, sur l'estrade de l'école?   (OCD 10:464)

What is there in common between the man who draws water from the well in your courtyard and the one who—not having the same burden to stem his weight against, clumsily simulates this action, his two arms held aloft, upon the stage at the art school?

The antidote Diderot sees to this excessive mannerism is to de-emphasize the role of academic training in the formation of young artists and instead to encourage them to "imit[er] scrupuleusement la nature" (OCD 10:467; scrupulously imitate nature). But while for him the key to beauty in art is to be found in nature, for Goethe the opposite is true. Goethe objects to the notion that raw nature makes a good model for art, noting that what is beautiful in nature and what is beautiful in art overlap but nonetheless differ decisively. As he writes elsewhere,

> Nach unserer Überzeugung sollte der junge Künstler wenig oder gar keine Studien nach der Natur beginnen, wobei er nicht zugleich dächte, wie er jedes Blatt zu einem Ganzen abrunden, wie er diese Einzelnheit [sic], in ein angenehmes Bild verwandelt, in einen Rahmen eingeschlossen, dem Liebhaber und Kenner gefällig anbieten möge. (MA 17:803, *Maximen und Reflexionen*)

> It is our conviction that the young artist shouldn't produce any studies from nature at all, or only very few, without at the same time considering how he might round out each drawing into a whole, how he might present the individual object, transformed into an agreeable picture and enclosed in a frame, so as to please the art lover and connoisseur.

It isn't that the beauty of nature cannot serve as a basis for the sort of beauty that resides in art, but the presence of natural beauty in no way guarantees the production of a beautiful work. Nature must be transformed if the resulting picture is to be aesthetically pleasing. While Diderot might have reached similar conclusions, his line of reasoning is quite different.

For Diderot, the "scrupulous imitation" of a form found in nature is the most direct way to produce beauty in art. This doesn't mean he equates artistic merit with the ability to produce a perfect or near-perfect reproduction, rather that the aspect of a work of art that produces the illusion of reality also has the ability to make an impression on the viewer. If nature produces stronger impressions than art, it is clear that art which creates the illusion of being part of nature will produce the strongest response. In Herbert Dieckmann's explanation, "For Diderot, pleasure taken in art is pleasure taken in an appearance

(*Schein*), yet this appearance gives him the illusion of the real (Diderot calls it nature or truth); that is, this pleasure is directed toward the object via the imitation."[28] For Goethe, the appreciation of the beautiful in art is inherently separate from the beautiful in nature—he differentiates strictly between the *Naturwahre* and the *Kunstwahre* (what is true in nature, what is true in art).[29] This is why he "corrects" the *inkorrekt* of Diderot's first sentence (Nature makes nothing that is incorrect) to *inkonsequent*:

> Korrektion setzt Regeln voraus, und zwar Regeln, die der Mensch selbst bestimmt, nach Gefühl, Erfahrung, Überzeugung und Wohlgefallen, und darnach mehr den äußern Schein als das innere Dasein eines Geschöpfes beurteilt; die Gesetze hingegen nach denen die Natur wirkt, fordern den strengsten, innern organischen Zusammenhang. (MA 7:521)

> Correctness presupposes rules, and these are rules that man himself determines based on feeling, experience, convictions and what he finds pleasing, and thus he judges more the outward appearance than the inner being of a work [created thing]; the laws according to which nature operates, on the other hand, demand the most stringent inner organic coherence.

For Goethe, in other words, there is a clear division between the rules of art and the laws of nature. And while for Goethe, as we will see, the *Genie* is the source of the rules that govern art, Diderot sees the *génie's* task as less one of invention than of discovery.

The second chapter of "Versuch über die Malerei," on the subject of color, undergoes an even more radical transformation than the first. Goethe not only continues in his method of citing a few lines of Diderot, which are then heavily amended and supplemented by his own commentary, but in this case slices up Diderot's essay into some two dozen short segments, which he then rearranges and incorporates into his own argument. As in the first chapter, Diderot praises the artist who is able to copy nature most precisely: "Quel est donc pour moi le vrai, le grand coloriste? C'est celui qui a pris le ton de la nature et des objets bien éclairés, et qui a su accorder son tableau" (OCD 10:471; Who,

CHAPTER 4

then, is for me the real, the great colorist? It is the one who has taken his tints from nature and well-lit objects, and who has been skillful in bringing harmony to this image). As before, Goethe emphasizes not fidelity to the natural world so much as the understanding of pictorial harmony that makes the portrayal of color "am richtigsten und reinsten" (MA 7:547; the most right and the purest). At the same time, Goethe's more advanced knowledge of the scientific mechanism of color comes into play. Take, for example, his gloss on the definition of the "grand coloriste" cited above:

> An wenig Gegenständen erscheint die Farbe in ihrer ursprünglichen Reinheit, selbst im vollsten Lichte, sie wird mehr oder minder durch die Natur der Körper, an denen sie erscheint, schon modifiziert und überdies sehen wir sie noch, durch stärkeres oder schwächeres Licht, durch Beschattung, durch Entfernung, ja endlich sogar durch mancherlei Trug auf tausenderlei Weise, bestimmt und verändert. (MA 7:547)

> There are few objects upon which color appears in its original purity, even in full light; it is always modified to a greater or lesser extent by the nature of the body upon which it appears, and on top of this we are seeing it both determined and altered in thousands of ways by stronger or weaker light, by shadow, by distance, indeed even by various sorts of illusions.

Goethe's understanding of the physical mechanisms by which colors appear to us in nature far outstrips Diderot's in sophistication, and the changes he makes to Diderot's comments on the use of color are in large part a matter of bringing up to date the work of a scholar writing thirty years earlier.[30] As a result, this chapter of the "Essais" is far less useful for the purposes of my discussion than the first, in which the two writers' disagreements are based not on a changing body of knowledge but on actually conflicting points of view.

Certainly Goethe's revision of these two sections of "Essais sur la peinture" constitutes a serious encounter with Diderot's work. Yet it cannot be assumed that these two chapters, taken in isolation, suffice to represent Diderot's complex, often contradictory ideas about the arts. To begin with, the final five sections of the "Essais," which Goethe omitted in his translation, present notions that complicate the views presented in the first two; this is above all true of the fourth and fifth sections, those on artistic expression ("Ce que tout le monde sait sur l'expression, et quelque chose que tout le monde ne sait pas" ["What Everyone Knows about Expression, and Something Not Everyone Knows"]) and composition ("Paragraphe sur la composition ou j'espère que j'en parlerai" ["Paragraph on Composition in Which I Hope I'll Speak about It"]). Particularly in the latter, Diderot relativizes much of what he wrote in the first section about the imitation of nature by emphasizing the distinction between "genre painting" (which includes still lifes, landscapes, and other static posed scenes) and "history painting." While most of his observations about the imitation of nature from the opening section are relevant primarily to the former category, it is only in the latter that, in his view, the painter can achieve the highest level of artistic achievement.

> Le peintre de genre a sa scène sans cesse présente sous ses yeux; le peintre d'histoire ou n'a jamais vu ou n'a vu qu'un instant la sienne. Et puis l'un est pur et simple imitateur, copiste d'une nature commune; l'autre est, pour ainsi dire, le créateur d'une nature idéale et poétique. (OCD 10:505)

> The genre painter has his scene constantly present before his eyes, while the history painter has either never seen his, or has seen it only for an instant. And so the one is purely and simply an imitator of and copyist from a common nature; while the other is, as it were, the creator of an ideal, poetic nature.

Certainly the successful process of creating this "ideal, poetic nature," which is to be carried out without the artist's having his model before his eyes, implies the previous study of "common nature" such as is argued for in the first section of the "Essais"; but it also involves the ability to achieve a level of abstraction that goes far beyond imitation. Even in more sophisticated forms of genre painting, as Diderot writes in the section of the "Essais" devoted to expression, more than simple copywork is involved: the artist is called on to select and arrange the elements that will make up his picture. A backdrop of ruins, for example, can be enhanced by the painter's adding figures in the foreground. These might include a traveler, a woman bent beneath the weight of the child she carries, or two men conversing on horseback—figures whose distinctive quality is that they are all fugitive, in the process of leaving the scene, since their presence in the painting is motivated only by an "affinité des idées" (affinity of ideas): "Tout passe, l'homme et la demeure de l'homme" (OCD 14:383; All things pass, man and human habitations alike").

Diderot's idea of "history painting" is not limited merely to the presentation of historical and mythological scenes. As Michael Fried has demonstrated in his important study *Absorption and Theatricality: Painting and Beholder in the Age of Diderot,* the term must be broadly understood in Diderot's work to include all sorts of works that imitate "la nature sensible et vivante" as opposed to "la nature brute et morte";[31] certainly it extends well beyond the portrayal of momentous events. Consider Diderot's praise of Jean-Baptiste Greuze's painting *Une jeune fille qui pleure son oiseau mort,* which is discussed in the *Salon* of 1765 (the *Salons*) Diderot's series of reports on the large annual exhibitions of paintings, included detailed descriptions of individual pictures to compensate for the fact that no direct technical means existed for reproducing the images themselves). This painting shows a young girl, tightly framed by the oval composition, resting her head in her hand with a sad, pensive expression; at the level of her breast lies a dead bird. Diderot reports in his *Salon* wishing to speak to the girl, to comfort her in her sadness.[32] The picture is historical in that it tells a story; it encourages the viewer to imagine the unfolding of the scene that resulted in the tableau captured on the canvas. It is also, as Fried argues, like many works of the period, inherently theatrical, since the girl's pose, her act of displaying the limp body of the dead bird, seems to imply the presence of an observer before whom this scene is being played out. Nevertheless, in the *Salons* Diderot can often be found praising painters, like Chardin, whose work cannot be described as historical even in this looser sense. Diderot saw merit, Fried writes, in Chardin's ability to "overcome the triviality of his subject matter by virtue of an unprecedented mastery of the means of imitation."[33] The artist's talent, in other words, made it possible for him to succeed even in an inherently inferior genre.

At the same time, Diderot's obvious preference for narrative-driven painting here and elsewhere put him at risk of being seen (by Goethe, for one) as embracing an understanding of art governed by the principle of *ut pictura poesis*—the Horatian dictum that "as is painting, so is poetry." This, however, is not—or not always—the case. In his *Salon* of 1767, he writes: "That which works well in painting always works well in poetry; but this is not reciprocal";[34] some narrative motifs, in other words, are well suited to portrayal on canvas, while others are not, demonstrating that the laws governing the artistic success of a painting do not correspond (or at least not fully) with those relevant to written forms of expression. And in his 1751 "Lettre sur les sourds et muets" ("Letter on the Deaf-Mutes"), Diderot draws a clear distinction between painting and the non-visual arts, noting that the mode of representation involved in painting is more immediate than that in either music or poetry: "C'est la chose même que le peintre montre; les expressions du musicien et du poète n'en sont que des hiéroglyphes" (OCD 4:185; It is the thing itself that the painter shows; the expressions of the musician and the poet are only hieroglyphs of it). To be sure, this often-cited dictum should not be taken to suggest that "la chose même" is necessarily an object present in nature. All paintings, even history paintings, have a "chose même"—though in the latter case they reside not in the painter's studio or outside his window, but in his imagination. Diderot's theoretical statements on art, then, may sometimes appear to contradict one another, but all consistently embrace the basic principle that effective painting is that which presents us vividly and credibly with its subject, whether it be an item found in nature or a scene of the artist's imagining. And the skills that allow the artist's work to be these things—vivid and credible—are developed by studying the only flawless model available to us: nature.

Diderot's ideas about representation in painting are also analogous to the mimetic principles put forth in his theory of acting. The actor's art resembles that of the painter—and differs from that of the poet or musician—in that the illusion created upon the stage presents itself to the spectator without a medium entailing necessary abstraction (words, musical notes); it offers a ringside view of the "chose même." And the account of artistic representation in Diderot's great essay on the theater, "Le paradoxe sur le comédien," sheds light on Diderot's writing on the visual arts. It describes a parallel situation, but cast in terms that offer less room for ambiguity.

CHAPTER 4

MIMETIC REPRESENTATION IN DIDEROT'S "PARADOX"

Diderot's essay on acting was not printed in its final form until 1830, but an earlier, briefer version, containing the same main points of argument, appeared in the 1770 issue of Grimm's *Correspondance littéraire*, and as the Diderot scholar Roland Mortier reports, there was at least one manuscript copy of "Paradox" in circulation in Germany by the 1790s, long after Goethe had become an enthusiastic reader of Diderot's work.[35] The central claim of Diderot's essay is that the greatest actor is not the one most filled with passion during his performance, but rather one who in a detached, calculated manner uses consciously applied gestures to achieve the desired dramatic effect. The paradox of the title, in other words, is that the actor best able to awaken the emotions of his spectators is the one who is himself free from emotion as he stands upon the stage. Diderot's essay was written to challenge the then widely held notion—expressed for example by the Abbé Du Bos in his 1719 *Reflexions critiques sur la poésie et sur la peinture*—that only emotion can produce emotion and that the actor who can move us is the one who himself is moved.[36] Instead, Diderot emphasizes the *conscious* effort with which the actor employs his craft to elicit the desired response from his audience. His essay anticipates both William Wordsworth's "powerful emotions recollected in tranquility" and Bertolt Brecht's estrangement effect.

Diderot's reasoning is based in large part on the fact that an actor whose performance depends on his ability to summon his emotions on the stage—today we would call him a "method actor"—is at the mercy of his emotions. How will the actor summoning feelings of grief to play a tragic scene be able to feel the same full-fledged sorrow during the hundredth performance of the play? The actor who maintains his detachment and concentrates on his craft, on recreating the expressions and gestures he has found to simulate grief when seen from the audience, will look and sound the same in every performance.

The good actor, for Diderot, does not restrict himself to copying an original found in nature. The basis for his performance is, rather, a model of his own envisioning, which he "a emprunté de l'histoire" (OCD 8:366; has taken from history) or which his imagination has "créé comme un grand fantôme" (8:366; created like a great phantom).[37] It is this combination of memory and imagination that—as in the work of the history painter—serves to produce the actor's conception of his role. This "phantom" is then copied, reproduced in every performance, with the success of the reproduction a function of the actor's technical skill. Clearly the first stage of the actor's task—the invention of a character to be portrayed—has a strong mimetic component. The actor "va sans cesse puisser dans le fonds inépuisable de la nature" (8:366; is ceaselessly delving into the inexhaustible wealth of nature, PA 104–5), while at the same time using his own experience of human behavior to determine which gestures, expressions and manners of speaking best evoke the character he is creating. Yet this phantom does not come into being through a purely imitative process. Rather, the form of this imitation is what Philippe Lacoue-Labarthe has described as "general" or "productive mimesis," which "reproduces nothing given" but rather "*supplements* a certain deficiency in nature, its incapacity to do everything, organize everything, make everything its work—*produce* everything."[38] It is the finest art to imitate something that does not exist, but which *might* exist—and, by dint of being imitated, *does*.

Lacoue-Labarthe's notion of general mimesis, defined against imitations of other sorts, goes back to the eighteenth-century distinction between the two forms of imitation: *imitatio* and *ritratto*. Whereas ritratto refers to a portrait or portrayal, something "re-taken" directly from nature, the notion of the imitatio is more complex: it implies the creation of "something that cannot exist independently from the *imitatio* . . . something is added to Nature that does not belong to Nature itself."[39] In fact the notion of general mimesis can be applied to imitations in a number of genres. Consider the case of John Myatt, an impecunious painter with great imitative skills, who was arrested as a forger in 1995 for painting and drawing on the order of two hundred pictures "by" artists including Giacometti, Chagall, Braque, Dufy, Matisse, Klee, Dubuffet, and Le Corbusier. Myatt, who first went into business with a classified ad in the British satirical magazine *Private Eye* offering "19th- and 20th-century fakes for $240," made his paintings using unverisimilitudinous emulsion paint (developed in the 1960s), which he cut with K-Y Jelly. The pictures—not copies of existing works but new paintings in the style of particular artists—were meant to adorn the living-room walls of relatively unexacting art lovers, much like posters of works by these artists, and Myatt did not attempt to make his pictures appear "old" or otherwise authentic. Producing these copycat paintings became criminal when Myatt went into business with a man

CHAPTER 4

named John Drewe, who over the course of nearly a decade provided phony "authentications" for Myatt's fakes and sold them through many of the world's best dealers and auction houses.[40]

The forger is, of course, himself an artist; what differentiates him from all other painters is his ability and willingness not only to imitate and abstract from nature but to do so in precisely the same manner (or close to it) as some other artist painting a similar motif. Like the actor, he is able to assume countless other personalities based on models he finds around him. John Myatt turned to painting imitations of great artists because he had been unable to sell his own artwork, which had been criticized for displaying no particular individual style. It may have been precisely this lack of personal identity as a painter that made Myatt so well suited to paint in the styles of other artists. Diderot's actor, too, is characterized by the absence of his own distinctive voice, which makes him all the better able to lend his voice to his different roles:

> Un grand comédien n'est ni un piano-forté, ni une harpe, ni un clavecin, ni un violon, ni un violoncello; il n'a point d'accord qui lui soit proper; mais il prend l'accord et le ton qui conviennent à sa partie, et il sait se prêter à toutes. (OCD 8:396)

> A great actor is neither a pianoforte, nor a harp, nor a harpsichord, nor a violin, nor a cello; he has no harmony of his own, but he can assume the harmony and the tone which fit his part, and he can lend his talent to all of them. (PA 133)

The analogy of the actor puts the forger in a category separate from that of most other painters, since the forger by definition "lends his talent" to the styles of others, while the painter's art in general is concerned with producing something whose like has never before been seen. Like the actor, too, the most masterful sort of forger, one whose work involves producing not a copy of a particular painting but rather a new work that shares the stylistic traits of a certain painter's oeuvre, is imitating something that did not previously exist. In effect, he is envisioning an unknown work by Braque or Giacometti, of which his painting is the copy.

The actor-forger link can serve to explicate Diderot's difficult but crucial notion of the "ideal" in mimetic art. The ideal is closely related to, but not identical with, the phantom in the actor's performance. When Diderot writes "La satire est d'un tartuffe, et la comédie est du Tartuffe. La satire poursuit un vicieux, la comédie poursuit un vice" (OCD 8:389; Satire is about a hypocrite, and comedy is about the Hypocrite. Satire attacks the vicious, comedy attacks vice, PA 127), he is distinguishing between a (hypocritical) individual, one of the numberless epigones of the great Tartuffe, and the personification of hypocrisy as a generalized concept.[41] The latter is an example of the ideal. And just as there is an ideal of the Proud Man, there is an ideal of Shakespeare's Falstaff—a model that serves the actor as a guide in the creation of his phantom. This ideal is abstract but not imaginary, Diderot tells us; it may take various forms, but the forms it can legitimately take are not infinite. He uses the visual arts to explain himself: it's easy to see that while there are (to follow his example) any number of beautiful women, none of them can be identical to the ideal of the beautiful, which allows for no defects or flaws. And yet this ideal must take into account the characteristics of these women; it is extrapolated from them. In other words, the ideal is arrived at empirically—the product of observations recorded in memory and processed by the imagination—but it itself is not directly drawn from nature. The ideal that guides the forger is the essence—abstracted from any particular work of the artist from whom he is copying—of what comprises the artist's style, his motifs and way of viewing them. It is his sense of what constitutes the ideal of Braqueness that allows him to envision the phantom Braque that he will then sit down to paint.

There exist, then, for Diderot, two intermediate layers that intervene between the fully realized work of art and its original natural model: the ideal and the phantom. This is a powerful model for the mechanisms of artistic creation—powerful because so general and thus widely applicable. This model allows Diderot to avoid all mention of naturalism in these discussions; he speaks instead of what he calls "truth."

> [L]e vrai de la scène [. . .] est la conformité des actions, des discours, de la figure, de la voix, du mouvement, du geste, avec un modèle idéal imaginé par le poète, et souvent exagéré par le comédien. (OCD 8:373)
>
> The truth of the stage is the conformity of the actions, the

speeches, the face, the voice, the movement, the gesture, with an ideal model imagined by the poet and often exaggerated by the actor. (PA 111)

It is the correspondence, in other words, between ideal and phantom. Since the ideal itself is already one representational step removed from real objects and persons in the world, the work of art is doubly mediated. Is this still a mimetic relationship? Yes, but not a simple one. And in a sense, Diderot's description of this representational model is a sort of shorthand for discussions of representation that will follow two hundred years later. It anticipates, for one thing, Christopher Prendergast's model of the "logical matrix of mimesis [. . .] formed from the combination, and confusion, of three (heterogeneous) kinds of sentences: a descriptive ["this is how things are"], a prescriptive ["you must accept that this is how things are"] and a normative ["there is an authority validating the two previous sentences"]."[42] Diderot's ideal is descriptive, his phantom more or less prescriptive, and his "truth" normative. And if representation, as Azade Seyhan writes, always "begins with a duplication or repetition of identity" and the "form of this repetition [. . .] is difference, that is, a split in subjectivity and identity,"[43] then the vexed identical-yet-different character of all mimetic structures verges on paradox. The double mediation of Diderot's "ideal" and "phantom" is, in effect, a strategy for addressing the virtual impossibility of representation itself.

Diderot's ideas about acting stand in stark contrast to Goethe's own set of instructions for dramatic performance, "Rules for Actors." These were guidelines compiled by Johann Peter Eckermann in 1824 in consultation with Goethe, on the basis of notes prepared by Goethe in 1803 for coaching young actors at the theater in Weimar. Goethe's "Rules" were conceived in opposition to the naturalistic acting style called for by Lessing. As an alternative, he seeks to elicit a more stylized performance (he includes instructions as to how to stand, what to do with one's hands while speaking, and so forth) with directives that at points recall certain terms used in Diderot's "Paradox." In section 35, for example, Goethe posits a complex mimetic relationship between nature and performance:

Zunächst bedenke der Schauspieler, daß er nicht allein die Natur nachahmen, sondern sie auch idealisch vorstellen solle und er also in seiner Darstellung das Wahre mit dem Schönen zu vereinigen habe. (MA 6.2:734)

First of all the actor must consider that his task is not only to imitate nature but also to represent it ideally [*idealisch*], and that he therefore must unite the true and the beautiful in his performance.

But the overlapping terminology notwithstanding, Goethe's intention here is quite different from Diderot's. The actor who represents nature "ideally" is, for Goethe, the one who succeeds in conjoining the "true" with the "beautiful" in his presentation, finding a middle ground between accurate imitation and the aesthetically pleasing. "Ideally" represented nature in Goethe, then, is portrayed in a way palatable to the observer. For Diderot, on the other hand, the "ideal" of something present in nature is the most characteristic representation of its essence—its portrayal may be altered, but only so as to amplify, underscore its essential features.[44] Thus for Diderot a "true" performance might involve emphasizing the grotesqueness of a conventionally unsightly figure on the stage. We should remember the satisfaction with which he begins his "Essais sur la peinture" by invoking the—presumably beautiful—correctness of nature which causes the face of a blind woman whose eyeballs have receded in their sockets to shift over time, in such a way that the harmony of the face as a whole is preserved. One might say that for Diderot only the unnatural is ugly. Goethe, on the other hand, appears to wish to have his actors add a harmonious touch to even the cruelest scenes. Their performances are not to be merely "true"—meaning true to nature or verisimilitudinous—but beautiful in the sense of displaying grace. This insistence on the pleasing is confirmed in the paragraph that follows the one just quoted:

§36. Jeder Teil des Körpers stehe daher ganz in seiner [the actor's] Gewalt, so daß er jedes Glied gemäß dem zu erzielenden Ausdruck frei, harmonisch und mit Grazie gebrauchen kann. (MA 6.2:735)

§36. Every part of [the actor's] body should thus be completely under his control, so that he can use each of his limbs freely, harmoniously and with grace in accordance with the

CHAPTER 4

expression he wishes to achieve.

Most of this directive might have appeared verbatim in Diderot's "Paradox," with the likely exception of the phrase "with grace." Certainly Goethe shares Diderot's sense of the importance of the actor's craft, which allows him to use his entire body consciously, letting "les larmes du comédien descendent de son cerveau" (OCD 8:370; tears pour down from his mind [PA 108]), as Diderot writes, to achieve the desired effect ("gemäß dem zu erzielenden Ausdruck"—Goethe). But Goethe's desire to make the stage a scene pleasing to the eye is for him equally important. Thus he urges his actors to play only near the center of the stage, not off toward the wings, which would disturb the general symmetry of the spectacle. Actors standing to the right of the stage are to gesture with their left arms, and vice versa (MA 6.2:738). (According to Diderot's *Encyclopédie*, on the other hand, symmetry employed outside of architecture is risky: "La symétrie qui est le fondement de la beauté en architecture, en est la ruine dans la plupart des autres beaux-arts" [The symmetry which is the basis of beauty in architecture spells its ruin in most of the other fine arts]).[45]

Diderot emphasizes that a good actor will be able to slip in and out of a role with little effort (given his emotional detachment vis-à-vis the labor he is performing) and notes that "le comédien dans la rue ou sur la scène sont deux personages si different, qu'on a peine à les reconnaître" (OCD 8:373; the actor in the street and the actor on the stage are two people so different that it's hard to recognize them [PA 111]). Goethe, on the other hand, urges the actor to "auch im gemeinen Leben bedenken, daß er öffentlich zur Kunstschau stehen werde" (MA 6.2:742; even keep in mind in his everyday life that he is on public display as an art object). The grace that the actor must cultivate so as to flourish on the stage, then, will mark him in all other areas of life; he is to embody the persona of "The Actor" everywhere he goes.

Diderot's actor is anything but a flamboyant public personality. Literally selfless, he is a shell, a cipher until the moment when he embodies the character he is portraying. This form of creative humility—the willingness to serve not just as maker but also as medium—corresponds to the humility toward nature implied in Diderot's essay on painting. In claiming that nature is never "incorrect," Diderot is arguing for the artist's assumption of a basic rightness in the ways of nature, and the trust that what was suitable for the grand work of art known as Life will also be worthy to stand as model for the lesser sort produced by man. It appears as if—on the face of things at least—it is Goethe's basic discomfort with the artistic portrayal of the disagreeable, the malformed and disturbing, that motivates both his response to Diderot and his own theory of representation. In fact this is a question with which he is confronted again and again in *Le neveu de Rameau*—and his response to this confrontation accounts for a number of the adjustments in the translation discussed earlier in this chapter ("Pantomime and Transformation: *Rameaus Neffe*"). At the same time, the question of the extent to which the repulsive is acceptable in art is raised by Diderot himself at several points in the novel. The story of the treacherous renegade, for example, involves the indeed rather shocking suggestion (implied by the obvious glee with which the title character recounts the tale) that one can take pleasure in the virtuoso perversity of a wicked deed, much as one can appreciate a virtuoso performance in music. The renegade in Rameau's story is playing the part of the villain, and triumphing in the role.

The renegade's role-playing in *Le neveu de Rameau* is part of the leitmotif of acting found throughout the novel. We have only to recall the enthusiasm with which Rameau relates the story of Bouret, who wishes to curry favor with the Keeper of the Seals by making him a present of his little dog, which the Keeper admires. He trains the dog to love this man and to hate him, the current owner—a feat he accomplishes by dressing up as the Keeper (complete with mask) before showing kindness to the dog, and then, in his own guise, abusing him. Even when Bouret is playing the role of himself, he is acting (since shouting at and striking the dog is not part of his ordinary behavior). He has invented a phantom (in the terms of the "paradoxe") loosely based on himself, and then acted it out admirably to fool what can be assumed to be the toughest of audiences.[46]

Rameau, relating this scene, is full of admiration: "Die Maske! Die Maske! Einen meiner Finger gäbe ich drum, die Maske gefunden zu haben!" (MA 7:609; The mask! the mask! I'd give one of my fingers to have discovered the mask!) He adds, "Diese Muster [ces modèles-là] nehmen einem den Mut" (7:609; These models destroy one's courage). Not only is he drawing our attention to the fact that the man working so hard to deceive his pet is indeed a sort of actor, but he is also marking this act of thespian guile as a "modèle," and thus worthy of being admired and emulated. The scene of Bouret, disguised as

CHAPTER 4

himself, striking his little dog thus becomes an exemplary scene of theater. The nature of his audience (animals do not dissemble) provides a more or less objective measure of his success, and the actor is imitating a particular model (himself as dog-hater) that is not found in nature, but certainly could be.

The closest Goethe comes to acknowledging the theatrical aspect of Rameau's character is in the passage under the heading "Rameaus Neffe" in the notes to the translation, in which he discusses the differences between German and French society:

> Hat also der Deutsche nur mit Ernst und Redlichkeit sein Verdienst zu steigern, wenn er von der Nation früher oder später begriffen sein will, so kann er dies auch um so gelassener abwarten, weil bei dem unzusammenhängenden Zustande unsres Vaterlandes jeder in seiner Stadt, in seinem Kreise, seinem Hause, seinem Zimmer ungestört fortleben und arbeiten kann, es mag draußen übrigens stürmen, wie es will. Jedoch in Frankreich war es ganz anders. Der Franzose ist ein geselliger Mensch, er lebt und wirkt, er steht und fällt in Gesellschaft. (MA 7:687)

> So if the German can only increase his own merits with earnestness and honesty if he wishes, sooner or later, to be understood by his nation, he can wait for this moment all the more calmly as—given the disconnected state of our fatherland—everyone can live and work undisturbed in his city, his community, his house, his room, regardless of what storms may be raging outside. In France, however, things were quite different. The Frenchman is a social creature—he lives and acts, he stands and falls in society.

The life of a Frenchman, then, is played out before an audience (for whom he *wirkt*, acts, makes an impression), while the German lives a more secluded existence that allows him to ignore the storms that may be in full blast out of doors. Ironically, the storms buffeting Germany at the moment Goethe was writing this were Napoleonic soldiers whose presence certainly did have quite an impact on German interiority, German isolation notwithstanding. But the relevance of this historical state of affairs (translating a Frenchman while besieged by the

French) seems not to have affected Goethe particularly—though eventually it would prevent the original text of *Le neveu de Rameau* from being published in Germany. Even in 1796, with French soldiers stationed in Würzburg, Stuttgart, and Ulm, Goethe could write a letter that mentioned troop movements briefly before going on to give some personal advice and then report on reading Diderot's "Essais sur la peinture" with no acknowledgment of any connection whatever.[47] It is as if he were fulfilling his own self-definition as an insular German.

The intersection of the themes of theatricality and music in *Le neveu de Rameau* involves not only their implied comparison (as two mimetic arts—a claim Diderot makes for music as though it were indisputably true) but also the odder means of pantomime. At various points in the dialogue, Rameau imitates the players of musical instruments. At its climax, he imitates not only the players but also the very instruments of an entire orchestra. At first these imitations are mere illustration and unproblematically realistic: after mentioning his envy of his uncle's success and naming particular pieces he admires, he adds: "Das sind Augenblicke, die vorübergehen. (Dann sang er die Ouvertüre der Galanten Indien [. . .])" (MA 7:579; These are moments that pass. [Then he sang the overture to *Les indes galantes* . . .]). A moment later, he is fantasizing in the second person about having enough talent to have composed a number of pieces himself: "Die andern wiesen mit Fingern auf dich. Das ist der, sagte man, der die artigen Gavotten gemacht hat. (Nun sang er die Gavotten [. . .])" (7:579–80; The others would point their fingers at you. That is the one, they would say, who did those charming gavottes. [Now he sang the gavottes . . .]). This realism is unproblematic since there is no significant difference between singing a piece of music and imitating someone who does so. Later, however, Rameau pantomimes the playing of a violin, tuning the imaginary instrument before applying the bow and humming the notes so convincingly that his listener "glaubte so gut die Akkorde zu hören als er" (7:588; thought he was hearing the chords just as [Rameau] did) (never mind that the human voice cannot produce more than one note at a time). Praised for his performance, he immediately sets about playing a fictional piano: "Seine Stimme ging wie der Wind, und seine Finger flatterten über den Tasten" (7:589; His voice went like the wind, and his fingers fluttered across the keys). As compared with the first set of pantomimes, he is now imitating not only a sound but the person producing the sound—including the errors,

CHAPTER 4

apparently, since "er manchmal tastete, sich schalt, als wenn er gefehlt hätte, sich ärgerte, das Stück nicht geläufig genug in den Finger zu haben" (7:589; he sometimes groped about, scolding himself as though he'd missed, annoyed not to have the piece more completely at his fingertips).

These musical pantomimes culminate in a tour-de-force of several pages in which Rameau goes from singing a series of individual pieces to singing dozens at once: "Er häufte und verwirrte dreißig Arien, italienische, französische, tragische, komische von aller Art Charakter" (MA 7:633; He combined and confused thirty arias, Italian, French, tragic, comic, of all sorts). His voice rises and falls from bass to falsetto, and his gestures portray now a young girl weeping, now a tyrant issuing orders, now a slave carrying them out. A moment later he has added to the performance all the supporting instruments: "Mit aufgeblasenen, strotzenden Wangen und einem rauhen, dunkeln Ton stellte er Hörner und Fagott vor, einen schreienden näselnden Ton ergriff er für das Hautbois, mit unglaublicher Geschwindigkeit übereilte er seine Stimme, die Saiteninstrumente darzustellen [. . .]" (7:634; With puffed-out, inflated cheeks and a raw, dark tone, he presented the horns and bassoon, he assumed a shrieking, nasal sound for the oboe, with incredible speed he pushed his voice faster than it could go to represent the string instruments . . .). And once he has supplemented his repertoire with the rest of the orchestra, he goes on to add, it seems, all of nature to the spectacle:

> Es war eine Frau, die in Schmerz versinkt, ein Unglücklicher, seiner ganzen Verzweiflung hingegeben, ein Tempel, der sich erhebt, Vögel, die beim Untergang der Sonne sich im Schweigen verlieren. Bald Wasser, die an einem einsamen und kühlen Orte rieseln oder als Gießbäche von Bergen herabstürzen, ein Gewitter, ein Sturm, die Klage der Umkommenden, vermischt mit dem Gezisch der Winde, dem Lärm des Donners, es war die Nacht mit ihren Finsternissen, es war der Schatten und das Schweigen, denn selbst das Schweigen bezeichnet sich durch Töne. (MA 7:635)

> It was a woman collapsing in pain, an unhappy man who had surrendered to the sum of his despair, a temple rising up, birds losing themselves in silence at sunset. Now it was water

trickling in some lonely, cool spot or plunging down mountainsides as rushing streams, a storm, the laments of those who perished, mixed with the whistling of the wind, the crash of thunder, it was the night with all its darknesses, it was shadow and silence, for even silence is marked by notes.

This apotheosis of representation takes Rameau's performance as an occasion to compress virtually all the arts in a moment of unprecedented expressive intensity. It is, in Leo Spitzer's words, "a world orchestra, echoing the music of the universe."[48] This explosion of synesthesia meant to convey the effect of Rameau's musical/theatrical performance is, ironically, a work of written literature—of poetry, that is—framed in a descriptive medium in which the argument for music's mimetic powers can be made much more strongly than in music itself. Rameau's "birds losing themselves in silence before sunset," communicated ostensibly through sound alone, challenge our capacity to imagine a form of musical expression rich enough to account for a scene more visual than aural. The scene is not so much a parody[49] as it is a tribute to the mimetic principle which, for Diderot, in music as in the other fine arts, provides the basis for artistic expression.

Ironically, perhaps, it is through these *musical* excursions that Rameau most forcefully demonstrates his prowess as an actor. The nephew is an artist in many mediums, not the least of which is the art of acting out his own role, which he does cynically, but with great skill. While he critiques others (like the renegade) for their performances on the stage that surrounds us, his role is the most difficult of all, for "nichts gleicht ihm weniger als er selbst" (MA 7:570; nothing resembles him less than he resembles himself). It is only natural that the range of his self-contradictory conduct is bound to include acts of questionable moral worth (causing Goethe to revile him in his notes to the book as "eine entschieden abhängige, zu allem Schlechten auf äußern Anlaß fähige Natur" who "unsere Verachtung, ja sogar unsern Haß erregt" [7:686; a clearly parasitical figure ready to take any occasion to indulge in low behavior, who provokes our contempt, indeed even our hatred]). Yet by treating all of life as an artwork of sorts, the nephew seems to be proposing an alternate form of integrity, a standard of worth: to act one's role well, to be the one to invent the mask, to captivate among one's audience not only lapdogs and nervous Jewish merchants but doubting philosophers as well. In fact, as Spitzer notes,

CHAPTER 4

what Goethe seems not to have realized about the nephew's character is that his "characterlessness [. . .] is only a consequence of his artistic mutability";[50] he is like the paradoxical actor who can shape himself to any role. In playing his role well, the nephew gives as well as takes pleasure. The greatest mistake one can make, he seems to suggest, would be to approach the world with naiveté, to remain oblivious to the actors and swindlers all around one, the parasites and sycophants who, like himself, live off their skill at working the crowd.

Goethe's rejection of the character of the nephew and his softening of certain of the novel's episodes have to do with his sense of taste, his feeling that certain subject matters are simply unsuitable for artistic representation. As it turns out, he disagrees with Diderot on the subject of taste (*Geschmack, goût*) in theoretical as well as practical terms. Diderot writes at length on this topic near the end of his "Essais sur la peinture" (in the last of the five sections not translated by Goethe), as does Goethe in the notes he appended to his translation of *Le neveu de Rameau*. The discrepancy is quite striking. For Diderot, the work of the genius is fated to be almost always rejected by his contemporaries because it does not conform to previously established conceptions (taste) of what constitutes beauty in art. Taste, for Diderot, is formed on the basis of that which already exists:

> Qu'est-ce donc que le goût? Une facilité acquise par des expériences réitérées, à saisir le vrai ou le bon, avec la circonstance qui le rend beau, et d'en être promptement et vivement touché. (OCD 10:519)
>
> So what is taste? A facility, acquired through repeated experience, to grasp what is true or good along with the circumstances that make it beautiful, and to be swiftly and powerfully moved by it.

But since taste (a matter of judgement) and sensibility are often at odds, it often happens that the first reactions to a work of art (the reactions of sensibility) are later shown by reason to have been mistaken—and so taste comes paradoxically into existence only as it is being exercised over time.

Goethe comes to a quite different conclusion about the development of taste, though he agrees with Diderot in considering it a special characteristic of the genius. While for Goethe "Der Geschmack ist dem Genie angeboren" (MA 7:665; Taste is an inborn quality of the genius), Diderot insists:

> Il [le génie] est seul. On ne l'apprécie qu'en le rapportant immédiatement à la nature. Et qui est-ce qui sait remonter jusque-là? Un autre homme de génie. (OCD 10:520)
>
> He is alone. He will not be appreciated unless it is by drawing a direct link between his work and nature. And who is capable of rising to such a height? Another man of genius.

In Diderot's view, then, only the genius has the ability immediately to recognize and to appreciate a work of genius. Goethe does not exclude the possibility of persons who are not themselves geniuses possessing taste, but he also acknowledges that the vast majority of people do not in fact have any: it "wäre freilich zu wünschen, daß die Nation Geschmack hätte, damit sich nicht jeder einzeln notdürftig auszubilden brauchte" (MA 7:665; it would be desirable for the nation to have taste so that each individual would not have to go through the labor of acquiring it as best he can).

Whereas taste for Diderot is absolute, something one either has or doesn't, Goethe recognizes the existence of various levels and degrees of taste: "Doch leider ist der Geschmack der nicht hervorbringenden Naturen verneinend, beengend, ausschließend [. . .]" (MA 7:665; But unfortunately the taste of those who are not creative is negative, limiting, excluding . . .). This faulty taste, which causes those who are not themselves creatively inclined to reject too much—innovative art along with the simply bad—would, for Diderot, not count as taste at all. At the same time, this sliding scale of tastes permits Goethe to avoid arriving at a logical conclusion such as the one drawn by Diderot (on the basis of his absolute understanding of taste): that the genius is doomed to suffer at least initial lack of recognition for his work because society is not comprised of taste-possessing fellow geniuses—a notion he deems so crucial that he ends his essay on it. Goethe, in contrast, suggests that it is part of the genius's task to play to the tastes of his fellow men such as they are and, in the process, gently develop the tastes prevalent in society. The work of the genius is determined, Goethe writes,

> teils durch innern Trieb und eigne Überzeugung [. . .], teils auch durch die Nation, durch das Jahrhundert, für welche gearbeitet werden soll. Hier trifft das Genie freilich nur allein den recten Punkt, sobald es Werke hervorbringt, die ihm Ehre machen, seine Mitwelt erfreuen und zugleich weiter fördern. (MA 7:665)

> partially by an inner drive and personal convictions, but partially also by the nation, by the century for which the work is intended. And here, to be sure, the genius only hits his mark when he produces works that bring him honor, give pleasure to his fellow man and foster the development of those around him.

This vision is made possible by a notion that is, in fact, inherently contradictory: that the genius (who by definition possesses the ultimate good taste) should cater in his art to the (by definition inferior) tastes of society. The work that establishes his genius, then, is to be determined less by his own tastes than by the tastes of his audience, which he is supposed to be developing through this work. How can a work of genius arise on the basis of imperfectly developed tastes? Moreover, since the true genius, as Goethe suggests, can be expected to enjoy success in his own lifetime, we must assume that the artist who does not succeed in gaining social approval for his work is not really a genius after all—a claim diametrically opposed to Diderot's.

Certainly one can imagine why it might have been uncomfortable for Goethe to have been forced to accept or reject outright a view of genius that basically precluded the possibility of the artist's enjoying success during his own lifetime. At the same time, Goethe's own conception of taste concords well with his ideas about representation—including the question of what constitutes a suitable subject for artistic portrayal.

Imitation of the Beautiful

Goethe's beliefs about art that prompt his rewriting of Diderot's "Essais" are most succinctly stated in his 1789 essay "Einfache Nachahmung der Natur, Manier, Stil" (Simple Imitation of Nature, Manner, Style). This essay appeared as part of a complex of short essays he published in Wieland's journal *Teutscher Merkur* on his return from Italy;

they combine reflections on a number of cultural and scientific topics. As Goethe wrote to Wieland in early September 1788, "Natural history, art, social conventions, etc., all these things are becoming amalgamated for me" (MA 3.2:422). In this essay, he divides the artistry of painters into three categories, which can also be understood as stages of development (3.2:186–91). In the first of these, the "simple imitation of Nature," the painter merely copies and records what he sees upon careful study of an object present before him as he paints. When he progresses beyond this stage, he enters the area of "manner," in which he illumines the harmony of many objects in his subject matter and "macht sich selbst eine Sprache, um das, was er mit der Seele ergriffen, wieder nach seiner Art auszudrücken" (3.2:187; creates his own language with which to express, in his own way, that which he has grasped with his soul). His subject is not present to him at the moment of painting—even his memory of it need not be particularly vivid. Finally, the artist may attain the highest level of artistic development, "style," the most synthetic stage in which his art reaches the point where it "die Eigenschaften der Dinge und die Art, wie sie bestehen, genau und immer genauer kennen lernt" (3.2:188; becomes increasingly familiar with the characteristic and essential features of things) and "die Reihe der Gestalten übersieht und die verschiedenen charakteristischen Formen nebeneinander zu stellen und nachzuahmen weiß" (3.2:188; can survey the range of figures and understand how to arrange the various characteristic forms and imitate them). The artist of the third stage no longer relies on the direct imitation of objects as they exist in nature to create his pictures. Rather, he himself has an active role in shaping compositions that may have no natural precedent. At the same time, it is crucial that these compositions grow out of the characteristic and essential features of the objects he represents. If it is only the state of his own soul he is representing, he will remain trapped within the confines of the mannered and never cross "die Schwelle des Heiligtums" (3.2:190; the threshold of the holy). The perfect work of art, Goethe writes in "Über Wahrheit und Wahrscheinlichkeit der Kunstwerke" (On Truth and Probability in Works of Art), is "supernatural" (*übernatürlich*) but not "extranatural" (*außernatürlich,* outside of nature); it is "ein Werk des menschlichen Geistes, und in diesem Sinne auch ein Werk der Natur" (MA 4.2:94; a work of the human spirit, and in this sense also a work of nature).

Unlike Diderot's analysis of the beauty of the artwork, in which the history of the portrayed objects plays at least an indirect role (the face of the blind woman is marked by her physical history and development), Goethe understands artistic representation as timeless. The "Eigenschaften der Dinge" (qualities of things) are, for him, "Eigenschaften" as they exist at the moment of their portrayal. This standpoint provides the position from which Goethe, unlike Diderot, rejects painting that uses narrative content for effect, as can be seen as early as 1797 in his rejection of the work of Johann Heinrich Füßli, which he viewed on a trip to Switzerland. For Goethe, Füßli's weakness as a painter is that he bases his pictures on subjects that are "abenteuerlich" and "entweder tragisch oder humoristisch; they speak either to the viewer's "Einbildungskraft und Gefühl" (imagination and feeling) or "Einbildungskraft und Geist" (imagination and spirit). In both cases, Goethe writes, the "sinnliche Darstellung" (representation to the senses) is only a "Vehikel": "Kein echtes Kunstwerk soll auf Einbildungskraft wirken wollen, das ist die Sache der Poesie" (MA 4.2:89; No genuine work of art should aim to impress the imagination, that should be left to poetry).[51] Goethe's belief that narrative elements have no place in the painter's art explains his comment to Schiller in a letter of 17 December 1796 that the volume containing Diderot's "Salon" and the "Essais sur la peinture" is "ein herrliches Buch und spricht fast noch mehr an den Dichter als an den bildenden Künstler, ob es gleich auch diesem oft mit gewaltiger Fackel vorleuchtet"[52] (a splendid book and speaks to the poet almost more than to the visual artist, although it often lights the way with a powerful torch for the latter as well). Imagination, in this case, implies the ability to construct a story, a scenario—clearly the domain of the poet and writer.

The question of the narrative content of the visual arts (history painting) is the axis around which many of Goethe's reservations about Diderot's views on mimetic representation are organized, and it is quite clear that on certain points (the portrayal of stories in painting, the artworthiness of the grotesque, the social acceptance of genius) the gulf between their viewpoints cannot altogether be bridged. Nonetheless, I wish to argue that Goethe's essay "Einfache Nachahmung, Manier, Stil" also contains the seeds for a reconciliation with several major elements of Diderot's aesthetic theory—a reconciliation that can be carried out by way of the model of representation described in Goethe's notes on translation from the *Divan* taken in conjunction with his concept of the *Genie*.

The essay "Einfache Nachahmung" is linked directly to Goethe's notes on translation through the parallel threefold path of development that characterizes the aesthetic education of painter and translator alike. In fact, the passage through multiple stages or epochs of development is a model Goethe applies to other fields as well. (In his *Maximen und Reflexionen*, for example, he writes of there being four epochs of development in science[53]—giving weight to his claim cited above about the "amalgamation" of these various realms.) Goethe's painter and translator both begin their careers with a stage of representation involving a direct, literal relationship between model and portrayal. Just as first-epoch translation informs us of the content of the foreign work, the artist's "simple imitation" is the product of diligence and technical skill: it records the physical content of a scene or landscape, and the painted image contains that which any reasonable person would agree to be the components of the scene it portrays.

In the second epoch of painting—as of translation—quite the opposite is the case. It is no longer absolute objectivity that is being asymptotically approached, but rather the subjectivity of the artist. Just as the second-epoch translator immerses himself in the foreign world so as to bring back with him the "foreign sense" which he then represents in his "own terms" (MA 11.1.2:263), the painter of "manner" creates his own language to express in his own terms that of his subject which he has grasped with his soul. The aim of this art is to document not the model but the painter's state upon perceiving it. As art, it is most often preferable to that of the first stage, Goethe writes, since it is a more sophisticated response to the raw material of an artwork; but it is confined to the limited sphere of individual psychology rather than being generalizable in more universal terms.

The quality of universality is reserved for the third level of both the translator's and the painter's art. The translator who strives to make his translation "identical to" the original text so that it can "take its place" rather than standing "instead" of it (MA 11.1.2:264) has gone beyond his own subjective reception of the original to reach a more generalizable reading of it. His translation, in its accuracy of form as well as content and its sensitivity to the expressive potential of the original, is designed to elicit a similar response—and not just in him, but in as many readers as possible. This resembles the situation of the painter whose work has reached the mastery of "style"—his presentation of his model reflects not only his subjective painterly view of it, but the essential attributes of the portrayed objects. This painter creates juxtapositions of objects that show us the secret truth of the objects themselves; in his art, the personal provides access to the universal.

The work of the third-epoch painter can be said to "stand in the place" of its subject insofar as it reveals something essential, intrinsic about the subject itself. Like a scientist, the painter of style labors to reveal the secrets of nature, to give us access to them—his project is part of an "amalgamated" common venture that unites efforts in any number of spheres. Fully realized style is "der höchste Grad wohin sie [die Kunst] gelangen kann; der Grad, wo sie sich den höchsten menschlichen Bemühungen gleichstellen darf" (MA 3.2:188; the highest level that art can achieve; the level where it can consider itself the equal of the highest/noblest human effort). At the same time, "style" of this level is, like the perfected third epoch of translation, an absolute state to be strived for, one that may never fully be achieved. Achieving it, in fact, would be enough to define the one who does so as a *Genie;* Goethe does not say so explicitly in this essay, but it is implied by the absoluteness of the language he uses to describe style (the "höchst[e] Grad [. . .] welchen die Kunst je erreicht hat und je erreichen kann" [3.2:191; the highest level . . . art has ever reached and can ever reach]).

The role of the genius brings Diderot and Goethe closer together at the same time that it separates them. Since Goethe understands the laws of nature as analogous to but separate from the rules of art, he is obliged to trace the origins of these rules back to the genius, who observes nature but stands apart from (above) it. Diderot's genius, on the other hand, is assigned the task of revealing, making visible certain qualities already present in nature. As Hans Robert Jauß explains, "The making-visible in Diderot [that which the genius performs] is no longer aiming at something transcendental, but rather at the harmony that inhabits the visible things themselves, the concordance of the parts to form the whole." The main difference between the two in their conception of the genius—and the point where Jauß sees Goethe as having misunderstood Diderot—has to do with the fact that "for Goethe the beautiful in art is no longer, as in Diderot, conceived of as already present in the things, but rather it must be brought forth by the artist as a *second Nature.*"[54]

So what is this "second Nature"? Certainly it is linked directly to nature itself, since it involves the portrayal of "die Eigenschaften der

Dinge und die Art wie sie bestehen" (MA 3.2:188), as Goethe writes of third-epoch painting. And if the portrayal provides a full enough insight into the "Eigenschaften der Dinge"—in other words, if the painting is the work of a genius—then this "second Nature" can complete the circle of representation by "standing in the place of" nature itself: serving as its translation. Since the attainment of this highest level of representation (by the genius) is determined through a comparison with things in nature, this determination does not differ substantially from the determination of the "truth" of a representation (the coincidence of "ideal" and "phantom") in Diderot's model. In both cases it is a matter of a mediation that through a combination of skill, intuition, and aesthetic prowess gives us the best possible understanding of the "chose même." And since Goethe's genius is human and the works of the "human spirit," as he tells us, are also "works of nature" (MA 4.2:94), then it stands to reason that even for Goethe the rules of art (born of and in the mind of the genius) belong to nature as well. The creation of beauty on the basis of nature and the discovery of beauty already present in nature are, in the end, not so far removed from one another.

Must we conclude that Goethe and Diderot are merely using different sets of metaphors to describe what is in fact the very same model of artistic representation? Not at all; the points of real difference enumerated above still hold. But we are nonetheless confronted with the irony—paradoxical, as it were—of Goethe's going to such lengths to distance himself from an aesthetic system large parts of which he might as well, in the end, have called his own.

IMITATION AND ILLUSION: THE TRANSLATOR AS ACTOR

Goethe is regularly criticized in the literature on Diderot for not having appreciated the full complexity and quality of Diderot's texts. Roland Mortier suggests that Goethe was, in the end, "incapable, in his intellectual rigor and his concern with method, of comprehending the sinuous, skipping, impulsive movement of Diderot's thought and his complete indifference to possible contradictions that might arise from this."[55] It is certainly true that Diderot is not always logical, and it is not terribly surprising that his impulsiveness, his indirectness of approach coupled with sudden flashes of brilliance, failed to meet with Goethe's approval. Herbert Dieckmann, on the other hand, stresses the fundamental similarities between their views and regrets that Goethe often became hypercritical in his assessment of Diderot's ideas: "Indeed, he often judges him far more harshly, dogmatically and theoretically than his own point of view requires."[56] Dieckmann attributes this oversight to the importance the theoretical questions under discussion held for Goethe; he was less interested in situating Diderot's views in their historical framework—they were, after all, thirty years old by the time he encountered them—than in establishing his own viable theory of aesthetic representation.

Much of the difficulty for Goethe in reconciling his views with those of Diderot may well have lain in the very structure of his developmental sequence of "epochs," the common motif of journeying *through* personal subjectivity to arrive at an objectivity that is no longer simple—the universal, mystical, infinitely suggestive richness of reference that characterizes the realm of the genius, the highest level of art. This fundamental pattern that for Goethe underlies all artistic development can help us in understanding his rejection of the displeasing as a subject for art. The second stage of the artist's journey to mastery—which remains present, encapsulated in the third—implicates his subjectivity in its direct response to the portrayed object, and so the artistic glorification of the maimed, corrupted, disfigured would imply the presence of a subjectivity that was drawn to these things. This would present a moral crux before which art, in Goethe's view, would fail outright. How could the artist emerging from the realm of second-epoch subjectivity to ascend to the heights of third-epoch art as a newly minted genius hold the title of genius with the taint of a soiled subjectivity upon him? Surely the genius must remain free of all such unsavory business. And it is precisely this awareness of an underlying defilement that so troubles Goethe in *Rameaus Neffe,* the perverse pleasure taken, say, in the deeds of the villainous renegade, not to mention the passages Goethe refused to translate at all, "die äußersten Gipfel der Frechheit, wohin wir ihm [Diderot] nicht folgen dürfen" (MA 7:686; the highest pinnacles of impertinence where we may not follow him). Add to this the suggestion that the nephew, with his multiple talents, might himself be a candidate for the rank of genius, and we have reached an area of speculation that would surely have caused Goethe the most profound discomfort.

But if we are to be troubled by the moral ambiguity of the "second Nature" offered us by the artist, surely it is the result of what Herbert Dieckmann calls a "too narrow" view of both Diderot's work and the idea of imitation: for Goethe, he writes, this was almost never *imitatio* and almost always *ritratto*.[57] It is above all in the sphere of ritratto that the artist's subjectivity is in danger of being compromised, receiving a moral taint. The artist of *imitatio* is shielded by the buffering capacity of the imagination that imposes itself between him and brute nature. Like the actor of Diderot's "Paradox," he is laboring in pursuit of a truth that may be far removed from naturalism, since the mimetic relationship between the actor's performance and nature is mediated by an abstract middle link whose presence haunts each performance. As Diderot has the interlocutor in "Paradox" object:

> À vous entendre, ne ressemblerait tant à un comédien sur la scène ou dans ses études, que les enfants qui, la nuit, contrefont les revenants sur les cimetières, en élevant au-dessus de leurs têtes un grand drap blanc au bout d'une perche, et faisant sortir de dessous ce catafalque une voix lugubre qui effraye les passants. (OCD 8:367)

> To listen to you, there's nothing so much like an actor when he's on stage or working on his part than those children who pretend to be ghosts in cemeteries at night by lifting a big white sheet over their heads with a pole and then making a mournful voice come out from under this catafalque to frighten passers-by. (PA 105)

What is this bedsheet ghost devised by children? Certainly it is not "naturalistic," insofar as ghosts one might expect to encounter, if one believes in such things, will hardly resemble the sheet-on-a-bedpole variety. Nor is the performance of these children in any way mimetic. They do not identify with the ghost; for them, its evocation and the intention to frighten can awaken only hilarity. The production of terror is, for them, a calculated comic act, and the more fear they elicit, the funnier they're likely to find it. The children have also not rooted their creation of the ghost's character in any sort of empirical observation. Rather, they are obeying the conventions of phantom portrayal familiar to today's children from television and to the children of Diderot's age from printed illustrations in books or magazines. Once the ghost performance has been perfected, it can be repeated as often as the actors' patience permits.

CHAPTER 4

Like these children, the history painter has no model "constantly present before his eyes," and the success of his representation cannot be verified by a direct comparison with the things whose "Eigenschaften" it reveals. In fact, it cannot be accounted for at all using the system presented in Goethe's "Einfache Nachahmung"—which is neither surprising nor an internal flaw in the system, since Goethe wishes to exclude such art from consideration in any case. The "truth" (for Diderot) of history painting must by necessity remain a mystery of sorts—something to be intuited rather than objectively verified. In Dieckmann's words, this truth is "the illusion of the real," a sense of verisimilitude that clearly resides in the eye of the beholder—which makes the most "truthful" history painting the most convincing sort, the sort that gives the viewer the strongest sense of gazing directly at the "chose même." And since the "ideal" of the history painting is a scene to which the viewer does not have direct access, his sense of the extent to which its representation is "truthful" is bound to be circular, derived from the painting itself.

The ideal of the history painting, finally, can be differentiated from its phantom only in terms of the painting's conception and execution. Seen from the perspective of the viewer of the finished work, phantom and ideal are collapsed one upon the other and exist only as a subjective (and as likely as not unreliable) reconstruction of what the painter was hoping to achieve. At the same time, this collapsing of the intermediate steps of representation brings the artist closer and closer to what, for Goethe writing about translation, is the ultimate mimetic achievement: the creation of a copy able to stand "in the place of" its original, the place of the other. What is this "place of the other"? Clearly translation and original can never be identical, strictly speaking, since they are written in two different languages. Thus it is also clear that one could never perfectly substitute for the other, that is, serve as an alternative to it. (Arguably, Goethe's translation of *Le neveu de Rameau* was an exception to this as long as the original was lost; Diderot's French audience was able to read the back-translated German text "instead of" the unavailable original.) But this "standing in the place of" is something different from actual identity. This place is the site of the phantom that stands behind Diderot's actor's performance, a site that, in a sense, does not exist at all. Yet insofar as the ghost is made actual—summoned into retroactive existence as a model for a performance we can see, a text we can read—the site, the place of the other, is made actual as well. It is this same invisible ghost that the translator is attempting to discover with the help of the original, his memory, and his imagination. The text's ghostly double *is* the text as it would exist, perfectly and without seams, in the translator's own language. This perfect, linguistically transplanted text cannot, does not exist. Yet this is precisely what the translator, in Goethe's third epoch, in turn-of-the-nineteenth-century service translation, and in the day-to-day toils of the best turn-of-the-twenty-first-century translators, is attempting to find. He is creating—paradoxically—a replica of something that never existed, but whose existence his work presupposes.

Thus these various art forms—acting, painting, and translation—come together in the theoretical terms expressed explicitly by Diderot and implicitly by Goethe. In the end, it is the existence of this eternally absent object of mimetic desire, the empty but essential middle term of representation, that characterizes, for both of them, all mature artistic expression. Whether we take the notion of the "ideal" in the sense of Diderot or Goethe (extrapolation from nature or refinement of nature), the fundamental role played in both cases by the natural world and the things we expect to find there implies that these two terms must eventually converge, at the point where the refinement of nature in art reaches its outer limit and gives way to a more empirical, scientifically oriented view of nature's aesthetic transformation (translation). Though Goethe is clearly not prepared to concede the role of disfigurement in art,[58] much less what he sees as the disfigurement of aesthetic sensibility in Diderot's theory of art—which he himself disfigures in translation—he shows himself in his notes on translation to be far closer to standing in the place of Diderot than he himself might have realized.

And so the Goethe who as translator-author put his mark on Diderot's text was, in the end, struggling to resolve issues that lay within the sphere of his own authorial production. In doing battle with the aesthetic theories articulated by Diderot, Goethe was in fact fighting the contradictions inherent in his own work. His translation project, then, was a way of confronting artistic difficulties of his own with the help of the friendly stranger who, interrupting his labors, offered him a way out of his dilemma. Goethe can be seen as the ultimate authorial translator, one for whom the translated author was not only—as with Kleist's Molière—a source of material to be incorporated into the translator's own work or—as with Hölderlin's Sophocles—one in

CHAPTER 4

whom the translator could attempt to lose himself altogether, but rather one through whose intervention Goethe was able find his way back to his own writing, his own art. In this sense, his translations are exemplary. Finally, every authorial translation is a work of original writing, a directly indirect means for the translating author to express in the clearest possible terms the things that matter to him most, using his own artistic skill and with the help of foreign words.

We have seen, then, in the course of these pages, three different ways in which the great *Goethezeit* authorial translators appropriated the texts they were translating to make them their own. By spinning a tale about translation in the form of a translated work, Kleist's *Amphitryon* presents itself as a model of a text that, as it were, consumes its own ghost and returns to haunt its original. Hölderlin, the most haunted of these masters, translates like an actor whose phantom is the one thing still animating his limbs—a phantom at times powerful enough to redefine "truth" in its own terms. And Goethe, the sovereign valiantly battling his ghost, engages it in conversation to produce thereby a work of art of which he himself is the author. All three of them dazzle with their mastery, all three of them—standing together to define an epoch—show us what a revolution in literature can look like.

Coda:
From the Nineteenth to the Twenty-First Century

In his paper "Sending: On Representation," Jacques Derrida asks whether "translation [is] of the same order as representation," whether it "consist[s] in representing a sense, the same semantic content, by a different language".[1] This question is not answered explicitly in his further remarks, but his discussion does imply that for him translation is at least *a* form of representation, as it clearly is for Goethe, even if the terms and nature of this representation remain subject to negotiation. But in fact this definition involves (in Derrida's case as well) redefining a problematic concept in terms equally problematic. A translation is a representation of an original text (and of the semantic content that text sought to express), yet the thickness of the description, the slant of the prism, remains an open question. If this book has demonstrated one thing, it is surely the precariousness of the assumptions that allowed for the development of service translation in the first place. Service translation implies the belief in the possibility of accurate representation in a medium—literary language—whose indeterminacy is profound. In the end, all translation is, to some extent and of necessity, authorial; service translation exists merely as a goal to be pursued, but a goal that provides the basis for most approaches to modern translation. What distinguishes—now, that is, since 1800—an emphatically authorial translator from one who is merely *bad* is the vision and skill that enable him to make his translation a thing apart—a text worthy of consideration as a primary work, one that in Appiah's terms is, like an "original," worth teaching.

The great authorial translators whose work has been analyzed here cannot serve as our models in the strictest sense: these translating renegades violated the rules of translation, indeed of the very reception of literary works, the respect for authorship, that have helped to constitute our modernity. Yet the artistic violation of authorial rights they perform with such virtuosity is perhaps itself—in this post-Benjaminian, post-Barthesian, post-Foucauldian age when everything is ruled by the vast and vastly productive anonymity of the electronic media, when all is "information"—pointing the way to new forms of translation, of reception, that can lead to a new post-authorial conception of writing as a social/communal endeavor. This is a mode of reception that asks not only "What is there?" and "Why is it there?" but "What can be made of it?" It is a way of catapulting works into a new era, not by erasing their characteristics, but by searching out the constitutive nub of the work that, grafted onto a new branch, will produce marvelous blossoms of a sort never before seen. Not the erasure of the older work, but its rebirth in a new form. Naturally all such projects carry with them the danger of reducing all works to the common denominator of readily transmissible mediocrity. For the endeavor not to be in vain—or, worse than that, destructive—the highest possible level of artistry (what Goethe would call "genius") is called for, such that the authorial prowess of the translator in no way lags behind that of the original author. Thus, while the translators-authors who have been examined here offer us a lesson in freedom, they also offer lessons in responsibility, since the further the translator ventures from the fold of service-oriented fidelity, the greater the risks become and the higher the stakes. The translator who approaches a text enters into a compact with the original author (not the historical person, of course, but the author such as can be extrapolated from the work), and certainly there is more than a literary reputation to uphold. The great authorial translators of the nineteenth century show us how it is possible to translate great works as great works, in translations that possess their own internal coherence, their own concerns, their own moral, social, political, artistic validity.

CODA

If finally, as Novalis tells us, all writing is translation, it is equally true that all translation is writing, and writing is an art form whose development has by no means come to an end.

Abbreviations

Abbreviations for multivolume works refer to the complete edition, rather than individual volumes.

FBA	Helmut Sembdner, *Johann Daniel Falks Bearbeitung des Amphitryon-Stoffes. Ein Beitrag zur Kleistforschung* (Berlin: Erich Schmidt, 1971).
FrA	Friedrich Hölderlin, *Sämtliche Werke* (Frankfurter Ausgabe), edited by D. E. Sattler with Michael Franz and Michael Knaupp, vols. 15 and 16 (Basel: Stroemfeld/Roter Stern, 1987).
GS	Walter Benjamin, "Die Aufgabe des Übersetzers," in *Gesammelte Schriften* 4:1, edited by Tilman Rexroth (Frankfurt am Main: Suhrkamp, 1991), 9–21.
HKn	Friedrich Hölderlin, *Sämtliche Werke und Briefe*, edited by Michael Knaupp, 3 vols (Munich: Hanser, 1992–93).
Kse	Heinrich von Kleist, *Sämtliche Werke und Briefe*, edited by Helmut Sembdner, 9th ed., 2 vols (Munich: Hanser, 1993).
MA	Johann Wolfgang von Goethe, *Sämtliche Werke nach Epochen seines Schaffens* (Münchener Ausgabe), edited by Karl Richter with Herbert G. Göpfert, Norbert Miller, and Gerhard Sauder, 21 vols (Munich: Hanser, 1985–).
OCD	Denis Diderot, *Oeuvres complètes*, edited by J. Assézat, 20 vols (Paris: Garnier, 1875–77).
OCM	Jean Baptiste Poquelin Molière, *Oeuvres complètes* 2 (Pléiade), edited by Georges Couton (Paris: Gallimard, 1971).
OeK	"Oedipus the King: Friedrich Hölderlin's Rendering of Sopho-

	cles," translated by David Constantine, *Comparative Criticism* 20 (1998), 223–36.
PA	Denis Diderot, "The Paradox of the Actor," in *Selected Writings on Art and Literature*, translated by Geoffrey Bremner (New York: Penguin, 1994), 100–158.
SW	August Wilhem Schlegel, *Sämmtliche Werke*, edited by Eduard Böcking, 12 vols (Leipzig: Weidmann'sche Buchhandlung, 1846–47).
TT	Rainer Schulte and John Biguenent, eds., *Theories of Translation: An Anthology of Essays from Dryden to Derrida* (Chicago: University of Chicago Press, 1992).

Notes

Preface

1. "Instead of merely transferring someone else's work faithfully and self-effacingly, the auteur transforms the material into an expression of his own personality." Edward Buscombe, "Ideas of Authorship," in *Theories of Authorship: A Reader*, ed. John Caughie (London: Routledge, 1986), 23.
2. For an example of the practical application of this mode of translation, see *Passion*, Lawrence Venuti's 1994 translation of Tarchetti's novel *Fosca*, and the preface in which he discusses his reasons for the decision to translate thus. Iginio Ugo Tarchetti, *Passion*, trans. Lawrence Venuti (San Francisco: Mercury House, 1994).

Chapter 1

1. Berman, *Experience of the Foreign*, 5.
2. Venuti, *The Translator's Invisibility*, 18.
3. Ibid., 20.
4. "Translation is also an offense against a still prevailing concept of scholarship that rests on the assumption of original authorship. Whereas this scholarship seeks to ascertain the authorial intention that constitutes originality, translation not only deviates from that intention, but substitutes others: it aims to address a different audience by answering to the constraints of a different language and culture. Instead of enabling a true and disinterested understanding of the foreign text, translation provokes the fear of error, amateurism, opportunism—an abusive exploitation of originality." Venuti, *Scandals of Translation*, 31.

5. Fränzel, *Geschichte des Übersetzens,* 29–30, 34–38, 47–48. See also Senger, *Deutsche Übersetzungstheorie,* 47–53. My account of the historical development of translation in this period relies heavily on Fränzel's exhaustive study, which is still considered definitive.
6. Gottsched, "Nachricht von neuen hierher gehörigen Sachen," 516.
7. All translations are my own unless otherwise noted.
8. Fränzel, *Geschichte des Übersetzens,* 60.
9. Breitinger, *Critische Dichtkunst,* 61.
10. Lessing, "Briefe, die neueste Literatur betreffend," 19.
11. Petersen, "Einleitung des Herausgebers," 11: 15.
12. Wittmann, *Geschichte des deutschen Buchhandels,* 129; Bruford, *Germany in the Eighteenth Century,* 275–79; Fränzel, *Geschichte des Übersetzens,* 86–87.
13. Fränzel, *Geschichte des Übersetzens,* 90–92.
14. Ibid., 108.
15. Ibid., 114.
16. Ibid., 126–27.
17. Ibid., 127.
18. Ibid., 130.
19. Ibid.
20. Ibid, 135.
21. Ibid., 138.
22. Ibid.
23. Herder, *Sämtliche Werke,* 25:34.
24. There had been considerable resistance to the use of the trochaic hexameter line in German even after the appearance of Friedrich Gottlieb Klopstock's *Messias* (1748–51), which was written entirely in this form—and despite the tradition of the alexandrine, an iambic hexameter form, used in the Baroque *Trauerspiel* just a century before. (Klopstock himself, translating an excerpt from *The Iliad* in 1776, did so in prose.)
25. Klopstock himself declared a Homer translation in hexameters impossible and produced a translation in prose. Herbst, *Johann Heinrich Voß,* 84, 95.
26. In a letter to Voß on 6 December 1796, Goethe writes, "Ich werde nicht verschweigen, wie viel ich bei dieser Arbeit unserm Wolf und Ihnen schuldig bin. *Sie* haben mir den Weg gezeigt, und *er* hat mir Mut gemacht ihn zu gehen." Goethe, *Goethes Briefe,* 2:581; I will not hesitate to say how much I owe to our Wolf and yourself regarding this project. See also 2:608.
27. Catalogued in Schroeter, *Geschichte der deutschen Homer-Übersetzung,* 253–54.
28. Schlegel, "Homers Werke von Johann Heinrich Voss" (1796), in

Sämmtliche Werke, 10:140. This standard edition of Schlegel's works is hereafter cited in the text as SW.
29. For a discussion in English of Voß's Shakespeare translations, see Bernofsky, "Schleiermacher's Translation Theory," 175–92, esp. 182–84.
30. Schlegel explains his change of opinion in detail in a letter to Goethe of 4 February 1799: "Es ist mir mit den Grundsätzen über die Übersetzungskunst aus den Alten eigen gegangen. Bey Beurteilung des Voßischen Homer lehnte ich mich stark auf die Seite der Opposizion. Ich hatte damals nur noch aus modernen Dichtern, Dante und Shakespeare übersetzt, ich wußte sehr gut, welche Freyheiten die Sprache zu diesem Gebrauche nöthig habe, und war darauf bedacht mich in ihren Besitz zu setzen. Daß die Annäherung an die Alten Befreyung von Fesseln einer konvenzionellen Grammatik in ganz entgegengesetzer Tendenz fodre hatte ich noch nicht erfahren." Quoted in Huyssen, *Die frühromantische Konzeption,* 86; I had a curious experience in attempting to derive principles for the art of translation from the ancients. When I judged Voß's Homer, I placed myself firmly on the side of the opposition. At the time, I had myself only translated from modern writers, Dante and Shakespeare; I knew very well what liberties of language were required for this purpose and I was set on acquiring this facility. I hadn't yet learned that approaching the ancients required quite an opposite sort of liberation from the fetters of conventional grammar.
31. Shakespeare, *Der Sturm,* 18:

> Five fathoms deep lies father your [= your father].
> His bones are turning into coral,
> Pearls are the eyes of him.
> Nothing about him that should decay,
> That is not transformed, ocean's treasure,
> into a rich and rare thing.
> Nymphs ring the bell for him hourly,
> Listen there! their little bell—Ding! ding! ding!

32. Variants quoted in Bernays, *Zur Entstehungsgeschichte,* 16. Wieland translated:

> Fünf Faden tief dein Vater ligt,
> Sein Gebein ward zu Corallen,
> Zu Perlen seine Augen-Ballen,
> Und vom Moder unbesiegt,
> Wandelt durch der Nymphen Macht
> Sich jeder Theil von ihm und glänzt und fremder Pracht.

Christoph Martin Wieland, *Gesammelte Schriften*, Zweite Abteilung: Übersetzungen, ed. Ernst Stadler (Berlin: Weidmannsche Buchhandlung, 1909–11), 1:328.

And Herder included a translation of these lines in Volume 1 of his *Volkslieder* (1778):

> Fünf Faden tief der Vater dein
> Liegt; sein Auge Perle ward,
> Zu Korallen sein Gebein
> Liegt im Meeresgrund' erstarrt;
> Unversehret, reich und schön
> Ist er verwandelt da zu sehen.
> Herder, *Sämtliche Werke*, 25:207.

33. In order: "Sir, I must speak with you"; "I must speak with you, sir"; "Sir, let [me] tell you something"; "I'd like to tell you something, sir"; "Sir, a word with you." Quoted in Bernays, *Zur Entstehungsgeschichte*, 238.
34. This myth has, bizarrely, lived on, with even scholars of the stature of Antoine Berman declaring the Shakespeare translations to have been a collaborative effort. Berman, *Experience of the Foreign*, 11.
35. Fränzel, *Geschichte des Übersetzens*, 136.
36. Christoph Martin Wieland, *Attisches Museum* 1 (1796), xxviii.
37. J. H. Voß (1821) and Droysen (1832) also published translations of Aristophanes's collected works.
38. Eigler and Kord, *Feminist Encyclopedia of German Literature*, 461. See also Hahn, *Unter falschem Namen*.
39. Paulin, "Luise Gottsched und Dorothea Tieck."
40. Eigler and Kord, *Feminist Encyclopedia of German Literature*, 6.
41. Bernays, "Vorrede und Nachwort zum neuen Abdruck." See also Bernays, *Entstehungsgeschichte*.
42. Berman, *Experience of the Foreign*, 131.
43. Schlegel, "Kritische Fragmente," 23.
44. Huyssen, *Die frühromantische Konzeption*, 93.
45. Norbert Greiner notes, for example, that Wieland became more critical of Shakespeare in the course of translating his plays: "*Before* beginning his translation activity (1758) he had termed dramatically essential all the playwright's peculiarities, later declaimed errors—the mingling of tragical and comical, the irregular unfolding of the plot, the baroque diction." Greiner, "Comic Matrix," 207.
46. This is a point that has been emphasized by many critics, notably Gebhardt and Habicht: Habicht, "The Romanticism of the Schlegel-Tieck

NOTES TO CHAPTER 1

Shakespeare," 45. Gebhardt, *A. W. Schlegels Shakespeare-Übersetzung.*

47. Schlegel, "Etwas über William Shakespeare bei Gelegenheit Wilhelm Meisters" (1796), published in Schiller's journal *Die Horen.* SW 7:61.
48. Goethe, *Sämtliche Werke,* 5:295. The complete edition (21 vols.) is hereafter cited in the text as MA (Münchener Ausgabe).
49. Be a good spirit, be a damned goblin, bring the perfumes of Heaven with you or the vapors of Hell, whether your intentions be good or evil, you come in such a worthy form, yes, I will speak with you, I will call you Hamlet, King, Father, oh answer me!
50. Shakespeare, *Complete Works,* 743.
51. Schleiermacher, "Ueber die verschiedenen Methoden des Uebersetzens," 47. For the English, I quote from my own translation in *The Routledge Translation Studies Reader,* 2nd ed., ed. Lawrence Venuti, forthcoming (2004).
52. Schleiermacher, "Ueber die verschiedenen Methoden," 58–59.
53. *Dolmetschen, Paraphrase,* and *Nachahmung.* The first term refers not only to oral translation but also to written translation with a purely communicative emphasis, as in multilingual business transactions. Schleiermacher uses *paraphrase* in the usual sense and *imitation* to refer to a translation that makes free with the original text in an attempt to achieve the same "effect" (*Wirkung/Eindruck*) in the target language by different means.
54. Ibid., 60. The organic/artificial theme is later continued in the metaphor Schleiermacher uses to describe the multilingual small talk of courtiers: "wie die Kresse, die ein künstlicher Mann ohne alle Erde auf dem weißen Tuche wachsen macht" Ibid., 62; like the watercress that an artful man causes to sprout without soil on a white cloth.
55. Ibid., 65.
56. Ibid., 57.
57. Ibid., 69. The French, on the other hand, are singled out for their cultural intolerance: "Wer wollte behaupten, es sei jemals etwas weder aus den alten Sprachen noch aus den germanischen in die französische übersezt worden!" Ibid; Who would claim that anything has ever been translated, whether from an ancient or a Germanic tongue, into French. He had alluded to this language more gently earlier in the essay, noting that his preferred method of translation "nicht in allen Sprachen gleich gut gedeihen kann, sondern nur in solchen die nicht in zu engen Banden eines klassischen Ausdrukks gefangen liegen, außerhalb dessen alles verwerflich ist." Ibid., 56; [It] cannot flourish equally well in all tongues, but rather only in those that are not confined within the narrow bounds of a classical style beyond which all else is deemed reprehensible.
58. "Jeder Mensch ist auf der einen Seite in der Gewalt der Sprache, die er

redet; er und sein ganzes Denken ist ein Erzeugniß derselben. Er kann nichts mit völliger Bestimmtheit denken, was außerhalb der Grenzen derselben läge." Ibid., 46; "Every human being is, on the one hand, in the power of the language he speaks; he and his whole thinking are a product of it. He cannot, with complete certainty, think anything that lies outside the limits of [this] language," Schulte and Biguenet, *Theories of Translation*, 38. English translations of Goethe and Humboldt provided from this anthology will be cited in the text hereafter as TT.
59. Goethe, "Noten und Abhandlungen zu besserem Verständniß des West-östlichen Divans: Übersetzungen," in MA 11.1.2:262–65.
60. Humboldt, "Einleitung," 14.
61. Ibid., 16.
62. Ibid., 14.
63. Benjamin, "Die Aufgabe des Übersetzers," 12; hereafter cited in the text as GS. English translation: Benjamin, "The Task of the Translator," 17.
64. Harry Zohn translates this as "the end of their time." Benjamin, "Task of the Translator," 18.
65. de Man, "Conclusions," 92.
66. Ibid., 80.
67. Tejaswini Niranjana argues that de Man reads the history "out" of Benjamin's essay, reading "in" an emphasis on poetics and language. Her own reading underemphasizes the importance of Benjamin's "pure language," which, however, could in fact be seen—via Romantic theory—to bear upon her own project. Niranjana, *Siting Translation*, 110–40.
68. de Man, "Conclusions," 92.
69. Fränzel, *Geschichte des Übersetzens*, 40.
70. Benjamin, "Task of the Translator," 18.
71. Ibid., 21 (translation amended).
72. Though I would argue that while de Man is clearly justified in saying that the meaning of the sentence is not encapsulated in any of its words or phrases, but rather in the relations between them, the words are meaningful with respect to their sentences in a way that letters, with respect to the words they form, are not: individual words, like sentences, have semantic value, while individual letters do not.
73. The metaphor of reading as *flânerie* provides the opening images of *Berliner Kindheit um Neunzehnhundert:* "Sich in einer Stadt nicht zurechtfinden heißt nicht viel. In einer Stadt sich aber zu verirren, wie man in einem Walde sich verirrt, braucht Schulung. [. . .] Diese Kunst habe ich spät erlernt; sie hat den Traum erfüllt, von dem die ersten Spuren Labyrinthe auf den Löschblättern meiner Hefte waren." Benjamin, *Gesammelte Schriften* 4.1:237; Not to find one's way in a city doesn't mean much. But to lose one's way in a city the way one loses

NOTES TO CHAPTER 2

one's way in the woods requires training. . . . I learned this art late; it fulfilled the dream whose first traces were the labyrinths on the blotting paper in my notebooks.
74. de Man, "Conclusions," 92.
75. Middleton, "Translation as a Species of Mime," 55, 56 (my italics).
76. Hirsch, *Übersetzung und Dekonstruktion*, 145.
77. Ibid., 150–51.
78. Ibid., 136.
79. Ibid., 131.
80. Ibid., 162.
81. Berman, 4.
82. Robinson, *Translator's Turn*, 88–89.
83. In addition to the authors discussed in the next few pages, the reader is referred in particular to the articles collected in Bassnet and Trivedi, *Postcolonial Translation: Theory and Practice*.
84. Spivak, "The Politics of Translation," 403.
85. Ibid., 400.
86. Appiah, "Thick Translation," 426–27.
87. Ibid., 425.
88. Niranjana, *Siting Translation*, 2.
89. Ibid., 167.
90. Friedrich Schlegel, "Athenäums-Fragmente," in *Schriften zur Literatur*, ed. Wolfdietrich Rasch (Munich: Deutscher Taschenbuch Verlag, 1972), 37.
91. Of course, not all that sounds odd is good—certainly there are cases in which the epithet "translatorese" is regrettably well deserved. At the same time, as Venuti argues, there tends to be a direct correlation between the desire—viewed on a national scale—to downplay cultural difference and the belief that foreign domination might somehow be beneficial for another country.
92. Quoted in Fränzel, *Geschichte des Übersetzens*, 138.
93. Barthes, "Death of the Author," 148.
94. Novalis, *Schriften*, 4:213.
95. Foucault, "What Is an Author?" 608.
96. Spivak, "The Politics of Translation," 398.

Chapter 2

1. On the difficulties of dating Kleist's play, see note 14.
2. Szondi, "Vorwort," 12.
3. The prologue to Plautus's play, spoken by Mercury, declares its genre as tragicomedy, noting that

> It wouldn't do to make it only comedy,
> not with gods and kings parading on the stage,

but asserting that the servant characters will provide a comic strand. Plautus, *Amphitruo,* trans. Charles E. Passage, in Passage and Mantinband, *Amphitryon,* 42.
4. Molière, *Oeuvres complètes* 2 (Pléiade), 1989–99. Lines from Molière's play will be cited hereafter in the text as OCM, with line number(s) from this Pléiade edition. All English translations are my own.
5. Mann, "Amphitryon," 66.
6. Kleist, *Sämtliche Werke und Briefe* 1:249, lines 78-83. References to this edition of Kleist's work, edited by Helmut Sembdner, will be cited hereafter in the text as KSe, followed by the volume and page numbers. Quotes from *Amphitryon* itself are cited with the line numbers as well, to simplify locating them in other editions.
7. Hans Robert Jauß notes that Kleist's Sosias is decidedly more physical and materialistic a character than Molière's. Jauß, "Poetik und Problematik," 237–38.
8. It more strongly recalls, in fact, Schlegel's translation of Bottom's transformation in *A Midsummer Night's Dream:* "Thou art translated" appears as "du bist verwandelt."
9. "But the decisive step over and beyond Molière that changes the entire set of problems at stake here lies in the fact that for both Alcmena and Amphitryon, whom Kleist implicates in the problem of unhappy consciousness, the question of identity must be decided not only on the basis of consciousness of self but on the basis of the *you,* i.e. of that certainty of self that the subject can find only in the relationship to another subject." Jauß, "Poetik und Problematik," 234–35.
10. The term *Wir-Identität* (we-identity) is provided by Karlheinz Stierle in his response to Jauß's paper: Stierle, "Amphitryon," 736.
11. Szondi, "Vorwort," 12.
12. The lexicon contains entries for both Amphitryon and Alcmena (cols. 213–15, 159–60).
13. Rose, *Handbook of Greek Mythology,* 206.
14. Hölderlin, *Sämtliche Werke und Briefe* 2:356, 1084.
15. The suggestion that Falk's play influenced Kleist was first made by Wilhelm Ruland in 1897, a claim later opposed by Erich Schmidt. The argument was further pursued in 1956 by the Swedish Germanist Örjan Lindberger in a monograph on *Amphitryon,* and has since been reprised by Helmut Sembdner, who has compiled a catalogue of the lines Kleist took from Falk and used this evidence to support his claim that the translation was completed in 1803. Nonetheless, the editors of the most

recent Kleist edition, Roland Reuß and Peter Staengle, contend that the play was written several years after the period of Kleist's acquaintance with Falk, during Kleist's tenure in Königsberg (May 1805–January 1807), citing the evidence of a contemporary chronicler, Wilhelm von Schütz. But Schütz's commentary is vague, and there is no indication of what evidence it is based on. Since *Amphitryon* was published only in 1807, while Kleist was imprisoned in Fort Joux, Schütz might well have assumed the play to have been a recently completed work. I find Sembdner's account, based as it is on extensive textual evidence, more convincing. Helmut Sembdner, "Kleist und Falk." Roland Reuß, "Zu dieser Ausgabe," *Amphitryon, Heinrich von Kleists Sämtliche Werke: Berliner Ausgabe,* ed. R. Reuß and P. Staengle (Frankfurt am Main: Stroemfeld/Roter Stern, 1991), 143–45.

16. Molière's text was itself believed in the nineteenth century to be a pièce-a-clef referring to Louis XIV, Mme de Montespan, and M. de Montespan—a notion that has since been discredited. Passage and Mantinband, *Amphitryon,* 129.
17. As Zschokke relates the episode: "There was a French engraving hanging in my room, 'La cruche cassée.' In the figures there depicted, we identified a sad pair of lovers, a bickering mother holding up a broken majolica jug, and a judge with a large nose. The assignment was for Wieland to write a satire, Kleist a comedy, and myself a story. Kleist's 'The Broken Jug' was the winner." Sembdner, *Heinrich von Kleists Lebensspuren,* 58–59.
18. Sembdner, *Falks Bearbeitung des Amphitryon-Stoffes,* 18. Reuß and Staengle's Königsberg thesis would imply that Kleist brought a copy of Falk's book with him, despite the fact that, given his acquaintance with Falk, he is more likely to have read it soon after its appearance in 1804.
19. Ibid., 572. Sembdner's 1971 *Falks Bearbeitung des Amphitryon-Stoffes* contains a complete text of *Amphitruon,* which is cited hereafter in the text as FBA, with line number(s).
20. "Es hatte allen Anschein, daß die Schweiz sowie Zisalpinien, französisch werden wird, und mich ekelt vor dem bloßen Gedanken. —So leicht indessen wird es dem Allerwelts-Konsul mit der Schweiz nicht gelingen." KSe 2:718, letter to Ulrike, 19 Feb. 1802; It looks very much as if Switzerland, as well as the cisalpine region, are going to become French, and the very thought fills me with disgust. —But the commonplace consul won't have it that easy either.
21. Berman, *Experience of the Foreign,* 136.
22. This dialectic will appear in quite different form in Hölderlin: the one thing the all-powerful gods cannot do is to worship (acknowlege) themselves—for this they need Man.

23. Bloom, *The Anxiety of Influence*, 14. Jauß speaks rather of "daemonization" in the Bloomian sense—a reading with which I would take issue, as it would seem to imply that the "power in the parent-poem that does not belong to the parent proper" (Bloom 15) was not already part of a Kleistian constellation. Kleist was no longer a youth when he encountered Molière. Cf. Jauß, "Poetik und Problematik," 241.

Chapter 3

1. See Louth, *Hölderlin and the Dynamics of Translation*, 104.
2. Hölderlin, *Sämtliche Werke und Briefe*, ed. Michael Knaupp, 1:866 (my emphasis). Although I will later cite the Greek originals of Hölderlin's translations from the Frankfurter Ausgabe, I am using Knaupp's excellent edition throughout this chapter, in part because of his use of modernized spellings, and in part because I refer to his commentary. But since all quotes from Hölderlin's Sophocles and Pindar translations will be identified by line number as well as by page, they can easily be located in either the Frankfurter or the Stuttgarter Ausgabe, as the reader prefers. References to Knaupp's edition will be cited hereafter in the text as HKn.
3. Novalis, *Schriften*, 4:213.
4. Beissner, *Hölderlins Übersetzungen*, 134.
5. Hölderlin is known, for example, to have owned a copy of Friedrich Gedike's translations of Pindar, but no one has been able to trace the influence in his translations. Hellingrath notes, "Während oder kurz vor der Zeit seiner eigenen Pindarübertragung hat er sie keinesfalls eingesehen." Norbert von Hellingrath, "Pindarübertragungen von Hölderlin: Prolegomena zu einer Erstausgabe," in *Hölderlin-Vermächtnis*, 27; During or immediately before his own Pindar translations he most certainly did not consult them. See also Seifert, *Untersuchungen zu Hölderlins Pindar-Rezeption*, 26n22.
6. Constantine, *Hölderlin*, 2.
7. For a list of the hexameter lines in the translation, see Michael Knaupp's commentary, HKn 3:407.
8. Hellingrath is convinced that "Die Pindarübertragung ist ein Versuch, niemals zum Druck bestimmt und ohne sicheres Anzeichen, daß je eine Absicht zur Veröffentlichung bestand." Hellingrath, *Hölderlin-Vermächtnis*, 66; The Pindar translation is an experiment never intended for print and without any definite sign that plans for a publication ever existed. Later commentators have maintained that the translations went through more than one draft, suggesting that Hölderlin was in fact interested in a final product for others to read. Friedrich Beissner argues that the manuscript should been seen as "eine planvoll angelegte Reinschrift

[. . .], aus verstreuten Konzepten, Entwürfen, Notizen zusammengeschrieben." Beissner, *Hölderlins Übersetzungen,* 30; a well-planned fair copy . . . assembled out of assorted sketches, drafts and notes. Beissner's claim is supported by Günther Zuntz's earlier observation that the manuscripts of the poems appear to have been written swiftly and fluently, without the interruptions that would have been caused, for example, by stopping to consult dictionaries. Zuntz, *Über Hölderlins Pindar-Übersetzung,* 2.

9. This is suggested by Michael Knaupp (HKn 3:430), who may well have been thinking of Hölderlin's dedication of the plays to Princess Auguste von Homburg: "Jezt hab' ich, da ein Dichter bei uns auch sonst etwas zum Nöthigen oder zum Angenehmen thun muß, diß Geschäft gewählt, weil es zwar in fremden, aber festen und historischen Gesezen gebunden ist." HKn 2:248; I have now, since poets among us are required also to produce something useful or pleasurable, chosen this business, because it is bound by laws that, though foreign, are also fixed and historical.

10. English translations of quotes from the first two acts of Hölderlin's translation of *Oedipus the King* are taken from "Oedipus the King: Friedrich Hölderlin's Rendering of Sophocles," trans. David Constantine, *Comparative Criticism* 20 (1998), 223–36, 224, which will be cited hereafter in the text as OeK.

11. Notably, Lönker, "Unendliche Deutung," 288–89, see especially n2.

12. Bernard Knox, "Commentary." In Sophocles, *Three Theban Plays,* 406.

13. Lönker, "Unendliche Deutung," 289.

14. My source for the Greek texts of Sophocles and Pindar are the bilingual editions of Hölderlin's translations in volumes 15 and 16 of the Frankfurter Ausgabe: Hölderlin, *Sämtliche Werke,* ed. D. E. Sattler, cited hereafter in the text as FrA. I am grateful to Naomi Rood for her assistance in reading and appraising the Greek text—though any errors of interpretation are mine alone.

15. Schleiermacher, "Ueber die verschiedenen Methoden des Uebersetzens," 55.

16. In the fragment of *The Iliad* translated by Hölderlin, Achilles, favorite of Apollo, figures prominently along with his attribute *podas okus,* which Hölderlin translates by turns "der schnellfüßige Achill" and "der schnelle Läufer Achilles." HKn 2:120–24. Fleetfooted Achilles is an ironic foil for the limping Oedipus. Hölderlin quotes from Voß's *Ilias* in an essay written for his planned journal *Iduna* (HKn 2:60).

17. Beissner, cataloging the many verbs translated by Hölderlin as *treffen* (to strike), links the use of the word to Hölderlin's own raptness before the Alps: *betroffen* (struck, 144). While this is clearly a valid resonance, it does not adequately account for the frequency of the word in the translation.

18. This line is echoed by an important pair of lines in "Wie wenn am Feiertage . . ." (As on a feast day). The first refers to the myth of Semele, who was burned to ashes when her lover Zeus appeared to her, at her own request, in his true form:

> So fiel, wie Dichter sagen, da sie sichtbar
> Den Gott zu sehen begehrte, sein Bliz auf Semeles Haus
> Und die göttlichgetroffne gebahr [. . .]

> So, as poets say, when she desired to see the god visibly, his thunderbolt fell on Semele's house, and the one struck by the god gave birth.

Equally fertile and equally imperiled by divine presence are the poets, whose representative speaks in the final fragmentary stanza:

> Und sag ich gleich,
> Ich sei genaht, die Himmlischen zu schauen,
> Sie selbst, sie werfen mich tief unter die Lebenden
> Den falschen Priester, ins Dunkel, daß ich
> Das warnende Lied den Gelehrigen singe (HKn 1:263)

> And if I say that I have come to gaze upon the heavenly ones, they themselves, they hurl me far down among the living, me the false priest, into the darkness, that I may sing the song of warning to scholars.

19. The play's opening exchange invokes the particular—Antigone summons her sister Ismene: "Darum, daß du's besonders hören könntest" [HKn 2:319, 20], though the Greek *mone* ("you alone") could have been translated quite differently. This use of the term emphasizes Hölderlin's understanding of particularity as separating out isolated instances of specificity: *besonders* means "you alone" only in the strong sense of "you, sundered from all others." This passage links the *Antigone* translation to that of *Oedipus*, which, as will be discussed below, is in many ways quite different.
20. Beissner, *Hölderlins Übersetzungen*, 142.
21. Rainer Nägele notes, in a reading of the poem "Die Scheinheiligen Dichter," that the line "ihr glaubt nicht an Helios, / noch an den Donnerer und Meergott" (juxtaposing divine name and function) "can be read not only as a denial of faith in all of these gods but also as a denial of two different kinds of faith: belief in a Greek god as a mythical entity named Helios, and belief in a modern version of natural forces that

might be representable in allegorical personifications like "Donnerer und Meergott." Nägele, *Echoes of Translation*, 59.
22. Allemann, *Hölderlin und Heidegger*, 31.
23. Santner, *Friedrich Hölderlin*, 59–60.
24. Thus "our relation to the Greeks is structured not like the relation of consciousness to the object of its knowledge but like a trope—chiasmus, a reversal concerned only with the relation of the terms and not their constitution." Warminski, *Readings in Interpretation*, 33.
25. Ibid., 19.
26. Szondi, *Hölderlin-Studien*, 108. This corresponds also to the mutual dependence of the genres discussed in Hölderlin's poetological texts: "im tragischen liegt die Vollendung des epischen, im lyrischen die Vollendung des tragischen, im epischen die Vollendung des lyrischen." "Der tragische Dichter," HKn 2:110; in the tragic lies the perfection/completion of the epic, in the lyric the perfection of the tragic, in the epic the perfection of the lyric), and thus the poet specializing in each genre does well (*thut wohl*) to study the others.
27. In Robert Fagles's translation: "Nor did that Justice, dwelling with the gods / beneath the earth, ordain such laws for men" (line 501–2); "No, / Justice will never suffer that" (605). Sophocles, *Three Theban Plays*, 82, 87.
28. Rose, *Handbook of Greek Mythology*, 175.
29. In Fagles's translation: "Protect your rights? / When you trample down the honors of the gods?" (line 834–35). Sophocles, *Three Theban Plays*, 98.
30. An. orosi ch' oide. soi d'upillousi stoma. / Kre. su d' ouk epaide tonde choris ei phroneis.
31. se d' autognotos oles' orga. In Fagles's translation: "Your own blind will, your passion has destroyed you" (line 962). Sophocles, *Three Theban Plays*, 104.
32. Benjamin, "Die Aufgabe des Übersetzers," 21. English translation: Benjamin, "The Task of the Translator," trans. Harry Zohn, 23.

33. en d' aloxoi
    poliai t' epimateres
    aktan parabomion
    allothen allai logron ponon
    ikteres epistonaxousi.
    paian de lampei, stonoessa te geros
    omaolos.

34. Constantine, *Hölderlin*, 238.

NOTES TO CHAPTER 3

35. Nisetich, *Pindar's Victory Songs,* 16.
36. Ibid., 31. See also 36–37.
37. Hellingrath, *Hölderlin-Vermächtnis,* 20.
38. Adorno, "Parataxis: Zur späten Lyrik Hölderlins," in *Noten zur Literatur,* 187.
39. Ibid., 191.
40. Albrecht Seifert has traced a passage from "Der Rhein"

    so, daß er [. . .] die Sprache der Reinesten giebt
    Verständlich den Guten, aber mit Recht
    die Achtungslosen mit Blindheit schlägt

    so that he gives the language of the purest ones, comprehensible to the good, but rightfully strikes the respectless with blindness

    to a verbatim translation of these lines as a demonstration that Hölderlin was certainly able to translate them literally. Seifert, *Untersuchungen zu Hölderlins Pindar-Rezeption,* 29–30).
41. In Nisetich's translation:

    There are in my quiver
    many swift arrows, striking
    to the wise, but the crowd needs interpreters.
    (*Pindar's Victory Songs,* ed. Nisetich, 91)

42. Manuscript variant recorded in FrA 15:84.
43. Inside are in-the-quiver / Resounding to-the-knowledgeable
44. *Pindar's Victory Songs,* ed. Nisetich, 23.
45. Hölderlin reads "Agesidamus" for "Ainesidamos," meaning, in this case, the son of Ainesidamos, i.e. Theron. Cf. FrA 15:149.
46. *Pindar's Victory Songs,* ed. Nisetich, 90.
47. Literally, "judges someone with-inimical [necessity] the-word pronouncing with-necessity."
48. Segal, *Sophocles' Tragic World,* 181.
49. See especially Nickau, "Die Frage nach dem Original," 274–76. Nickau contests Beissner's reading of the passage, which construes *notisai* ("treibe zurük") as a conjunctive, intransitive verb form, as it is now generally taken to be by commentators on the passage, though this passage of Hölderlin's translation makes sense only when "das rükgängige Wesen" is read as appositive to "den Ares" and "treibe zurük" as transitive imperative.
50. "[D]er goldenen Kind, / Der Hoffnung, du, unsterbliche Sage!" struc-

turally resembles, for instance, the opening lines of "Friedensfeier":

> Der himmlischen, still wiederklingenden,
> Der ruhigwandelnden Töne voll,
> Und gelüftet ist der altgebaute,
> Seeliggewohnte Saal (HKn 2:361)

> Full of heavenly, silently echoing, peacefully wandering sounds, and well aired-out is the old-built, blissfully inhabited hall.

51. aglaas ebas thebas, eipe moi o teknon / elpidos ambrote fama.
52. Fagles's translation. Sophocles, *Three Theban Plays*, 76.
53. apotryetai, pallomenon arotron / etous eis etos hippei- / o genei poleyon
54. Bernard Böschenstein extends the activities invoked in Hölderlin's translation of the stasimen to translation itself, which, he writes, is "als ein eigentliches Über-Setzen mitreflektiert, als ein Über-Setzen, das durch die Nacht führt, in Verbindung mit einem Durchgang durch den Winter, durch das Meer, vielleicht auch durch das Gebirge." Böschenstein, "Die Nacht des Meers," 105; reflected as a true trans-lation [crossing-over], as a trans-lation that leads through the night, in connection with a passage through winter, through the ocean, perhaps even through the mountains. This "journey," marked by a "Tendenz zu konkreterem, rauherem, alltäglicherem Wortschatz und zur Rückverwandlung übertragener in 'eigentliche' Bedeutung" (tendency to use more concrete, unrefined, more quotidian vocabulary and to change figurative meanings back into "real" ones) in Hölderlin's revision of this passage exemplifies the "vaterländische Umkehr" described in Hölderlin's notes to the play. Ibid., 107.

Chapter 4

1. Gespräch mit Kanzel von Müller, 24 April 1830, quoted in the editorial material on "Goethe and Diderot" in Goethe, MA 7:1033.
2. I will be using the term *mimesis* throughout this chapter to indicate an imitating representation (*Nachahmung*)—W.J.T. Mitchell calls it an "iconic" form of representation because, like imitation, it is a mode of representation based on resemblance—while remaining mindful of the term's complexity. As Arne Melberg has noted, "*Mimesis* is *never* a homogeneous term, and if its basic movement is towards similarity it is *always* open to the opposite." Erich Auerbach's classic study of this topic includes a brief discussion of Goethe. Auerbach describes the realism of Goethe's novels as stemming largely from the fact that Goethe accurately

depicts the rigidity of a social order under which he himself has had to suffer. *Rameaus Neffe* is also mentioned in passing, but only for the sake of noting Goethe's remarks on the function of taste in French culture. Mitchell, "Representation," 14. Melberg, *Theories of Mimesis*, 3. Auerbach, *Mimesis*, 330–31.

3. The same question is posed explicitly, however, in Derrida's "Sending: On Representation," which I return to in the coda to this book. Derrida, "Sending: On Representation," 294–326.
4. Fuhrmann, "Goethes Übersetzungsmaximen," 30.
5. Ibid., 38.
6. See commentary to *West-östlicher Divan* in the Hamburger Ausgabe: Goethe, *Werke*, 2:550ff.
7. Ibid., 2:121.
8. Said, *Orientalism*, 19.
9. Although Goethe's first formulation of this concept, in an 1827 essay for the journal *Über Kunst und Altertum*, is made with a sweeping gesture of objectivity, describing the emergence of an international space of "world and human relationships" as something "one" perceives, in the next sentence he speaks of his own personal desire to bring the attention of "my friends" to the emerging phenomenon of world literature. See Pizer, "Goethe's 'World Literature' Paradigm," 215.
10. "Goethe makes easy reference to the Orient as a world of presence, voice, and origin, but seems at the same time aware that the source is always already erased, deferred, bracketed, or, to put it more positively, that the Orient can always be appropriated for an Occidental masquerade." Kontje, "Goethe's Multicultural Masquerades," 7.
11. Walser, "Energisch," in *Das Gesamtwerk*, IX: 350.
12. Note also the resemblance of this "one" to the anonymous universal subject discussed by John Pizer, "Goethe's 'World Literature,'" 215.
13. Until "zuletzt der ganze Zirkel abgeschlossen [ist], in welchem sich die Annäherung des Fremden und Einheimischen, des Bekannten und Unbekannten bewegt."
14. Diderot, *Oeuvres complètes*, ed. J. Assézat, 380; hereafter cited in the text as OCD.
15. The German word had already acquired its connotation of "prostitute," but was still in wide use in the sense of "young girl" or "female servant." Grimm's *Wörterbuch* cites examples from Voß, Schiller, Mörike, and others in which the word refers to virtuous young women.
16. As Goethe wrote to Carl Friedrich Zelter in October 1831, the Schlegel brothers were guilty of having "in Kunst und Literatur viel Unheil angerichtet" (done a lot of damage in the areas of art and literature) and Novalis had wished to see Goethe wiped out: "deliert (ausgelöscht)"

(eradicated). Goethe, *Goethes Briefe*, 4:455.

17. To this day it is not known what became of the particular copy of the manuscript Goethe used for his translation, though it is presumed to have been returned to Russia as part of Diderot's literary estate, which Diderot himself sold to Catherine the Great. The Monval manuscript, famously discovered by scholar Georges Monval at a *bouquiniste's* stall along the Seine, is in Diderot's own hand and taken to be authoritative. It now resides at the Pierpont Morgan Library in New York. One other edition, the 1875 Assézat edition, contains a text variant that appears also in Goethe's translation: "glücklich derjenige unter uns, der ein Vierundzwanzig-Sous-Stück in seiner Tasche hat, um den Wagen zu bezahlen." MA 7:616; happy is the one among us who has a twenty-four-sous coin in his pocket for cab-fare. The phrase "pour payer le fiacre" appears only in this edition. But whether this edition might be based on the manuscript Goethe saw is a claim not pressed even by Assézat himself, who notes in his foreword only that "des circonstances particulièrement heureuse mirent entre nos mains une copie sans date, mais évidemment de la fin du siècle dernier, du *Neveu de Rameau*." OCD, 380; particularly fortunate circumstances placed in our hands a copy of *Le neveu de Rameau* that has no date but clearly is from the end of the past century.

18. It appears in the 1740 edition of the *Dictionnaire de l'Academie* in the sense of the smallest bit of a thing—a more specific chemical definition was not to come until the early nineteenth century.

19. German etymological dictionaries disagree on the exact date, but all consulted place the word's first appearance toward the end of the eighteenth century.

20. "Ces gens qui se [perchent] à chevauchons sur l'epicycle de Mercure, [qui voïent si avant dans le ciel,] ils m'arrachent les dens." Montaigne, *Oeuvres Complètes*, 4:193. Those people who bestraddle the epicycle of Mercury and see so far into the heavens make me grind my teeth. Michel de Montaigne, *Essais,* trans. J. M. Cohen (London: Penguin, 1993), 193.

21. See MA 7:569, 570, 582, 585, 595–56, 601, 612–13, 622, 627, 639.

22. The French word is also discussed in Goethe, *Wilhelm Meisters Lehrjahre*, 377.

23. Goethe's notes on the translation acknowledge this, speaking of "die äußersten Gipfel der Frechheit, wohin wir ihm nicht folgen durften." MA 7:686; the highest pinnacles of impertinence where we were not free to follow him.

24. An obvious misreading (either on Goethe or the copyist's part) of *à voir* as *avoir*.

NOTES TO CHAPTER 4

25. These are the *Histoire de Dom B*****, portier des Chartreux, écrite par lui-même* (anonymous), and Pietro Aretino's *Postures (Sonetti lussuriosi)*, whose original accompanying etchings by Marcantonio Raimondi were destroyed by order of the pope. Note by Günter von Metken in *Rameaus Neffe*, ed. Günter von Metken (Stuttgart: Reclam, 1986), 163, note to p.40, line 7.
26. "Au demuerant, de ces mauvais contes, moi, je n'en invente aucun; je m'en tiens au rôle de colporteur. Ils disent qu'il y a quelques jours, sur les cinq heures du matin, on entendit un vacarme enragé; toutes les sonnettes étaient en branle; c'étaient les cris interrompus et sourds d'un homme qui étouffe: 'A moi, moi, je suffoque; je meurs.' Ces cris partaient de l'appartement du patron. On arrive, on le secourt. Notre grosse créature dont la tête était égarée, qui n'y était plus, qui ne voyait plus, comme il arrive dans ce moment, continuait de presser son mouvement, s'élevait sur ses deux mains, et du plus haut qu'elle pouvait laissait retomber sur les parties casuelles un poids de deux à trois cents livres, animé de toute la vitesse que donne la fureur du plaisir. On eut beaucoup de peine à le dégager de là. Que diable de fantaisie a un petit marteau de se placer sous une lourde enclume." OCD 5:452. "After all, I don't invent any of these scandalous tales myself, I stick to the job of carrier. They say that a few days ago, at five o'clock in the morning, a furious din was heard: all the bells were jangling and there were broken and muffled cries of a man being strangled. 'Help, help! I'm suffocating, I'm dying.' These cries came from the master's room. Help arrives. That huge creature of ours, who was quite out of her mind and had lost all idea of time and place, as happens at such a moment, was still going at full speed, lifting herself up on her hands and dropping on old Casual Parts a weight of two to three hundred pounds with all the violent animation that frantic enjoyment can give. It was very difficult to extricate him. What a fantastic idea for a little hammer to put itself under a heavy anvil!" Denis Diderot, *Rameau's Nephew and D'Alembert's Dream*, trans. L. W. Tancock (Harmondsworth: Penguin, 1971), 92.
27. Mortier, *Diderot en Allemagne*, 306.
28. "Diderots Gefallen an der Kunst ist ein Gefallen am Schein, doch dieser Schein gibt ihm die Illusion des Wirklichen (Diderot nennt es Natur oder Wahrheit), d.h. durch die Nachahmung hindurch zielt das Gefallen auf den Gegenstand." Dieckmann, "Die Wandlung des Nachahmungsbegriffes," in *Nachahmung und Illusion*, 48.
29. For example, in "Über Wahrheit und Wahrscheinlichkeit der Kunstwerke. Ein Gespräch" ("On truth and probability in works of art. A conversation"). MA 4.2:89–95, 93.
30. Though one might note that this movement to correct the text accord-

ing to scientific advances is the opposite of the strategy Goethe employed in his translation of *Le neveu de Rameau*, in which he systematically eliminated the scientific terminology—whose use, admittedly, was in large part ironic.
31. Fried, *Absorption and Theatricality*, 75, citing Diderot's "Essais."
32. His remarks also suggest, as Fried notes, that he wishes to understand the death of this little bird as a metaphor for lost virginity. Ibid., 59.
33. Ibid., 74.
34. Dieckmann, *Nachahmung und Illusion*, 57–58.
35. The *Correspondance littéraire* was a periodical in manuscript form, founded by Friedrich Melchior Grimm in 1753, by means of which German royal and learned circles kept abreast of new developments in French literature and philosophy. According to Mortier, there is no firm evidence that Goethe read "Paradox" before its first print appearance in 1830, but certainly he must at least have heard about the copies of "Paradox" being passed around. (Hamann saw one before his death in 1788, as did Herder.) Goethe had been an ardent admirer of Diderot since discovering *Jacques le fataliste* in the *Correspondance littéraire* in 1778, and is known to have read several of the works by Diderot published there in the early 1780s. Mortier, *Diderot en Allemagne*, 239 and 329–31; also MA 7:1032.
36. Dieckmann, *Nachahmung und Illusion*, 43.
37. English translation: Diderot, "The Paradox of the Actor," trans. Geoffrey Bremner, 104; hereafter cited in the text as PA.
38. Lacoue-Labarthe, "Diderot: Paradox and Mimesis," 255.
39. This explanation comes from Max Imdahl: "Der Begriff der Nachahmung ist in der Geschichte der Ästhetik mehrdeutig verwendet. *Imitatio* im Unterschied zu *ritratto* meint bereits, daß etwas hergestellt wird, was unabhängig von der *imitatio* nicht existieren kann. *Imitatio* bedeutet eine qualitative Verbesserung im Sinne des Aristoteles: der Natur wird etwas hinzugefügt, was ihr selbst nicht angehört." Quoted from the discussion session recorded in Dieckmann, *Nachahmung und Illusion*, 222; The concept of imitation has been used in different senses in the history of aesthetics. *Imitatio*, in contrast to *ritratto*, already means that something is being produced that cannot exist independently of the *imitatio*. *Imitatio* signifies a qualitative improvement in the sense of Aristotle: something is being added to nature that does not belong to nature itself. Compare also Dieter Heinrich: "*Imitatio* bedeutet nicht reine Abbildung. Sie wird seit Aristoteles verstanden als Vervollkommnung der Natur, da diese an der Ausfaltung des ihr prinzipiell Möglichen gehindert sein kann." Ibid.; *Imitatio* does not signify pure depiction. Since Aristotle, it has been understood as a perfecting of nature, since

nature can be hindered in developing all that is theoretically possible for it.
40. Landesman, "A 20th-Century Master Scam," 31.
41. This is the distinction also made by Diderot's Rameau, who notes that it is fine to be a miser as long as you don't sound like one (in other words: to be truly offensive, one must personify stinginess).
42. Prendergast, *The Order of Mimesis*, 5.
43. Seyhan, *Representation and Its Discontents*, 4.
44. Ernst Osterkamp has even described the mediation of the object found in nature by the "ideal model created by the genius" as a source of the moral content of art as understood by Diderot. Osterkamp, *Im Buchstabenbilde*, 24–25.
45. *Encyclopédie ou dictionnaire raisonné des sciences, des arts et des métiers*, 15:735a.
46. This scene is bizarrely misreported in Kenneth Burke's *A Rhetoric of Motives* (143), in which Burke supposes Bouret himself has been promoted to the rank of Keeper of the Seals and attributes the dog's fear to a condemnation of social climbing.
47. Letter to J. H. Meyer, 1 August 1796, in Goethe, *Goethes Briefe*, 2:232–33.
48. Spitzer, "The Style of Diderot," 160.
49. As suggested by John Neubauer in "Absolute and Affective Music," 122.
50. Spitzer, "The Style of Diderot," 157.
51. In his earlier days, on the other hand, Goethe revered Füßli's art after having been made acquainted with it by his friend J. C. Lavater. In 1779 he attempted to recruit Füßli to design a monument; Füßli refused. MA 4:2, 987; see also Goethe's letter to Lavater of 3–5 December 1779, in Goethe, *Goethes Briefe*, 1:287.
52. Goethe, *Goethes Briefe*, 2:250.
53. The four epochs of science Goethe names in the *Maximen und Reflexionen* are the "kindliche, poetische, abergläubische; empirische, forschende, neugierige; dogmatische, didaktische, pedantische; ideele, methodische, mystische." MA 17:912; childish, poetic, superstitious; empirical, researching, curious; dogmatic, didactic, pedantic; idea-centered, methodical, mystical.

These epochs are to be understood as developmental, like the epochs of translation and painting. The childish/poetical epoch is the simple relationship to the object (as seen in both the content-reporting translator and painter). The empirical/enquiring stage delves into the causes and effects of a phenomenon like a painter preparing to develop a subjective manner of painting or the translator immersing herself in a foreign culture—after which preparation they produce second-epoch work reminis-

cent of the dogmatic/pedantic stage of science that insists on the validity of its own subjectivity. The highest epoch of science, the ideal/methodical/mystical stage, achieves the general, the universally applicable, as in the two art forms Goethe elucidates in more detail.
54. "Das Sichtbarmachen Diderots [that which the genius performs] zielt nicht mehr auf etwas Transzendentes, sondern auf die den sichtbaren Dingen selbst innewohnende Harmonie, das Zusammenstimmen der Teile zum Ganzen [. . . während] bei Goethe das Schöne der Kunst nicht mehr, wie bei Diderot, als in den Dingen schon vorliegend gedacht ist, sondern erst vom Künstler als eine *zweite Natur* hervorgebracht werden muß." Dieckmann, *Nachahmung und Illusion*, 223.
55. "[I]ncapable, dans sa rigueur intellectuelle et son souci de méthode, de comprendre la démarche sinueuse, sautillante, primesautière de la pensée de Diderot et son indifférence absolue aux éventuelles contradictions qui en surgiraient." Mortier, *Diderot en Allemagne*, 316.
56. "Ja, er urteilt oft sehr viel schärfer, dogmatischer und theoretischer, als es seinem eigenen Standpunkt entspricht." Dieckmann, "Goethe und Diderot," 483–84.
57. Dieckmann, *Nachahmung und Illusion*, 222.
58. Though as Osterkamp reveals in his analysis of over five decades' worth of Goethe's essays describing works of art, the later Goethe (as of around 1820) was prepared to expand the boundaries of Classical art to include "das Nicht-Idealische und Natürliche, das Mißgebildete und Irreguläre" (the non-ideal and the natural, the misshapen and the irregular), though he continued to distance himself from a "romantischen Ästhetik des Häßlichen" (romantic aesthetic of the ugly). Osterkamp, *Im Buchstabenbilde*, 376.

Coda

1. Derrida, "Sending: On Representation," 297.

Bibliography

Adorno, Theodor W. *Noten zur Literatur.* Edited by Rolf Tiedemann. Frankfurt am Main: Suhrkamp, 1981.
Allemann, Beda. *Hölderlin und Heidegger.* Zurich: Atlantis, 1954.
Appiah, Kwame Anthony. "Thick Translation." In *The Translation Studies Reader,* edited by Lawrence Venuti with Mona Baker, 417–29. London: Routledge, 2000.
Auerbach, Erich. *Mimesis.* Translated by Willard R. Trask. Princeton, NJ: Princeton University Press, 1953.
Barthes, Roland. "The Death of the Author." 1968. Translated by Stephen Heath. *Image, Music, Text.* New York: Hill and Wang, 1977.
Bassnett, Susan, and Harish Trivedi, eds. *Post-colonial Translation: Theory and Practice.* London: Routledge, 1999.
Behler, Ernst. *German Romantic Literary Theory.* Cambridge: Cambridge University Press, 1993.
Beissner, Friedrich. *Hölderlins Übersetzungen aus dem Griechischen.* 2nd ed. Stuttgart: Metzler, 1961.
Benjamin, Walter. "Die Aufgabe des Übersetzers." In *Gesammelte Schriften* 4:1, edited by Tilman Rexroth, 9–21. Frankfurt am Main: Suhrkamp, 1991.
———. *Berliner Kindheit um Neunzehnhundert.* In *Gesammelte Schriften* 4:1, edited by Tilman Rexroth, 234–304. Frankfurt am Main: Suhrkamp, 1991.
———. *Deutsche Menschen: Eine Folge von Briefen.* Frankfurt am Main: Suhrkamp, 1972.
———. "The Task of the Translator." Translated by Harry Zohn. In *The Translation Studies Reader,* edited by Lawrence Venuti with Mona

Baker, 15–23. London: Routledge, 2000.

Benn, M. B. *Hölderlin and Pindar*. Anglica Germanica: British Studies in Germanic Languages and Literatures 4. The Hague: Mouton, 1962.

Berman, Antoine. *The Experience of the Foreign: Culture and Translation in Romantic Germany*. Translated by S. Heyvaert. Albany: State University of New York Press, 1992.

Bernays, Michael. "Der Schlegel-Tieck Shakespeare." *Jahrbuch der deutschen Shakespeare-Gesellschaft* 1 (1865): 396–405.

———. "Vorrede und Nachwort zum neuen Abdruck des Schlegel-Tieckschen Shakespeare." *Preussische Jahrbücher* 68, no. 3 (1891): 524–69.

———. *Zur Entstehungsgeschichte des Schlegelschen Shakespeare*. Leipzig: Hirzel, 1872.

Bernofsky, Susan. "Schleiermacher's Translation Theory and Varieties of Foreignization: August Wilhelm Schlegel vs. Johann Heinrich Voss." *The Translator: Studies in Intercultural Communication* 3, no. 2 (1997): 175–92.

Bloom, Harold. *The Anxiety of Influence: A Theory of Poetry*. Oxford: Oxford University Press, 1975.

Böschenstein, Bernard. "Die Nacht des Meers: Zu Hölderlins Untersuchungen des ersten Stasimons der Antigone." In *Studien zur deutschen Literatur: Festschrift für Adolf Beck zum siebzigsten Geburtstag*, edited by Ulrich Fülleborn and Johannes Krogoll. Heidelberg: Winter, 1979.

Breitinger, Johann Jacob. *Critische Dichtkunst*. 2nd ed. 1740. Reprinted with an afterword by Wolfgang Bender. Stuttgart: Metzler, 1966.

Bruford, W. H. *Germany in the Eighteenth Century: The Social Background of the Literary Revival*. 1935. Reprint, Cambridge: Cambridge University Press, 1959.

Burke, Kenneth. *A Rhetoric of Motives*. Berkeley: University of California Press, 1969.

Constantine, David. *Hölderlin*. Oxford: Clarendon, 1988.

———. "Hölderlin's Pindar: The Language of Translation." *Modern Language Review* 73 (1978): 825–34.

———, trans. "Oedipus the King: Friedrich Hölderlin's Rendering of Sophocles." *Comparative Criticism* 20 (1998): 223–36.

Crapanzano, Vincent. *Serving the Word: Literalism in America from the Pulpit to the Bench*. New York: New Press, 2000.

Delabastita, Dirk, and Lieven D'hulst, eds. *European Shakespeares: Translating Shakespeare in the Romantic Age*. Amsterdam: John Benjamins, 1993.

De Man, Paul. "Aesthetic Formalization: Kleist's 'Über das Marionettentheater.'" In *The Rhetoric of Romanticism*, 263–90. New York: Columbia University Press, 1984.

———. "Conclusions: Walter Benjamin's 'The Task of the Translator.'" In *The*

Resistance to Theory, 73–105. Theory and History of Literature 33. Minneapolis: University of Minnesota Press, 1986.

Derrida, Jacques. "Babylonische Türme. Wege, Umwege, Abwege." In *Übersetzung und Dekonstruktion*, edited by Alfred Hirsch, 119–65. Frankfurt: Suhrkamp, 1997.

———. "Sending: On Representation." Translated by Peter and Mary Ann Caws. *Social Research* 49, no. 2 (1982): 294–326.

Diderot, Denis. *Oeuvres complètes*. Edited by J. Assézat. 20 vols. Paris: Garnier, 1875–77.

———. "The Paradox of the Actor." In *Selected Writings on Art and Literature*, translated by Geoffrey Bremner, 100–158. New York: Penguin, 1994.

———. *Rameaus Neffe*. Translated by Johann Wolfgang von Goethe. Edited by Günter von Metken. Stuttgart: Reclam, 1986.

Dieckmann, Herbert. "Goethe und Diderot." *Deutsche Vierteljahresschrift* 10 (1932), 478–503.

———. "Die Wandlung des Nachahmungsbegriffes in der französischen Ästhetik des 18. Jahrhunderts." In *Nachahmung und Illusion, Kolloquium Gießen Juni1963. Vorlagen und Verhandlungen*, edited by Hans Robert Jauß, 28–59.München: Eidos, 1964.

Eigler, Friederike, and Susanne Kord, eds. *The Feminist Encyclopedia of German Literature*. Westport, CT: Greenwood, 1997.

Encyclopédie, ou Dictionnaire raisonné des sciences, des arts et des métiers, par une société de gens de lettres. Paris, 1751–66.

Fagles, Robert. See Sophocles, *The Three Theban Plays*.

Foucault, Michel. "What Is an Author?" Translated by James Venit. *Partisan Review* 42, no. 4 (1975): 603–14.

Fränzel, Walter. *Geschichte des Übersetzens im 18. Jahrhundert*. Beiträge zur Kultur- und Universalgeschichte 25. Leipzig: Voigtländer, 1914.

Fried, Michael. *Absorption and Theatricality: Painting and Beholder in the Age of Diderot*. Chicago: University of Chicago Press, 1988.

Fröschle, Hartmut. *Der Spätaufklärer Johann Heinrich Voß als Kritiker der deutschen Romantik*. Stuttgarter Arbeiten zur Germanistik 146. Stuttgart: Heinz, 1985.

Fuhrmann, Manfred. "Goethes Übersetzungsmaximen." *Goethe-Jahrbuch* 117 (2000): 26–45.

Gebhardt, Peter. *A. W. Schlegels Shakespeare-Übersetzung: Untersuchungen zu seinem Übersetzungsverfahren am Beispiel des Hamlet*. Göttingen: Vandenhoeck & Ruprecht, 1970.

Goethe, Johann Wolfgang von. *Goethes Briefe*. Edited by Karl Robert Mandelkow with Bodo Morawe. München: Beck, 1965–86.

———. *Sämtliche Werke nach Epochen seines Schaffens* (Münchener Ausgabe).

———. Edited by Karl Richter with Herbert G. Göpfert, Norbert Miller, and Gerhard Sauder. 21 vols. Munich: Hanser, 1985–98.

———. "Translations." In Schulte and Biguenet, *Theories of Translation*, 60–63.

———. *Werke* (Hamburger Ausgabe). Edited by Erich Trunz. Hamburg: Wegner, 1948–60.

———. *West-Östlicher Divan*. Vol. 3, bk. 1 of *Sämtliche Werke*, edited by Hendrik Birus. Frankfurt am Main: Deutscher Klassiker Verlag, 1994.

———. *Wilhelm Meisters Lehrjahre*. Frankfurt: Insel, 1998.

Goldsmith, Ulrich K. "Hamlet: From Shakespeare to Schlegel, to Gundolf, to Fried." In *Polyanthea: Essays on Art and Literature in Honor of William Sebastian Hechscher*, edited by Karl-Ludwig Selig. The Hague: Van der Heÿden, 1993.

Gottsched, Johann Christian. "Nachricht von neuen hieher gehörigen Sachen." *Beyträge zur kritischen Historie der Deutschen Sprache, Poesie und Beredsamkeit* 7, no. 27 (1741): 512–19.

Greiner, Norbert. "The Comic Matrix of Early German Shakespeare Translation." In Delabastita and D'hulst, *European Shakespeares*, 203–17.

Gundolf, Friedrich. *Shakespeare und der deutsche Geist*. Berlin: Bondi, 1922.

Habicht, Werner. "The Romanticism of the Schlegel-Tieck Shakespeare and the History of Nineteenth-Century German Shakespeare Translation." In Delabastita and D'hulst, *European Shakespeares*, 45–53.

Hahn, Barbara. *Unter falschem Namen: Von der schwierigen Autorschaft der Frauen*. Frankfurt: Suhrkamp, 1991.

Hart Nibbrig, Christiaan L., ed. *Übersetzen: Walter Benjamin*. Frankfurt: Suhrkamp, 2001.

Hay, Gerhard. "August Wilhelm Schlegels Beitrag zur *Jenaischen Allgemeinen Litteratur-Zeitung*. Mit einem unveröffentlichten Brief Schlegels." In *Teilnahme und Spiegelung. Festschrift für Horst Rüdiger*, edited by Beda Allemann and Erwin Koppen, 316–26. Berlin: de Gruyter, 1975.

Haym, Rudolf. *Die romantische Schule. Ein Beitrag zur Geschichte des deutschen Geistes*. Berlin: Gaertner, 1870.

Hederichs, M. Benjamin. *Gründliches Lexicon mythologicum*. 2nd ed. Leipzig: Johann Friedrich Gleditsch, 1741.

Heine, Heinrich. *Historisch-kritische Gesamtausgabe der Werke*. Edited by Manfred Windfuhr. Hamburg: Hoffmann und Campe, 1973–97.

Hellingrath, Norbert von. *Hölderlin-Vermächtnis*. Munich: Bruckmann, 1936.

Herbst, Wilhelm. *Johann Heinrich Voß*. 3 vols. Bern: Herbert Lang, 1970. Original edition: Leipzig: Teubner, 1872–76.

Herder, Johann Gottfried. *Sämtliche Werke*. Edited by Bernhard Suphan. Hildesheim: Olms, 1967–68. Reprint of earlier edition: Berlin: Weidmann, 1877–1913.

Hirsch, Alfred, ed. *Übersetzung und Dekonstruktion*. Frankfurt: Suhrkamp, 1997.

Hölderlin, Friedrich. *Sämtliche Werke* (Frankfurter Ausgabe). Edited by D. E. Sattler with Michael Franz and Michael Knaupp. Vols. 15 and 16. Basel: Stroemfeld/Roter Stern, 1987.

——. *Sämtliche Werke und Briefe*. Edited by Michael Knaupp. 3 vols. Munich: Hanser, 1992–93.

Humboldt, Wilhelm von. "Einleitung." *Aeschylos Agamemnon. Metrisch übersetzt*. In *Gesammelte Werke*. Vol. 3, 1–33. Berlin: Reimer, 1843.

——. "From the Introduction to His Translation of *Agamemnon*." In Schulte and Biguenet, *Theories of Translation*, 55–59.

Huyssen, Andreas. *Die frühromantische Konzeption von Übersetzung und Aneignung: Studien zur frühromantischen Utopie einer deutschen Weltliteratur*. Zurich: Atlantis, 1969.

Jauß, Hans Robert. "Poetik und Problematik von Identität und Rolle in der Geschichte des Amphitryon." In Marquard and Stierle, *Identität*, 213–53.

Kirkwood, G. M. *A Study of Sophoclean Drama*. Ithaca, NY: Cornell University Press, 1994.

Kleist, Heinrich von. *Sämtliche Werke und Briefe*. Edited by Helmut Sembdner. 9th ed. 2 vols. Munich: Hanser, 1993.

——. *Amphitryon*. Vol. 1, bk. 4 of *Sämtliche Werke* (Berliner Ausgabe), edited by Roland Reuß and Peter Staengle. Frankfurt am Main: Stroemfeld/Roter Stern, 1991.

Knox, Bernard. See Sophocles, *The Three Theban Plays*.

Kontje, Todd. "Goethe's Multicultural Masquerades." Paper presented at the convention of the Modern Language Association, Washington D.C., Dec. 30, 2000.

Lacoue-Labarthe, Philippe. "Diderot: Paradox and Mimesis." Translated by Jane Popp. In *Typologies*, edited by Christopher Fynsk. Stanford: Stanford University Press, 1998.

Landesman, Peter. "A 20th-Century Master Scam." *New York Times Magazine*, July 18, 1999, 31.

Larson, Kenneth E. "Pro und contra Schlegel: Die zwei gegensätzlichen Blankversübersetzungen des King Lear von Heinrich Voss (1806 und 1819)." *Deutsche Shakespeare-Gesellschaft West Jahrbuch* 1989: 113–33.

Lazenby, Marion Candler. "The Influence of Wieland and Eschenburg on Schlegel's Shakespeare Translation." PhD diss., Johns Hopkins University, 1924.

Lessing, Gotthold Ephraim. "Briefe, die neueste Literatur betreffend," Part 2 (1759). *Gesammelte Werke*, Vol. 2, 19–23. Munich: Hanser, 1959.

Lönker, Fred. "'Unendliche Deutung.'" *Hölderlin-Jahrbuch* 26 (1988–89):

BIBLIOGRAPHY

287–303.
Louth, Charlie. *Hölderlin and the Dynamics of Translation*. Studies in Comparative Literature 2. Oxford: Legenda, 1998.
Mann, Thomas. "Amphitryon: Eine Wiedereroberung." In *Heinrich von Kleist: Aufsätze und Essays*, edited by Walter Müller-Seidel, Wege der Forschung 147, 51–88. Darmstadt: Wissenschaftliche Buchgesellschaft, 1967.
Marquard, Odo, and Karlheinz Stierle. *Identität*. Munich: Fink, 1979.
Melberg, Arne. *Theories of Mimesis*. Cambridge: Cambridge University Press, 1995.
Michel, Wilhelm. *Hölderlins abendländische Wendung*. Jena: Diederichs, 1923.
Middleton, Christopher. "Translation as a Species of Mime." *Review of Contemporary Fiction: Robert Walser Number* 12, no. 1 (1992): 50–56.
Mitchell, W. J. T. "Representation." In *Critical Terms for Literary Study*, 2nd ed., edited by Frank Lentricchia and Thomas McLaughlin. Chicago: University of Chicago Press, 1995.
Molière, Jean Baptiste Poquelin. *Oeuvres complètes* 2 (Pléiade). Edited by Georges Couton. Paris: Gallimard, 1971.
Montaigne, Michel de. *Oeuvres Complètes*. Edited by A. Armaingaud. Paris: Conard, 1926. Text based on the Bordeaux manuscript.
Mortier, Roland. *Diderot en Allemagne*. Paris: Presses Universitaires de France, 1954.
Nachahmung und Illusion. Kolloquium Gießen Juni 1963. Vorlagen und Verhandlungen. Poetik und Hermeneutik 1. Edited by Hans Robert Jauß. München: Eidos, 1964.
Nägele, Rainer. *Echoes of Translation: Reading between Texts*. Baltimore: Johns Hopkins University Press, 1997.
Neubauer, John. "Absolute and Affective Music: Rameau, Diderot, and Goethe." In *Johann Wolfgang von Goethe: One Hundred and Fifty Years of Continuing Vitality*, edited by Ulrich Goebel and Wolodymyr T. Zyla, 115–31. Lubbock: Texas Tech University Press, 1984.
Nickau, Klaus. "Die Frage nach dem Original." *Hölderlin-Jahrbuch* 26 (1988–89), 269–86.
Niranjana, Tejaswini. *Siting Translation: History, Post-Structuralism, and the Colonial Context*. Berkeley: University of California Press, 1992.
Nisetich, Frank. See *Pindar's Victory Songs*.
Novalis [Friedrich von Hardenberg]. *Schriften*. 2nd ed. Edited by Paul Kluckhohn and Richard Samuel. Stuttgart: Kohlhammer, 1975.
Opitz, Martin. *Buch von der Deutschen Poeterey*. 1624. In *Gesammelte Werke*, edited by George Schulz-Behrend. Stuttgart: Hiersemann, 1978.
Osterkamp, Ernst. *Im Buchstabenbilde. Studien zum Verfahren Goethescher Bildbeschreibungen*. Stuttgart: Metzler, 1991.

Passage, Charles E., and J. H. Mantinband, eds. *Amphitryon: Three Plays in New Verse Translations*. Chapel Hill: University of North Carolina Press, 1974.

Paulin, Roger. "Luise Gottsched und Dorothea Tieck: vom Schicksal zweier Übersetzerinnen." *Shakespeare-Jahrbuch* 134 (1998): 108–22.

Petersen, Julius. "Einleitung des Herausgebers." *Lessings Werke*. Vol. 11, *Das Theater des Herrn Diderot*, edited by Julius Peterson, 7–30. Berlin: Bong, 1925.

Pindar's Victory Songs. Translated and edited by Frank J. Nisetich. Baltimore: Johns Hopkins University Press, 1980.

Pizer, John. "Goethe's 'World Literature' Paradigm and Contemporary Cultural Globalization." *Comparative Literature* 52, no. 3 (2000): 213–27.

Plato. *The Symposium*. Translated by Walter Hamilton. Harmondsworth: Penguin, 1951.

Platon. *Das Gastmahl*. Vol. 2, bk. 2, *Platons Werke*, translated by Friedrich Schleiermacher. 3rd ed. Berlin: Georg Reimer, 1857.

Prendergast, Christopher. *The Order of Mimesis*. Cambridge: Cambridge University Press, 1986.

Robinson, Douglas. *The Translator's Turn*. Baltimore: Johns Hopkins University Press, 1991.

Rose, H. J. *A Handbook of Greek Mythology*. New York: Dutton, 1959.

Said, Edward W. *Orientalism*. New York: Pantheon, 1978.

Santner, Eric L. *Friedrich Hölderlin: Narrative Vigilance and the Poetic Imagination*. New Brunswick, NJ: Rutgers University Press, 1986.

Schlegel, August Wilhelm. *Kritische Schriften und Briefe*. Edited by Edgar Lohner. Stuttgart: Kohlhammer, 1962–74.

———. *Sämmtliche Werke*. Edited by Eduard Böcking. Leipzig: Weidmann'sche Buchhandlung. 12 vols. 1846–47.

Schlegel, Friedrich. "Kritische Fragmente" (1797). In *Schriften zur Literatur*, edited by Wolfdietrich Rasch, 7–24. Munich: Deutscher Taschenbuch Verlag, 1972.

Schleiermacher, Friedrich. "Ueber die verschiedenen Methoden des Uebersetzens" (1813). In *Störig, Das Problem des Übersetzens*, 38–70.

Schroeter, Adalbert. *Geschichte der deutschen Homer-Übersetzung im 18. Jahrhundert*. Jena: Costenoble, 1882. Reprint, Hildesheim: Gerstenberg, 1978.

Schulte, Rainer, and John Biguenet, eds. *Theories of Translation: An Anthology of Essays from Dryden to Derrida*. Chicago: University of Chicago Press, 1992.

Segal, Charles. *Sophocles' Tragic World: Divinity, Nature, Society*. Cambridge, MA: Harvard University Press, 1995.

Seifert, Albrecht. *Untersuchungen zu Hölderlins Pindar-Rezeption*. Münchner germanistische Beiträge 32. Munich: Fink, 1982.

Sembdner, Helmut, ed. *Heinrich von Kleist's Lebensspuren. Dokumente und Berichte der Zeitgenossen.* 2nd ed. Frankfurt am Main: Insel, 1992.

———. *Johann Daniel Falks Bearbeitung des Amphitryon-Stoffes. Ein Beitrag zur Kleistforschung.* Berlin: Erich Schmidt, 1971.

———. "Kleist und Falk." In *In Sachen Kleist. Beiträge zur Forschung.* 2nd ed. Munich: Hanser, 1984.

Senger, Anneliese. *Deutsche Übersetzungstheorie im 18. Jahrhundert (1734–1746).* Bonn: Bouvier, 1971.

Seyhan, Azade. *Representation and Its Discontents.* Berkeley: University of California Press, 1992.

Shakespeare, William. *The Complete Works.* Edited by Stanley Wells and Gary Taylor. Oxford: Oxford University Press, 1988.

———. *Hamlet, Prinz von Dänemark.* Translated by August Wilhelm Schlegel. Stuttgart: Reclam, 1990. First published 1798.

———. *Der Sturm.* Translated by A. W. Schlegel. Stuttgart: Reclam, 1993. First published 1798.

———. *The Tempest.* Vol. 3, *The Works of William Shakespeare in Sixteen Volumes,* edited by Edmond Malone. London: 1816.

Sophocles. *The Three Theban Plays.* Translated by Robert Fagles, with commentary by Bernard Knox. New York: Penguin, 1982.

Spitzer, Leo. "The Style of Diderot." In *Linguistics and Literary History,* 135–91. New York: Russell and Russell, 1962.

Spivak, Gayatri Chakravorty. "The Politics of Translation." In *The Translation Studies Reader,* edited by Lawrence Venuti with Mona Baker, 397–416. London: Routledge, 2000.

Stierle, Karlheinz. "Amphitryon—Ein dialektisches Märchen der Identität." In Marquard and Stierle, *Identität,* 734–39.

Störig, Hans Joachim. *Das Problem des Übersetzens.* Darmstadt: Wissenschaftliche Buchgesellschaft, 1963.

Suerbaum, Ulrich. "Der deutsche Shakespeare: Übersetzungsgeschichte—Übersetzungstheorie." In *Festschrift Rudolf Stamm,* edited by E. Hasler and J. Kolb. Berne: Francke, 1969.

Szondi, Peter. *Hölderlin-Studien. Mit einem Traktat über philologische Erkenntnis.* Frankfurt am Main: Suhrkamp, 1977.

———. "Vorwort." In *Amphitryon,* edited by Joachim Schondorff. Munich: Langen-Müller, 1964.

Venuti, Lawrence. *Scandals of Translation: Towards an Ethics of Difference.* London: Routledge, 1998.

———. *The Translator's Invisibility: A History of Translation,* London: Routledge, 1995.

Venuti, Lawrence, ed. *The Translation Studies Reader.* With Mona Baker. London: Routledge, 2000.

Voß, Heinrich. "Vorrede." In Vol. 1, *Shakespeare's Schauspiele Von Johann Heinrich Voss Und Dessen Söhnen Heinrich Voss Und Abraham Voss. Mit Erläuterungen,* ix–lxxii. Leipzig: F. A. Brockhaus, 1818.

———. *Homer's Werke.* 2 vols. Stuttgart: Cotta, 1844.

Walser, Robert. *Das Gesamtwerk.* Edited by Jochen Greven. Zurich: Suhrkamp, 1978.

Warminski, Andrzej. *Readings in Interpretation: Hölderlin, Hegel, Heidegger.* Minneapolis: University of Minnesota Press, 1987.

Webster's New International Dictionary of the English Language. 2nd ed. Springfield, MA: Merriam, 1953.

Wittmann, Reinhard. *Geschichte des deutschen Buchhandels.* 2nd ed. München: Beck, 1999.

Zuntz, Günther. *Über Hölderlins Pindar-Übersetzungen.* PhD diss., Marburg University, 1928.

Index

Abeken, B. R., 104
Actor/acting, 168–69, 170, 171–73, 174, 175–79, 189
Adaptation, 47, 48, 51, 52, 86, 87, 94, 142
Adorno, Theodor, 125
Aesthetics, 45, 117, 217n. 39; education in, 2, 27, 149; in Goethe vs. Diderot, 157, 159, 162, 173, 184, 185, 187, 188, 191; in Kleist, 50–51, 75; and Venuti, 38. *See also* Art
Allemann, Beda, 113
Ambiguity, 31, 47, 151
Amphitryon, myth of, 49–50, 81
Appiah, Kwame Anthony, 194; "Thick Translation," 39
Aristophanes, 19
Aristophanes of Byzantium, 124–25
Art, 37, 139, 141, 160, 161, 162, 163–64, 165–67, 171, 174–75, 179, 180, 181, 182, 183–84, 185–86, 188. *See also* Aesthetics; Representation
Audience. *See* Reader/audience
August Boeckh, *Pindari Epiniciorum Interpretation Latina com Commentario Perpetuo*, 125

Authenticity, 73, 74
Author, x, 2, 3, 6, 24, 25, 28, 43, 109. *See also* Translation, authorial

Barthes, Roland, 43
Bassnett, Susan, 40
Baudelaire, Charles, *Tableaux parisiens*, 31, 35
Baudissin, Wolf Graf von, 18, 20
Beauty, 160–61, 162, 163, 171, 173, 174, 180, 183–84, 186, 187
Beckett, Samuel, *En attendant Godot*, 50
Beissner, Friedrich, 94, 112
Benjamin, Walter, xi, 25, 31–35, 36, 37, 40, 123, 135, 137, 148, 204n. 67, 204–205n. 73; "Die Aufgabe des Übersetzers," 25, 30, 91
Berman, Antoine, 2, 37, 87; *The Experience of the Foreign*, 21
Bernays, Michael, 20
Bible, 8, 91, 144, 145
Bloom, Harold, 89–90
Boccaccio, Giovanni, 20
Bodmer, Johann Jacob, 1, 6, 11
Böhlendorff, Casimir Ulrich, 113

INDEX

Borheck, August Christian, 81
Brecht, Bertolt, 137, 168
Breitinger, Johann Jacob, 14; *Critische Dichtkunst*, 5–6
Büchner, Georg, 18
Bürger, Gottfried August, 12

Cellini, Benvenuto, 141, 142
Cervantes, Miguel de, *Don Quixote*, 18
Chézy, Helmine von, 20
Colonialism, 38, 39–40. *See also* Culture; Foreign; Politics; Post-colonialism
Comedy, 49, 50, 52, 58, 59, 60, 68, 69, 89
Consciousness, 63, 74, 76
Constantine, David, 95, 124
Cramer, C. F., 159–60
Crapanzano, Vincent, 42
Culture: in Appiah, 39; and authorial translator, 41; in Benjamin, 33, 34; in Berman, 37; and contemporary theory, 43; differences in, 9; and foreignizing translation, 2, 3; in Goethe, 142, 149; in Hamann, 9; Hellenic, 93, 94; in Herder, 14; Hesperian, 93, 113–15, 137; in Hölderlin, 93, 94, 113–14, 115, 121, 127, 135, 137; in Humboldt, 30; and Kleist, 86; and language, 10, 14, 30; openness to foreign, 27; in Schlegel, 14; in Schleiermacher, 26, 28, 37; and service translation, 42; of translator, 144; in Venuti, 38. *See also* Colonialism; Foreign; Post-colonialism

Deconstruction, 40
De Man, Paul, 32, 34, 35, 40, 204n. 67
Derrida, Jacques, 40; "Des tours de Babel," 36–37; "Sending: On Representation," 193
De Staël, Madame, 20

Diderot, Denis: acting in, 168–69, 170, 171–72, 173, 174, 175–79, 189; art in, 139, 141, 160, 161, 162, 163–64, 165–67, 171, 174–75, 179, 180, 181, 182, 183–84, 186; beauty in, 160–61, 162, 163, 171, 173, 174, 180, 183–84, 186; ideal in, 170–71, 172, 173, 187; imitation in, 154, 158, 162, 163, 165, 166, 169, 177–78; Lessing's translations of, 7; materialism of, 153; mimesis in, 139, 141, 169, 172, 179, 184; misunderstanding of, 187–88; model in, 155, 158, 159, 160, 161, 162, 165, 167, 168, 170, 172, 175, 176, 184, 187; morality in, 150, 151, 153, 155–57, 159, 175, 179–80, 188, 189; nature in, 168, 171, 173, 174–75, 176, 178, 190; painting in, 140, 141, 142, 159, 161, 165, 166–67, 168, 183, 184, 190; phantom in, 168, 169, 171, 172, 175, 187; representation in, xi, 172, 173, 179, 187, 189; and Schiller, 140; truth in, 171–72, 180, 187, 189
———WORKS: *Encyclopédie*, 174; "Essais sur la peinture," xi, 140, 159–67, 173, 180, 181, 184; "Lettre sur les sourds et muets," 167; *Le neveu de Rameau*, xi, 140, 175–80; "Le paradoxe sur le comedien," 141, 168–75, 189; *Salon*, 166, 167, 184
Dieckmann, Herbert, 162, 187–89, 190
Distraction, productive, 147–48
Drewe, John, 170
Du Bos, Abbé, *Reflexions critiques sur la poesie et sur la peinture*, 168

Eckermann, Johann Peter, 172
Education, 2, 27, 29, 149, 160, 161–62

INDEX

Eichendorff, Joseph Freiherr von, 18
Eschenburg, Johann Joachim, 13, 24, 144
Euripides, 19
Experience, 49, 73, 89

Falk, Johann Daniel, 49; *Amphitruon*, 80–86, 206–207n. 15
Fichte, Johann Gottlieb, 73
Fidelity, 2, 4, 5–6, 11, 13, 17, 20, 23, 30, 44, 91, 131, 149
Fielding, Henry, 18
Foreign: and Benjamin, 31–32; and culture, 2, 3; in Goethe, 29, 145–46, 185; in Hölderlin, 94, 109, 131–32; in Humboldt, 29–30; in Pannwitz, 32; in Schleiermacher, 26, 27, 28, 29, 105; and service translation, 41; in Spivak, 38–39; in translation, 2–3; and Venuti, 38, 40–41, 42. *See also* Colonialism; Culture; Other; Post-colonialism
Forger, 170, 171
Form, 9, 11, 14, 18, 20, 104, 145. *See also* Syntax
Foucault, Michel, 42
Fouqué, Friedrich Baron de la Motte, 18, 80
Fried, Michael, *Absorption and Theatricality*, 166
Fuhrmann, Manfred, 141, 142
Füßli, Johann Heinrich, 184

Gedike, Friedrich, 208n. 5
Genius, 181–82, 184, 186, 187, 188
Gerstenberg, Heinrich Willhelm von, 8–9
Goethe, Johann Wolfgang von, x, xi, 43; acting in, 172–73, 174, 176; adaptation by, 142; art in, 139, 141, 160, 161, 162, 163–64, 165–67, 182, 183, 184, 185–86, 188; beauty in, 160–61, 162, 163, 173, 186, 187; and Benjamin, 36, 37; developmental epochs in, 28–29, 36, 143–46, 149, 185–86, 188, 217; and fidelity, 23; imitation in, 139, 141, 146, 159, 173, 185, 189; and Kleist, 51; mimesis in, 139, 141, 146, 172, 184, 189; model in, 155, 158, 159, 160, 161, 162, 175, 176, 184, 185–86, 190; morality in, 150, 151, 153, 155–57, 159, 175, 179–80, 188, 189; nature in, 139, 141, 159, 160, 161, 162, 163–64, 165–67, 172, 173, 186–87, 189, 190; original in, 28–29, 36, 141, 145, 149; other in, 143, 146, 148–49; painting in, 183, 184, 185–86, 190; pleasing in, 173, 174, 188; reader/audience in, xi, 29, 144–45, 173, 176, 181, 182, 185; representation in, xi, 145–46, 159, 175, 184, 185, 193; in Robinson, 37, 38; and Schleiermacher, 28–29; and service translation, x, 23–24, 159; theory of, xi, 25, 37–38, 142, 145, 146–48, 185, 187, 189–90; and Voß, 11, 23–24, 144; and Wieland, 28, 182, 183
———WORKS: Cellini translation, 141, 142; *Dichtung und Wahrheit*, 142, 144, 145; Diderot translations, 139, 142; Diderot's "Essais sur la peinture" translation, xi, 140, 141, 159–67; Diderot's *Le neveu de Rameau* translation, xi, 140, 141, 142, 149–59, 175–80; "Einfache Nachahmung der Natur, Manier, Stil," 182, 184–85, 189; "Geständnis des Übersetzers," 146–48; *Hermann und Dorothea*, 11; *Maximen und Reflexionen*, 185; "Notes on Translation," 142, 143–44; "Rules for Actors," 172; Shakespeare translation, 23–24;

233

INDEX

Goethe, WORKS (*continued*)
  "Über Wahrheit und Wahrscheinlichkeit der Kunstwerke," 183; Voltaire translation, 141, 142; *West-östlicher Divan*, 25, 28–29, 142–44, 145; *Wilhelm Meister*, xi, 22, 23–24
Gottsched, Johann Christian, 1, 5, 6, 8, 20
Gottsched, Luise, 1, 20
Grace, 74, 75, 76, 173, 174
Greuze, Jean-Baptiste, *Une jeune fille qui pleure son oiseau mort*, 166
Grimm, Friedrich Melchior, *Correspondance littéraire*, 168, 217n. 35
Grotesque, 155–56, 173, 175, 184, 190

Hafiz, 142, 143
Haller, Albrecht von, 153
Hamann, Johann Georg, 8, 9
Hammer, Josef von, 142, 144
Hederich, M. Benjamin, *Gründliches Lexicon mythologicum*, 77
Hegel, G.W.F., 63, 114
Hellingrath, Norbert von, 125
Herder, Johann Gottfried, 8, 9–10, 30, 43, 142; *Alte Volkslieder*, 10
Herz, Henriette, 20
Hesiod, 49
Hexameter verse, 9, 10–12, 96, 97, 200n. 24. *See also* Poetry/verse
Hölderlin, Friedrich: adaptation by, 94; allegory in, 114, 115, 117, 121; character in, 95, 111; community in, 110; on composition, 93; crisis of signification in, 121–22; demonstrable presentation in, 111–12, 113, 115, 117, 118, 126; fate in, 97, 98, 100, 101, 110, 111, 116, 127, 129, 132, 133; foreignizing translation of, 91; hubris in, 100, 101, 109, 128; interpretation in, 94, 97–98, 99, 100, 102, 103, 104, 109, 122, 130; irony in, 101; language hybridization of, xi; literalism in, 93, 94–95, 112, 120–21, 124; mediation in, 101–4, 109, 113, 129, 135; *miasma* in, 98–99, 110; mode of representation in, 112, 113, 115, 116, 117, 135, 137; *nefas* in, 94, 100, 101, 103, 104, 108, 109, 128; oracle in, 97, 98, 99, 100, 101, 103, 104, 108, 109, 132; particular in, 112; particular vs. general in, 110–11, 113; particular vs. infinite in, 98, 99, 100, 103; as poet, 133–34, 135; presumption in, 94, 99, 100, 104, 109; prophecy in, 100, 101, 106, 108; reception of, 137; themes in, 94, 106–9; theory of, 97; on *Totalempfindung*, 92, 93; translation in, x–xi, 92, 93, 96, 101, 114–15, 117, 118, 120, 135; *Urwort* in, 100, 101; *vaterländische Umkehr* in, 113, 115, 116, 117
———WORKS: "Allgemeiner Grund," 92; "Anmerkungen zum Oedipus," 94, 97, 98, 99; "Anmerkungen zur Antigonä", 94, 113, 118; "Brod und Wein," 102, 104, 135; *Empedokles*, 93, 97, 114; Greek translations, 91, 92, 93–94; "Der Grund zu Empedokles," 92; Homer translations, 93, 96, 108, 129; hymns, 129; *Hyperion*, 135–36; "Lehre vom Wechsel der Töne," 124; Lucan's *Pharsalia* translation, 96–97, 129; Pindar translations, 91, 92, 93, 94, 97, 100, 123–29, 133, 137, 208n. 5, 208–209n. 8; "Der Rhein," 101; Sophocles translations, xi, 90, 94, 97, 136, 137, 191; Sophocles' *Antigone* chorus translation, 91, 92, 93, 129–35; Sophocles' *Antigone*

INDEX

translation, 92, 93, 97, 110–24, 129, 137; Sophocles' *Oedipus Rex* translation, 92, 93, 97, 104–9, 118, 121, 129; *Die Trauerspiele des Sophokles,* 92, 97; "Über die verschiedenen Arten, zu dichten," 95–96

Homer, 4–5, 10–12, 93, 95, 96, 108, 129

Huber, Christiane Friederike, 20

Huillet, Danièle, 137

Humboldt, Wilhelm von, 25, 29–30, 43

Huyssen, Andreas, 22

Ideal, 170–71, 172, 173, 187, 189, 190, 219n. 58

Identity, 48–49, 56, 59, 60–69, 70–76, 77, 79, 88, 89, 100

Iduna, 95, 96

Imitation: in Diderot, 154, 158, 162, 163, 165, 166, 169, 177–78; by forger, 170; in Goethe, 139, 141, 146, 159, 173, 185, 189; in Hölderlin, 105, 106; in Humboldt, 30; *imitatio* vs. *ritratto* in, 169, 189, 217–218n. 39; in Kleist, 47, 76, 87; by Myatt, 170; in Schleiermacher, 26. *See also* Representation

Intertext, 76–86

Intertextuality, 91

Invisibility, 3, 28, 38, 43

Irony, 88, 154–55

Jauß, Hans Robert, 63, 74, 89, 186, 208n. 23

Jonson, Ben, 18

Kleist, Heinrich von, x–xi; adaptation by, 47, 48, 51, 52, 86, 87; alterations by, 51, 53, 54, 55, 56, 58, 59, 60, 63, 66–67; character in, 50, 52, 54, 55–56, 57, 58, 59, 63, 64–65, 69–70, 71, 78; and Falk, 81–84, 85, 206–207n. 15; and France, 84, 86; identity in, 48–49, 56, 59, 60–69, 70–76, 77, 79, 88, 89; irony in, 88; and Napoleon, 84, 86, 87; original in, x–xi, 49, 75, 87; and Rotrou, 50; themes in, 48, 51, 56, 58, 59
———WORKS: *Amphitryon: Ein Lustspiel nach Molière,* x–xi, 47, 48–49, 50–86, 87–88, 191; *Die Familie Schroffenstein (Die Familie Ghonorez),* 86; *Die Hermannsschlacht,* 52, 70, 84, 85–86, 87; *Das Käthchen von Heilbronn,* 52; "Katechismus der Deutschen," 74–75, 86, 87; *Die Marquise von O . . . ,* 70, 86–87; *Penthesilea,* 77, 78; "Über das Marionettentheater," 74; *Der zerbrochene Krug,* 80, 87

Klopstock, Friedrich Gottlieb, 1, 12; *Messiade,* 11

Knox, Bernard, 99

Kontje, Todd, 143

Krüdener, Juliane Freiin von, 20

Lacoue-Labarthe, Philippe, 169

La Fayette, Mme. de, 20

Language: ambiguity in, 31; in Appiah, 39; in Benjamin, 30, 31–37; convergence in, 31, 32, 33, 35; and culture, 10, 14, 30; defamiliarization of, 26; development of, 30, 31–32, 35, 37; differences in, 9, 32; in Falk, 80; and futurity, 32; in Goethe, 183, 185; in Hamann, 9; in Herder, 9, 14; and history, 31, 32, 37; in Hölderlin, xi, 92, 94, 105–7, 108–9, 124, 125, 137; in Humboldt, 30; *Irrationalität* of, 32; literatures transplanted into single, 26–27, 28; as living breath of speech, 13, 16; meaning vs. expression in, 31; and nation, 9, 30; of nature, 9; pure, 31, 32, 33, 35, 37, 38;

Language (*continued*)
  sameness of, 9; Schlegel on, 13–14; in Schleiermacher, 26–27, 28; sensual properties of, 13–14; synthesis of, 94; translation as native to target, 26; as transparent, 12. *See also* Syntax
Leibniz, Gottfried Wilhelm, 32–33
Lenclos, Ninon de, 20
Lessing, Gotthold Ephraim, 1, 6–7, 172
Lönker, Fred, 99
Louth, Charlie, *Hölderlin and the Dynamics of Translation*, 91
Lowe-Porter, Helen, 42
Luther, Martin, 28, 144, 145

Mann, Thomas, 52, 89
Mauvillon, Éléazar de, 5
Meaning, 13, 31, 42, 43
Melberg, Arne, 213–14n. 2
Mereau-Brentano, Sophie, 20
Meter, 16, 17, 52, 105, 124. *See also* Poetry/verse
Meyer, Heinrich, 160
Michel, Wilhelm, 113
Middleton, Christopher, "Translation as a Species of Mime," 35–36
Mime, 35–36, 177–78
Mimesis, 139, 141, 146, 169, 172, 179, 184, 189; defined, 213–14n. 2. *See also* Imitation
Misprision, 89, 98
Model, 155, 158, 159, 160, 161, 162, 165, 167, 168, 170, 171, 172, 175, 176, 184, 185–86, 187, 190. *See also* Original; Phantom
Molière, 150; *Amphitryon*, x, 47–48, 49, 50, 51–69, 70, 71, 76, 77–78, 81, 82–83, 84, 87, 88, 89–90
Montaigne, Michel de, "On Presumption," 154
Mortier, Roland, 168
Music, 158–59, 177–79

Myatt, John, 169–70

Nägele, Rainer, *Echoes of Translation*, 91
Napoleon, 75, 84, 86, 87, 140, 176
Nation, 9, 30, 43, 75, 113, 114, 115, 116, 117, 169. *See also* Politics
Nature, 9, 37, 139, 141, 159, 160, 161, 162, 163–64, 165–67, 168, 171, 172, 173, 174–75, 176, 178, 186–87, 188, 189, 190
Niranjana, Tejaswini, 204n. 67; *Siting Translation*, 39–40
Novalis, 4, 43, 93; *Heinrich von Ofterdingen*, 151

Objectivity, 42, 93, 185, 188
Oedipus, saga of, 77, 78, 79, 87, 100
Olearius, Adam, 142
Orientalism, 143
Original: alteration of, 26; author of, 2, 6, 25, 28; in Benjamin, 36; Breitinger on, 6; and copy, x–xi, 49, 72, 76, 88–89, 90; in Diderot, 168, 171; dislocation of, 146, 189; emulation of, 3; fidelity to, 2, 4, 5–6, 11, 13, 17, 20, 23, 30, 44, 91, 131, 149; Gerstenberg on, 8–9; in Goethe, 28–29, 36, 141, 145, 149; in Hölderlin, 93, 94, 104, 109, 118; in Humboldt, 30; identity with, 28–29, 144, 146; intent of, 2; in Kleist, x–xi, 49, 75, 87; language of, 28; and mimesis, 141; Schlegel's fidelity to, 12; in Schleiermacher, 26, 28; and translation, 14, 21, 22, 24, 69–76, 146, 192, 194; transparent communication of, 12. *See also* Model
Other, 2, 42, 114, 143, 146, 148–49. *See also* Foreign

Painting, 169, 170, 171; in Diderot, 140, 141, 142, 159, 161, 165,

INDEX

166–67, 168, 183, 184, 190; in Goethe, 183, 184, 185–86, 190
Pannwitz, Rudolf, *Die Krise der europäischen Kultur*, 32
Paraphrase, 1, 26, 144
Parataxis, 125, 130
Parody, 144, 145, 179
Perception, 73
Periphrasis, 5–6
Phantom, 168, 169, 171, 172, 175, 187, 189
Pindar, 91, 92, 93, 94, 97, 100, 123–29, 133, 137, 208n. 5, 208–209n. 8
Pizer, John, 214n. 12
Plautus, 49, 50, 77, 80, 81
Poetry/verse, 5, 9, 10–12, 13, 16, 17, 41, 52, 80, 92, 96, 97, 105, 113–15, 124, 200n. 24
Politics, 3, 25, 38, 41, 50–51, 80, 117. *See also* Nation
Post-colonialism, 28, 38. *See also* Colonialism; Culture; Foreign; Politics
Prendergast, Christopher, 172
Prose, 10, 13
Publication, 7–8

Reader/audience: accustomed to foreign texts, 27; in Diderot, 175, 176; Gerstenberg on, 8; in Goethe, xi, 29, 144–45, 173, 176, 181, 182, 185; of Hölderlin, 94; in Humboldt, 30; in Schleiermacher, 25, 27; and text as information, 10; of Voß, 14
Renegade, 156, 157, 158, 159, 173, 175, 179, 188
Representation, xi, 13, 116, 117, 135, 145–46, 159, 172, 173, 175, 179, 184, 185, 187, 189, 193, 213–14n. 2. *See also* Art; Imitation
Robinson, Douglas, *The Translator's Turn*, 25, 37, 38

Romanticism, ix–x, 4, 12, 21–22, 30, 32, 41–42, 43, 87, 151
Rotrou, Jean de, *Les Sosies*, 48, 50, 84
Rupp, Victoria von, 20
Rushdie, Salman, *The Satanic Verses*, 44

Saadi, 142, 143
Said, Edward, 143
Santner, Eric, 114
Schiller, Johann Christoph Friedrich, 11, 15, 17, 114, 140, 184
Schings, Hans-Jürgen, 24
Schlegel, August Wilhelm, 3, 20, 27; *Ion*, 17; Shakespeare translations of, ix, 4, 12–18, 21–23, 24
Schlegel, Caroline, 18, 20
Schlegel, Friedrich, 4, 21–22, 41–42; *Lucinde*, 151
Schleiermacher, Friedrich, ix, 2, 4, 8, 9, 10, 18, 20, 25–28, 29, 32, 36, 37, 38, 39, 43, 105, 149; "Über die verschiedene Methoden des Übersetzens," 25
Seeger, Ludwig, 19
Segal, Charles, 129
Sembdner, Helmut, 81
Seyhan, Azade, 172
Shakespeare, William, ix, 4, 10, 12–18, 13, 21–24
Sign, 9
Signification, 121–22, 123
Sophocles, xi, 90, 91, 92, 93, 94, 97, 104–9, 110–24, 129–35, 136, 137, 191
Spitzer, Leo, 179–80
Spivak, Gayatri Chakravorty, 40; "The Politics of Translation," 38–39
Stolberg, Leopold Graf, 11
Straub, Jean-Marie, 137
Subjectivity, 92, 93, 185, 188, 189
Subversion, x–xi, 41, 48, 69
Syntax, 10; in Benjamin, 32, 33, 34, 35, 36; in foreignizing translation, 3; in Goethe, 149; in Hölderlin, xi, 91, 93, 94, 104,

INDEX

Syntax (*continued*)
105, 107, 125, 127, 130, 131, 132, 134, 135, 137; in Middleton, 36; in Schlegel, 13, 14–17; in Schleiermacher, 26, 27, 36; in Voß, 11, 12, 13, 14, 16, 17. *See also* Language
Szondi, Peter, 49, 50, 68, 77, 113, 115

Tieck, Dorothea, 18, 20
Tieck, Ludwig, 4, 18, 20
Tone, 3, 10, 16, 17, 47, 95, 124
Tragedy, xi, 49, 50, 69, 99
Tragicomedy, x, 50, 89
Transformation, 60–63
Translation: and adaptation, 48; as allegory, 90; alteration in, 5; as approximation, 21, 22; as authorship, 19–20; as comprehensible and pleasing, 8, 9, 13; as debt/responsibility, 37; developmental epochs of, 28–29, 36, 143–46, 149, 217; as different, 14; domesticating, 2; dress metaphor of, 36; eighteenth century, 1, 4, 12; ethics of, 2, 3, 5; fidelity in, 2, 4, 5–6, 11, 13, 17, 20, 23, 30, 44, 91, 131, 149; foreignizing, 2–3, 38, 41, 42, 91, 95, 109, 131–32; fruit metaphor of, 36; Hamann on, 9; impossibility of, 9, 21, 32; as improvement, 24; interlinear, 29, 37, 91, 137, 144, 149; literal, 9; as mimesis, 139, 141, 146; moral imperative of, 37; as native to target language, 26; non-ethnocentric, 2; as opaque, 34; and original, 14, 21, 22, 24, 69–76, 146, 192, 194; and politics, 25; process of, 92–93, 146–48; prose, 5, 144–45; publication of, 7–8; reception of, 38; as redemptive, 38; as representation, 193; and Romanticism, 22; and theology, 37; theory vs. practice in, 45; as transaction series, 37; of translation, 5; as translucent, 34, 35; as transparent, 29; verbatim, 9, 93, 124, 129, 130, 134
Translation, authorial, 41, 44–45; defined, x; in Goethe, 140, 141, 159, 190; by Hölderlin, 95, 137; by Kleist, 47; as model, 194; and original, 192, 194; as representation, 139; and service translation, x, 44, 45, 193, 194
Translation, service, 18; and authorial translation, x, 44, 45, 193, 194; birth of, 10; defined, ix–x, 2; fidelity in, 41, 44; and foreignizing translation, 3, 41; as goal vs. product, 42, 193–94; in Goethe, xi, 23–24, 159; by Hölderlin, xi, 91, 137; by Kleist, xi, 47, 52, 90; and Lessing, 7; as norm, 4; perfect translation in, 21; and Romanticism, 4, 41–42; and Schleiermacher, 27–28; summation of, 41–44; and Voß, 4, 20
Translator: and author, 3; author as, x, 24; Breitinger on, 6; culture of, 144; as go-between, 145; as invisible, 28, 38, 43; language development by, 31–32; payment of, 7; presence of, 41; and service translation, ix; Venzky on, 5
Trivedi, Harish, 40
Trochaic verse, 96, 97, 200n. 24. *See also* Poetry/verse
Truth, 171–72, 173, 180, 187, 189
Tymoczko, Maria, 40

Universal, 21, 41, 185, 186, 188, 218–19n. 53

Venuti, Lawrence, 205n. 91; *The Translator's Invisibility*, 2, 25, 26, 28, 38, 40, 42
Venzky, Georg, 13, 14; "Bild eines

238

INDEX

geschickten Übersetzers," 5
Voltaire: *Mahomet*, 141, 142; *Tancred*, 141
Voß, Heinrich, 104–5
Voß, Johann Heinrich: and Goethe, 23–24, 144; and Hölderlin, 95–96; Homer translation of, 4–5, 10–12, 95, 96, 108; Klopstock on, 12; *Luise*, 11, 17; *Odüssee*, 96; Schlegel on, 12, 13, 14; service translation by, 20; Shakespeare translation of, 12; Vergil translation of, 12

Walser, Robert, 148

Warminski, Andrzej, 114
Wieland, Christoph Martin, 1, 12–13, 18–19, 24, 28, 80, 144, 182, 183, 202n. 45
Wieland, Ludwig, 80
Women, 19–20, 70
Word, 3, 26, 34, 36, 43. *See also* Language; Syntax
Wordsworth, William, 168

Zenge, Wilhelmine von, 73
Zschokke, Heinrich, 80; *Molières Lustspiele und Possen*, 81; "Der zerbrochene Krug," 81